MONDO TOKYO

MONDO TOKYO

Dispatches from a Secret Japan

PATRICK MACIAS

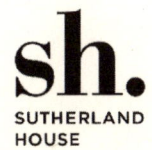

sh.
SUTHERLAND
HOUSE

TORONTO, 2024

Sutherland House
416 Moore Ave., Suite 205
Toronto, ON M4G 1C9

Copyright © 2024 by Patrick Macias

All rights reserved, including the right to reproduce this book or portions thereof in any form whatsoever. For information on rights and permissions or to request a special discount for bulk purchases, please contact Sutherland House at info@sutherlandhousebooks.com Sutherland House and logo are registered trademarks of The Sutherland House Inc.

First edition, January 2024

If you are interested in inviting one of our authors to a live event or media appearance, please contact sranasinghe@sutherlandhousebooks.com and visit our website at sutherlandhousebooks.com for more information about our authors and their schedules.

We acknowledge the support of the Government of Canada.

Manufactured in Turkey
Cover designed by Lena Yang
Book composed by Karl Hunt

Cover credits: Mitsume

Library and Archives Canada Cataloguing in Publication
Title: Mondo Tokyo : dispatches from a secret Japan / Patrick Macias.
Names: Macias, Patrick, 1972- author.
Description: Includes bibliographical references and index.
Identifiers: Canadiana (print) 20230557341 | Canadiana (ebook) 20230558461 | ISBN 9781990823299 (softcover) | ISBN 9781990823411 (EPUB)
Subjects: LCSH: Popular culture—Japan—Tokyo.
Classification: LCC DS896.5 .M33 2024 | DDC 306.0952/135—dc23

ISBN 978-1-990823-29-9
eBook 978-1-990823-41-1

Contents

Introduction   xi

TOKYO A GO-GO   1

The Ballad of Dasai Gaijin   3

Tales of the Psychic Snake   7

Boys' Love Café   13

Memo from the Maid Wars   18

It Is Only One Flower in the World   22

Female Android at Tokyo Department Store Looks for Love   25

Eye-Popping Robot Girls Restaurant Opens in Tokyo!   27

Tower Records Shibuya: No Music, No Life   30

SCENES FROM THE OTAKU-VERSE   37

Life and Death in an Otaku Paradise   39

The Shokotan Tapes: An Interview with Shoko Nakagawa   49

The World's Oldest Living Otaku: Twenty-Five Years of
Fred Patten   53

The Death of a Producer: Arrivederci, Yoshinobu Nishizaki   60

The Wild Frontier   65

A Bonkura Life   73

The Best Otaku Shops in Tokyo   78

More Anime, More Problems: An Interview with Terumi
Nishii   83

Taking It to the Streets: The Otaku Reclaim Akihabara   89

Leiji Matsumoto: Time Never Betrays a Dream   93

THREADS   99

The Men of *Host Knuckle*   101

Little Devil Swallowtail Butterflies: The Girls of *Koakuma
Ageha*   106

Shibuya 109-2 Elegy   112

Made in Japan: Harajuku Fashion Brands   120

On "Aymmy in the batty girls" and the Retro Adventures of
Ayumi Seto   126

Harajuku Burger Queen: An Interview with Ayumi Seto   130

GODAO: Fashion in the Dark   136

Sebastian Masuda and 6% DOKIDOKI: Colorful Anarchy   144

CONTENTS

TUNES AND VIBES — 149

The Feminine — 151

The Roots of J-Pop: Ten Bands to Explore — 155

Shinjuku Freakbeat — 163

R.I.P. (Rest in Pixar) Perfume — 167

On "PONPONPON" — 172

Making a Virtual Idol: A Conversation with the Creators of Hatsune Miku — 176

Masked Marvels: The Strange World of Kamen Joshi — 180

Idolized — 187

AKB48: Smells like Teen Spirit — 191

Eiichi Ohtaki: The Wizard of City Pop — 197

MONSTERS OF THE SCREEN — 205

Directing with Napalm: The Ryuhei Kitamura Interview — 207

We Will Be Rambo — 214

We Are the Japanese Fantasy Film Society: Kaiju 'Zines circa 1980 — 216

Outlaw Obituary: On Bunta Sugawara, 1933–2014 — 222

The Harajuku Line: Forgotten Fashion Monsters of Japanese V-Cinema — 226

My Top Five Godzilla Movies — 236

Shuji Terayama's Notes from Underground — 243

Kaiju Rhapsody — 249

Tetsuro Tamba: The Prince of the East 253

Sonny Chiba: The Last Action Hero 260

Kumi Mizuno: The Bride of Godzilla 266

Epilogue 272
Author Biography 276

For Julia . . .
Don't be afraid to explore an unfamiliar place.

Introduction

I wake up and I'm in Japan.

I'm exactly where I want to be, after decades of only dreaming about it. I live minutes from a train station that can take me to my favorite points on the map: Nakano, Akihabara, Harajuku, Shibuya, Shinjuku, to name just a few stops on the East Japan Railway line.

But I don't want to go outside.

As I write this, Tokyo is experiencing its highest-ever COVID-19 infection numbers. These are plague times and it's cold outside. So, until further notice, Japan is a place where I sit and think about a place called Japan.

* * *

I'm five years old and seeing Japan for the first time.

It's 1979. My dad tells me a Godzilla movie is on TV. I've never seen one before, but I like dinosaurs. He figures it's something I might enjoy. So I sit in front of a Sony cathode-ray television that beams out *Godzilla: King of the Monsters* from 1956, starring Raymond Burr and a guy named Hauro Nakajima in a rubber lizard suit.

That's all it takes.

From this point forward, I fall hard for Japan . . . or at least *an idea* of Japan, cobbled together in my young imagination from the monster movies, space battleships, and giant robots that I see on TV.

* * *

The more I saw, the more I wanted to learn. As I grew up, I wanted to visit Japan. Maybe it's because Japan seemed like a more exciting place than where I was born and grew up: in the Northern California suburbs of Sacramento. International travel seemed like a big dream for my little kid brain. It might not have been so ambitious as dreams go—not like becoming an astronaut, baseball player, or president—but it seemed huge to me.

I clung hard to any piece of Japanese culture I could find. My personal heroes as I grew up were *Godzilla* special effects director Eiji Tsuburaya and manga artist Leiji Matsumoto, who created the immortal Captain Harlock and his rebellious adventures through space. My bible was the book *Manga! Manga! The World of Japanese Comics* (1983). These works inspired me to make Super 8 films, to draw, to write; in other words, to create.

These days, a lot of American fans use the Japanese term *otaku* to refer to folks who love Japanese culture—it roughly translates to "obsessed nerd." But when I was a kid in the 1970s and 1980s, no one around me was into this sort of stuff. There weren't any words to describe what the heck was wrong with me as I entered my Japan-consumed adolescence.

Then (as now), I would annoy people with random facts about Godzilla and tell everyone how much I loved Japanese cartoons. But my enthusiasm was based in the very real and electric feeling that I had when I encountered all these things from Japan: the movies, the music, the anime, the games. It felt like something special was happening over there, far away, across the sea.

INTRODUCTION

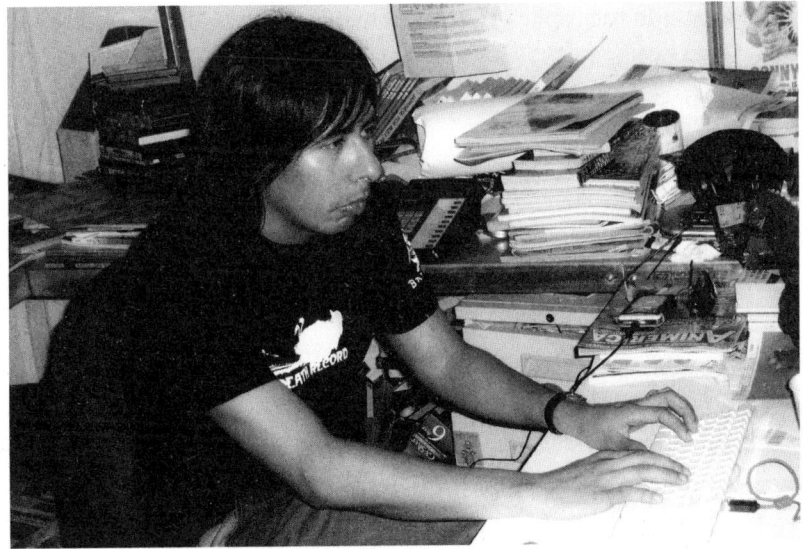

The author at his desk in San Francisco, early 2000s.

At the age of 19, I moved to San Francisco and started writing professionally for a syndicated news service. My life revolved around movies: I hung out with experimental filmmakers in the Mission District and wrote film reviews for free weekly papers and assorted 'zines. It was the 1990s: alternative culture was strong and Bay Area rents were still cheap.

Almost despite myself, something like an actual career began to take shape.

In 1997, I started working as a writer and editor at manga and anime company Viz Media. Viz began asking me to write and contribute to several books in short succession: *Japan Edge* (1999), *Fresh Pulp* (1999), and my first book as a solo author, *TokyoScope: The Japanese Cult Film Companion* (2001).

Once I had a couple of bonus paychecks in my pocket, I went to Japan for the first time. I can clearly remember seeing Tokyo Tower on the bus from the airport and thinking how small it looked in comparison to the replica I'd seen destroyed in movies by giant monsters like Mothra and Gamera. But it didn't matter that it was smaller. It was *real*.

Like many tourists before me, I was knocked out by Tokyo. I could not get the towering Shinjuku skyline—or the streets filled with people below—out of my mind. I wanted to go back to Japan as soon as I left. I spent the years that followed saving up money for flights and hotels, splurging on trips and travelling to Tokyo several times a year, coming back to the USA with suitcases filled with DVDs, CDs, books, magazines. I was trying to take Japan back to America with me, piece by piece.

One of the movies that I brought back made me a bit of money. These were the days of the J-Horror craze, the genre of creepy Japanese movies about ghost kids and undead girls who crawl out of your TV set (like Godzilla once emerged from mine). I got a finder's fee from a Hollywood producer for securing a copy of the J-Horror movie *Ju-On*, which was later remade as *The Grudge*.

With this new injection of cash, I quit my job and ran away to Tokyo.

I don't know what I was thinking. I was in my early 30s and I felt it was time to just live that dream, to dive in, to take that leap of faith.

I placed an ad looking for somewhere to stay while in Tokyo. It was answered by an anime screenwriter, and I moved in with him. I lived on and off in his tiny spare bedroom in a rundown apartment building in the Kichijoji area of Tokyo for several years.

It was 2005. I was writing. I was podcasting. I was blogging. I had my own blog, titled "An Eternal Thought in the Mind of Godzilla." I'd modeled it after the quote "Rome is an eternal thought in the mind of God," which I thought was something Saint Augustine had said; although, looking it up again, it seems to have been a line from the 1960 Stanley Kubrick film *Spartacus*. Go figure.

INTRODUCTION

Having a blog was useful because I was writing a lot. I was working on a book that became *Japanese Schoolgirl Inferno*, published in 2006. Most of my days were spent bumming around the city and grinding away in cafés trying to hit my word count. Blog entries helped me get the writing juices flowing and it was fun to see reader reactions and comments.

I tried not to overthink it. If there were inside jokes or personal references that only made sense to me, I'd keep them in. Every now and then, I would write longer pieces, like interviews or profiles with people I was hanging out with, event reports, deep dives into idol groups, flashbacks to obscure Japanese cultural ephemera, or whatever else was rattling around in my mind.

I also wrote a lot of stream-of-consciousness pieces, cobbling together an imaginary version of Japan drawn from my fantasies and obsessions, sometimes featuring recurring characters. I set these stories in a weird future era of Japan called the *Taishomei*

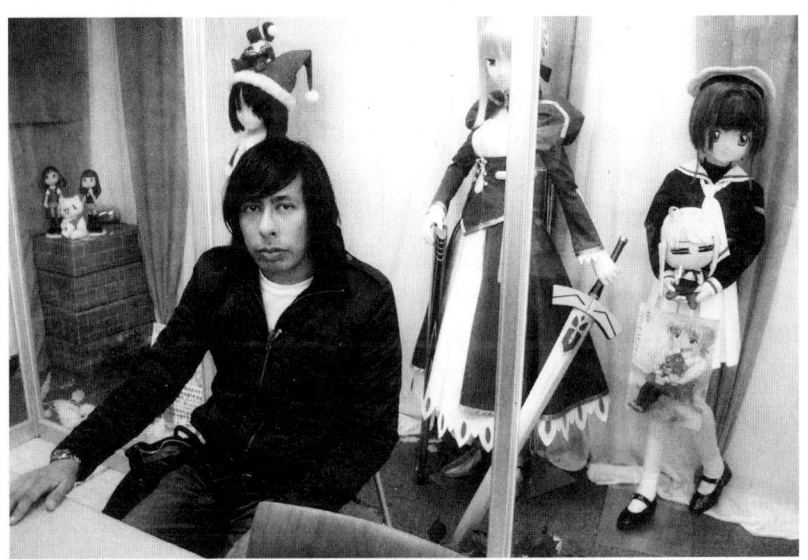

The author in Akihabara, Tokyo, 2006.

(a combination of the three imperial eras of 20th-century Japan: Taisho, Showa, Meiji). While other bloggers quickly figured out how to monetize content via ads or affiliate links, I used mine as a big messy sketchbook for my ideas. It led to something stranger and more fun and unique.

This was a great time to be in Japan, and Tokyo in particular. Akihabara, Tokyo's famously nerdy tech district, was in the middle of a renaissance of sorts, thanks to media buzz from movies like *Train Man* (based on a supposedly true story about a young otaku who saves a girl on a train and starts a romance) and the craze over maid cafés (places where you could order overpriced drinks and snacks from young women wearing French maid outfits who called you "master"). Across town in Harajuku, street fashion and youth culture were still buzzing.

However, I could tell that time was running out. There were more tourists. The real weirdos were retreating from their old haunts. The unique flavor of Japanese style was under threat from encroaching global brands like H&M and Forever 21, plus an influx of real estate speculation. Of course, Tokyo—like any major city or giant robot worth its salt—is always transforming. I'm glad that I was there to experience that moment before big chunks of the underground evaporated.

The book in your hands is a collection of my reflections on the Japanese life and culture that I experienced over the course of 15 years. Some of the things that I wrote about back then are gone now and some of them changed into something new and even wilder. The stories in this book will take you on a journey through all of it. I've divided them into sections based on the big themes that have always mattered to me: music, fashion, movies, and the unique and crazy inner life of Tokyo. I've remixed many of my essays, recontextualized them, and added new thoughts here and there.

Even when I get misty-eyed about how things have changed, I remember that there are some Japanese cultural pillars that will be around forever. I've ended each section with my personal profiles of icons: the actors, places, designers, musicians, and colorful characters who you should check out right now. They will always be Eternal Thoughts in the Mind of Godzilla!

I hope that wherever you are when you read this, you're in the place *you* want to be. I'll be in Tokyo, looking out the window, wondering when I can go outside again, to see what has changed and what will stay the same.

Patrick Macias

TOKYO A GO-GO

Wild scenes from the Tokyo underground: maid cafés, robots, and assorted freak-outs.

The Ballad of Dasai Gaijin

July 2005

Originally, I thought that *dasai gaijin* simply meant "uncool foreigner," like Schwarzenegger promoting instant ramen or Richard Gere enthusing "I love Tokyo!" But it's much, much worse than that. My friend Slasher corrects me: "It's more like *pathetic* foreigner."

At least 60 people are crammed into the Acid Panda Café in Ookayama tonight; they're here for Dasai Gaijin Night Vol. 2, a sequel to an event that was held a few months back.

A two-man techno band Leopaldon not only runs the Acid Panda Café, they're also dedicated to hunting down the most fucked-up foreigners they can find so that they can mercilessly mock them. They scour the Internet for pics and post them on an online Dasai Gaijin community, which currently numbers nearly 2,000 members.

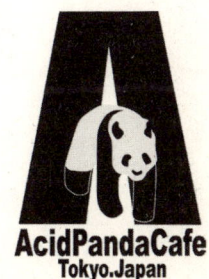

Now they sit on stage before me, breaking down their massive collection of JPEGs into categories:

The Royals—Awkward family portraits straight out of the Sears catalog.

The Gamers—Nerds, basically lined up at networked computers while happily trying to kill each other in virtual combat.

The Last Samurai—Pictures of wayward gaijin with their host families out in Bumfuck, Japan. Helps if they are wearing a stylish yukata robe.

The Creators—The proud owners of science fair projects, ugly clay sculptures, and homemade Star Trek props.

The Monsters—Oversized, hideous, and savage, eating giant hamburgers in clothes that are forever several sizes too small.

The Cosplayers—You know how that one goes: paint yourself blue and be a Smurf or dress up like a cardboard Transformer.

And so on. Each picture and category is greeted with hoots and shouts of "Dasai!!!" from the audience.

Next comes a PowerPoint presentation, with graphs and pie charts that help explain the aesthetics of Dasai Gaijin.

At the first level is a lack of concern for one's own self-image. The

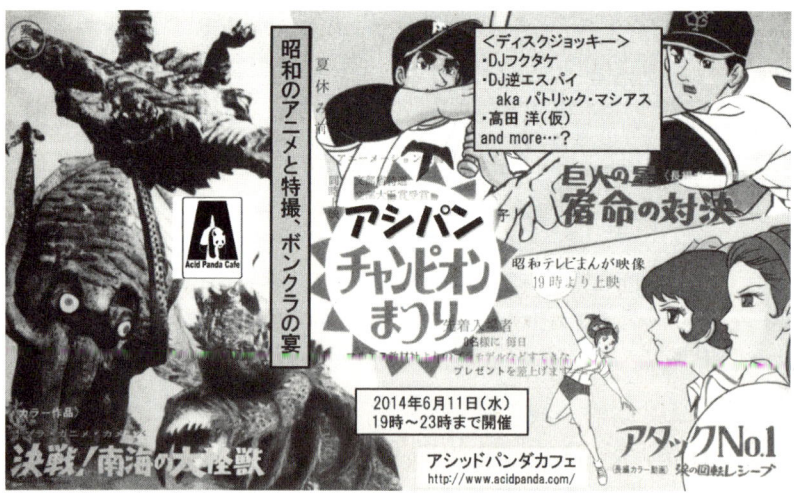

Flier for the Acid Panda Festival, 2014.

next level is ugliness, plain and simple. Overlapping both is humor. Dasai Gaijin have to be funny looking; otherwise, what's the point? But there is another shadow aspect. It's also not funny.

Next is a session of real-time hunting for Dasai Gaijin. Google is the best place to find their grazing pastures. The top keyword searches that yield bountiful harvests are "Party" and "Crazy Dancing."

Then they announce that there is a special guest in the house. An actual, for real, real Dasai Gaijin!

Naturally, it's me.

The hosts wave a mic in my face and ask, "What would Americans think if they found out about this event?"

"Maybe it would start a war," I say. "Americans don't want to be Dasai and don't want other people laughing at them. Eventually, they would start hunting for Dasai Nihonjin."

"What words do you recommend searching for when looking for Dasai Gaijin?"

"Let's face it: most Dasai Gaijin are white people. So just type 'white people' into the search engine and let it rip. 'Stoned' is also good. So is 'heavy metal fans.'"

We do a live search and find a dating site for men with long hair. Next, Leopaldon take some of most Dasai images they've found and do some culture jamming on the quick: using a computer to insert Dasai Gaijin images into places where normally "cool" gaijin reside, like ads for Apple products, magazine covers and billboards, sales campaigns for Tower Records. It's pretty satisfying to see the world turned upside down like this.

The rest of the evening is a blur of beers and bitter laughter. I ask a pair of girls: what brought you to this event? What is it about Dasai Gaijin that made you come all the way out to Ookayama?

"Dasai Gaijin are funny. They look so happy. They're cute."

It seems like Westerners have gone from being cool to being the Muppets.

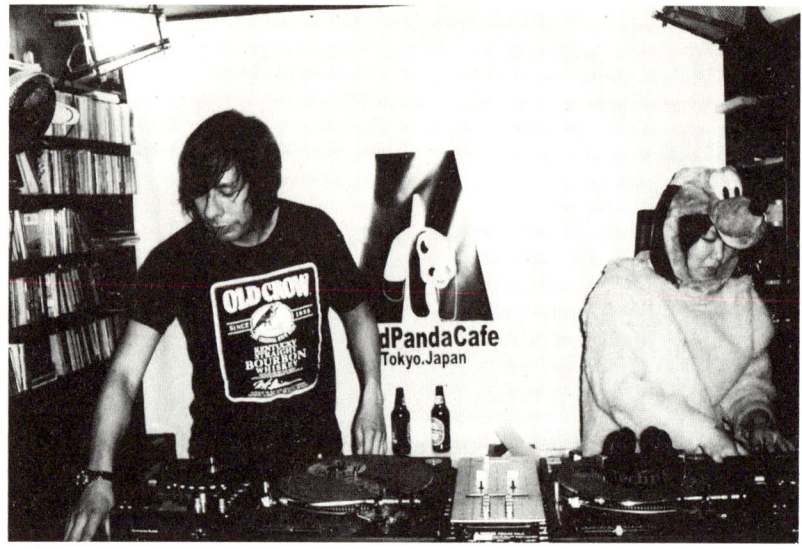

The author (at left), DJ-ing at the Acid Panda Cafe, 2008.

The DJs start spinning up for Dasai Gaijin dancing. Slasher takes over the turntables and plays the Ghostbusters theme, Kenny Loggins, Andrew W.K. Around 4 am, the set is almost exclusively culled from music that's several decades old: "Wake Me Up Before You Go-Go", "Mr. Roboto".

Slasher sits at the bar mulling it over. "This started out as Dasai Gaijin night, but somehow it's turned into '80s night."

Well, the 1980s was when gaijin iconography was at its zenith in Japan. But the passing of time has turned these works into laughable bits of crappy ear candy. Cool ages to fool.

At 5 am, it's all over, but the 30 or so survivors still have to pose for pictures. Everyone makes their best stupid grinning Dasai Gaijin faces, fingers spread out into Vs. They put me on a pedestal. Literally. At first, I refuse. But then I realize this my destiny.

I've been proclaimed a "Dasai Gaijin" just for showing up in Japan.

Tales of the Psychic Snake

November 2005

Tonight, Koyuki is the most beautiful girl in Japan; maybe even the world. She's all of 19 years old, clad in a red kimono, her big eyes framed by razor-sharp cheekbones. Right now, she is eating a snake, a real one, taking bites out of it like it's a whip of black licorice. The audience gasps, repulsed. A second later, they are screaming.

Koyuki has tossed her half-eaten viper into the center of the crowd. But it's only a rubber snake, a cheap gag. And the rubes fell for it, as they have for centuries. Koyuki smiles mischievously—only a little, mind you—and nods her head, begging forgiveness for the indulgence.

She goes back to eating her snake, the real one.

It sounds strange, but what she's doing is actually situation-appropriate. It's Wednesday night and there's a *matsuri* festival at the Hanazono, a Shinto shrine for businesspeople, entertainers, pimps, and probably con men, too. After all, the area is next to Shinjuku Kabukicho, Tokyo's time-honored Pleasure District.

Outside, Yasukuni-dori is crowded with *tekiya* stalls selling fan favorites like yakitori, takoyaki, okonomiyaki, and that most traditional of festival beverages: overpriced beer. The latter can be had any night of the year and the former never tastes better than during a festival. But we didn't come here for the booze and the chow. We want to get freaked out.

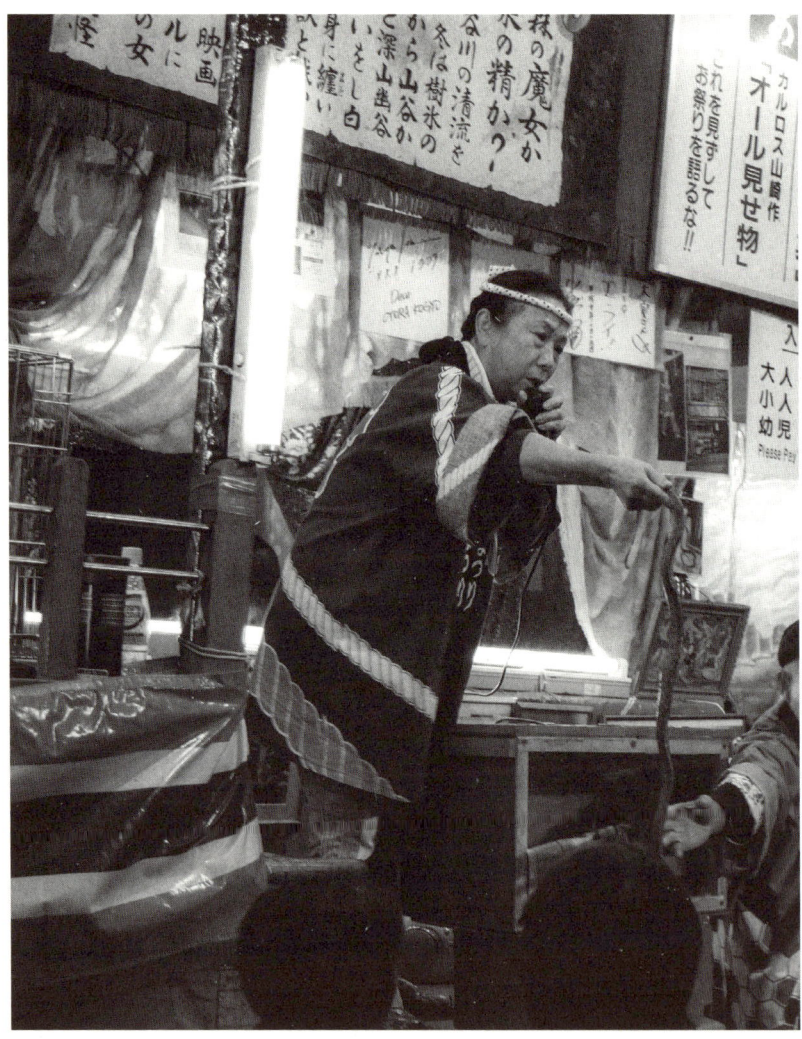

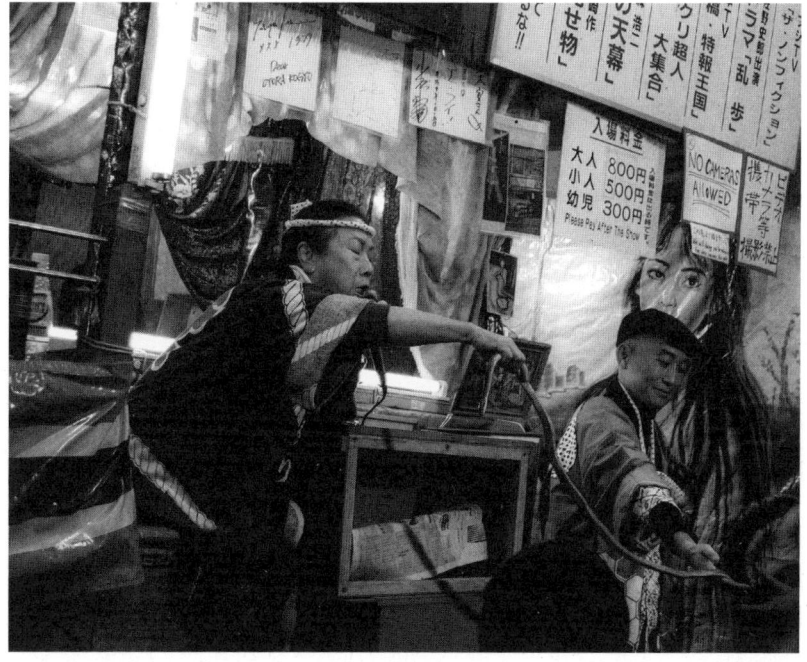

Outside the tent, the barker—an old woman who looks like Beat Takeshi—eggs us on, selling up the New Face in the show. She's a beauty! She's even been in a newspaper and was photographed for *Shonen Jump* magazine! To our right is an enormous painted mural of a woman in white, a hideous snake around her neck. She looks nothing like Koyuki, but that's who it's supposed to be. To the barker's left is a tiny metal cage. A white poodle in a tutu lies on its stomach inside. It's a dog's life. Mondo Cane meets Mondo Tokyo.

It's JPY 800 a peek. Pay after the show. We shuffle into the tent. Inside, a pair of middle-aged women are displaying a mummified two-headed calf to the crowd.

"Yeah, we saw that last year," says my friend Slasher, and indeed we did, but being the suckers that we are, we keep coming back. It's the same setup as before: stage with faded red curtain, audience standing on a rickety raised floor. Inside, someone who looks like the barker's sister does the announcing.

Oh, and there are snakes. Handfuls of poisonous vipers and a colossal boa constrictor slither across the floor, while dried scales are handed out for good luck.

The grand finale: an old woman with drag queen makeup, a veteran of the freak show scene and Koyuki's *sempai*, puts on a bib. She wads up a dozen or so white candles in one hand and ignites the wicks until there's a tiny inferno in her palm. Then she pours the hot wax into her mouth. There is no expression on her haggard, corpse-like face. Then she holds the candles in front of her mouth and blows. A Gene Simmons-sized jet of flame erupts. It's cold outside, but the force of the blast briefly cooks us.

Later, we sit at a yakitori stand and dig the real-time yakuza movie unfolding around us. Clouds of smoke and steam. Tall bottles of sake and beer. Tourists, old people, a crowd of hosts, couples, and an endless supply of gangsters stroll around. A festival in Shinjuku means members of the "dark society" will crawl out of their bars, dens, and dives and parade around the place, pausing—along with the commoners—to throw some money at the shrine.

A single, lonesome security guard patrols the area. "Look at that loser," says Slasher. "He knows he can't do shit here."

Then he breaks it down. Yakuza Type A favors expensive suits, diamond watches, and sunglasses at night. Two fat cats, massive with an air of menace, enter the tent, and the merchant does his best bowing and mincing. Yakuza Type B lives in a cheap jogging suit, like something you'd get at Ross (Dress for Less). These are the *tekiya* mostly, the guys running the booths and stalls. Both types saunter around clutching little briefcases full of cash. I see at least one hand-off go down for real and sense dozens more around me.

It's a gangster SimCity, but the V-Cinema cameras never come out. Everyone is on their best behavior. Much bowing and yelling ensues whenever members of different castes meet and greet each other.

"Goddamn, it's a yakuza zoo," I say.

Slasher is quick to make corrections. "Hey, don't call them that here..." Instead, we refer to them as "They Who Must Not Be Named." Several cups of hot sake later, we have to let our hens out. Then it's karaoke in Kabukicho until 6 am.

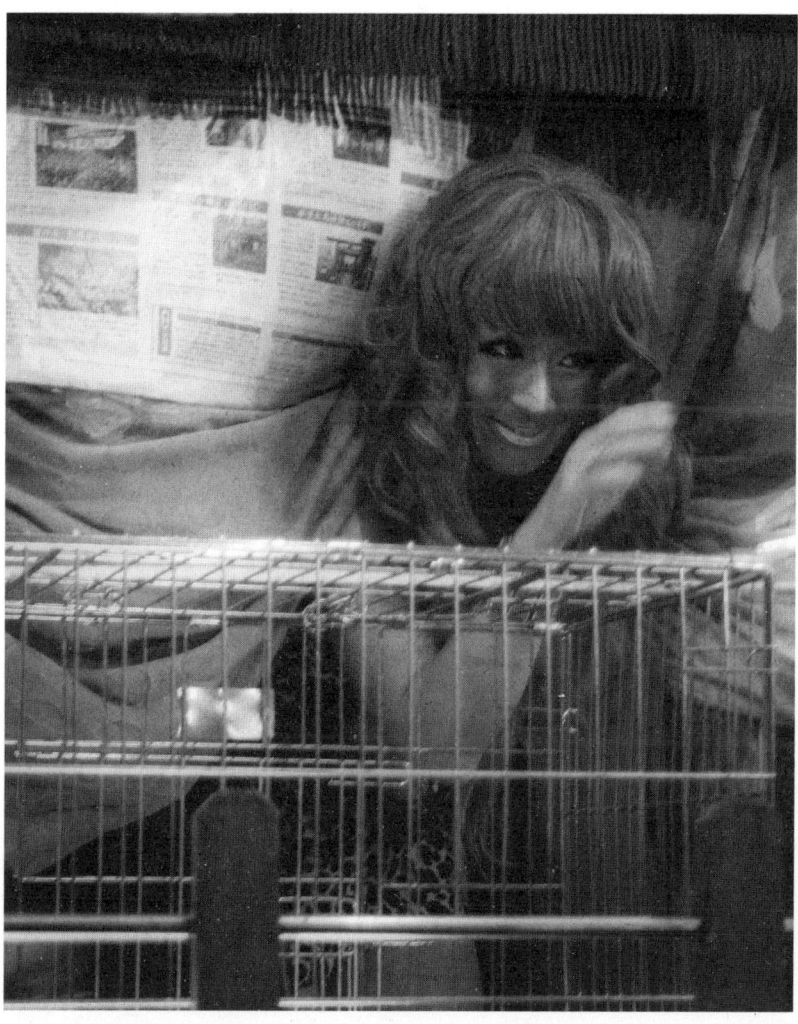

It's the usual long burnout ride back home, mouth like an ashtray, dreading the moment I'll have to wake up, knowing it will feel like someone hit me in the face with a baseball bat. But at least I didn't have to eat a snake for tips.

Boys' Love Café

March 2006

An Ikebukuro backstreet. Somewhere near the entrance to the Sunshine City shopping complex, formerly the site of fearsome Sugamo Prison. There's a ramen shop, another ramen shop, a yakitori stand, and then a storefront window framed by black lace curtains and violet drapes.

The sign outside reads "B:Lily-rose." A tall and elegant young man in a pinstripe suit welcomes us and takes our coats. It takes a second to settle in: "Dude, that dude isn't a dude, dude." Neither is anyone else working inside.

B:Lily-rose is a cafe staffed by women who cross-dress as men. Not just as any old Tom, Dick, or Harry, but "beautiful men" who represent the very ideal of Boys' Love, or *yaoi*, in manga and anime. The *yaoi* genre is all about pretty young guys who are into each other, and most of the fans are women. It is the female version of the maid cafes that cater to male tastes, mostly centered in the nerdy Akihabara district.

There's also a butler cafe named Swallowtail, which was our first choice for a late afternoon refreshment, but business there is so popping that they required a reservation in advance. Still, B:Lily-rose, which opened a scant three months ago, doesn't disappoint.

It's a small concrete bunker, made cozy by fake flowers and careful attention to detail. It is full of customers fresh from shopping sprees at the nearby Otome Road, Tokyo's designated district for young women interested in love between men, which hosts a row of shops selling amateur press *dojinshi* (thin pamphlets offering illustrated stories depicting relationships of various levels of intimacy, from mild to wild, between popular male characters). Billboards outside advertise the wares within: two blond and blue-eyed boys about to kiss, their lips almost touching . . . almost! . . . but not quite.

Our "garcon" gives us a choice for where to sit. The first option is a stainless steel table fringed with over-stylized black and red chairs smuggled in from the Mad Hatter's tea party, perhaps. The other

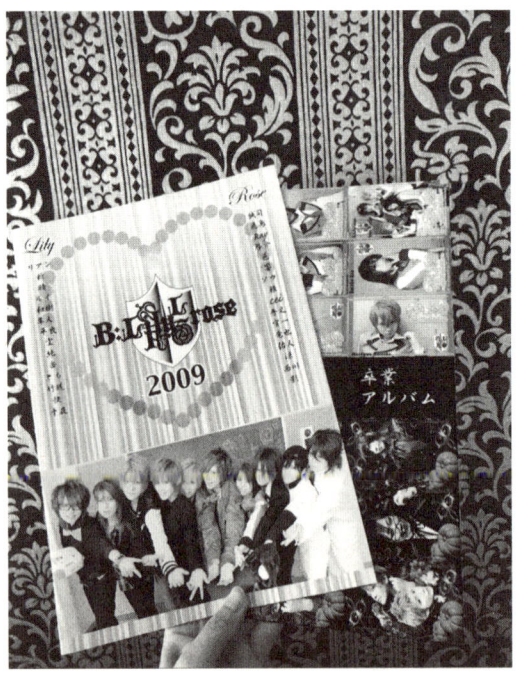

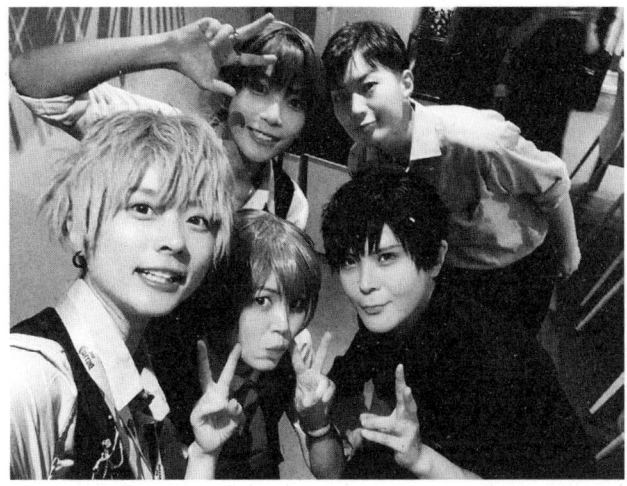

option is a gleaming white counter facing the wall, where a seat costs an extra JPY 500 (USD 4.50); this entitles you to the "Conversation System," an up close and personal chat with the bartender (in picture-perfect vest and bowtie) working the shift.

I count five "hosts" in all working the floor. Everyone is tall, thin, and impeccably dressed. Black trench coats, tailored jackets. Hair is dyed either reddish brown or dirty blond, styled with wax, just like the latest J-pop boy band idols. Colored contact lenses take us one step further away from reality and closer to some kind of ideal version of what it means to be male or female. Our waiter wears a sharp black pinstripe suit, just like the person outside. She leans in to ask what we'd like to drink. The voice is velvet androgyny.

A menu lists off alcoholic and soft cocktails with names like Baby Kiss, Cutie Boy, and Sweet Love. I order a Coke. A tiny bottle is produced, along with a glass. Someone is standing behind me. A thin hand crosses into my field of vision. The Coke is poured with a careful ritual finesse.

Time to scan the customers. It's mostly young women in their 20s dressed a little punk, a little goth. Plaid skirts and designer

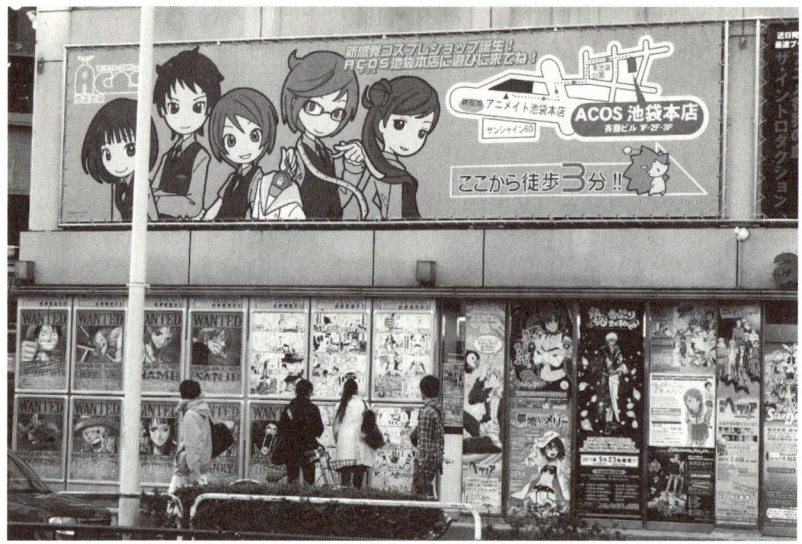

Otome Road in Ikebukuro, Tokyo, 2006.

black T-shirts with skulls on them, probably bought off the rack at Marui Young. Hair is black, straight. A lot of people wearing glasses. The girl sitting next to me is drawing something in a sketchbook. Beautiful pencil illustrations of characters from the anime and manga *Bleach* . . . who also, coincidentally, bears a striking similarity to the staff of B:Lily-rose.

Maybe it's pure paranoia, but I imagine the cold eyes of death on me. "What the fuck is this gaijin . . . this . . . this . . . MAN doing in here?" Hard to get too comfortable. I have to keep one eye on the clock. As the menu helpfully points out, "No men allowed after 4 pm."

I've only a few minutes to figure it all out before I'm thrown into the street. Coming here was my friend Yanagi's idea. She's a journalist who has been following the burgeoning female nerd scene in Ikebukuro. What is the appeal of a place like this, I ask her?

"It's peaceful, elegant, and clean. There's nothing dirty about this place at all."

Meanwhile, a widescreen television on the wall plays the Tom Cruise and Brad Pitt version of *Interview with the Vampire*, and it's at the scene where a naked woman is sacrificed on stage to a shocked audience. No one in the cafe even blinks an eye at this graphic depiction of sex and violence.

It's almost 4 pm. I'm about to turn into a pumpkin. Better make a run for the door. Our host gathers up our coats and bags. "It's cold outside," she (he?) purrs to us. "Please don't catch a cold. Please come again." Did she say it to me or was it only intended for my female companion?

The B:Lily-rose café closed in 2019, but the name and brand is still used for special events.

Memo from the Maid Wars

October 2006

The room looks like the entrance to a ride at Disneyland or a spaceport for a rocket to a maid-populated moon. People sit in church-like pews watching pretaped maid antics on a widescreen TV or browse through seemingly endless quantities of maid merchandise. Maids stand behind the reception desk, make notes in maid schedule books, and pause to robotically shout out numbers into a maid microphone. One by one, the customers depart for the upper floors and packs of new people shuffle through the door to take their place.

This is the lobby for Akihabara's oldest and, judging by the looks of things, single most popular maid establishment, @home Cafe.

@home Cafe itself is staffed by "fantasy maids" in brown uniforms that owe little to the Victorian and French tradition. The idea is that you'll be served by a fleet of beautiful young girls dressed as maids who will respond to your every whim. The customers are surprisingly stylish-looking young men. About ten of them sit in the back, puffing cigarettes and cracking jokes. I only count three or four stereotypical Akihabara otaku sitting by themselves, lost in private reverie. All chairs face forward to a stage where God only knows what is going happen.

Eventually, they call out the number for our little TV crew. The holy trinity of director, soundman, and cameraman scout out the mysterious upper floor where I am told I will have to "play games with a maid" as the cameras roll.

The music on the hi-fi is pretty amazing: Super Moe Pop sung by the in-house band Kanzen Maid-Sengen. The sugar sweet songs performed by the staff all seem to feature the word "goshujin-sama" ("master") at least one million times.

They seat me at a counter down front, right next to a *hime* gal ("rich princess type"; think Paris Hilton goes Cinderella) with bouffant hair who is having some gooey ice cream dessert with her mom. Other perfectly normal-looking women are seated throughout the restaurant, all beaming. Apparently, anyone and everyone wants to be called "master" these days.

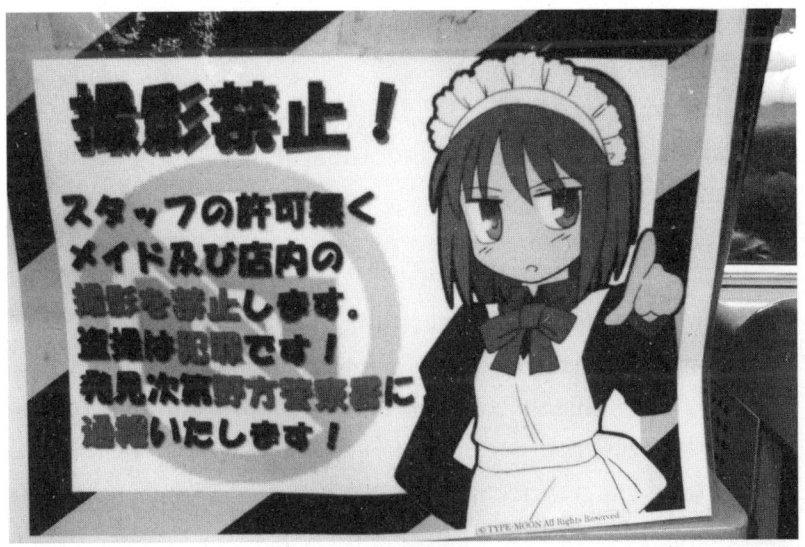

Sign reminding patrons that it is prohibited to take pictures of the maids without permission.

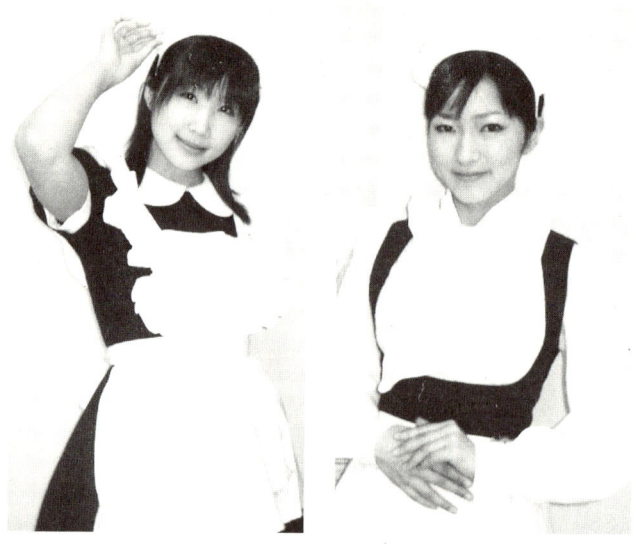

A maid appears before me. She is a perky, toothy little thing wearing gold-rimmed glasses that do not have any lenses (some folks just think that glasses, or *megane*, look cool), which is so dysfunctional that I can only assume it is supposed to induce *moe*—innocent cuteness—at some astral level.

I calmly inform her that she is not my maid. Rather, she is my enemy. I am going to wipe the floor with her at whatever silly game we wind up playing. No way am I going to lose to Miss Megane Moe on NHK World television.

We play the "Wani Wani Panic" game. Imagine a goofy plastic alligator head filled with tombstone-like teeth. The maid and I take turns pressing the teeth down, Russian Roulette style, until the jaw snaps on her dainty hand and she makes situation-appropriate squeaky little noises.

The *hime* gal and her mom have their backs firmly to us the whole time. They don't want any part of this.

Miss Megane Moe vanishes for a while, then reappears on stage with another maid. They lead the entire cafe into a rousing game of

Rock, Paper, Scissors. They sing in unison "@home, moe moe, jan, ken, pon!" The camera zooms in on my face. Hi, Mom?

I briefly and seriously contemplate jumping out the window to my right. I see myself falling seven stories down to my death, my splattering brains hitting both used computer parts and a vending machine selling instant *oden*. There really is nowhere else to go from here.

Instead, I wait for the maid to bring me my chow. It turns out to be a heart-shaped hamburger (framed by angel's wings made out of mayonnaise) and bunny ear cheesecake that our cameraman eagerly consumes after he takes his close-up.

I'm told later that what makes the food here so special is that "the maid puts her *moe* into it." Make of that what you will.

@home remains a popular destination in Akihabara, although the café made national headlines when 12 of their maids caught COVID-19 early in the pandemic.

It Is Only One Flower in the World

November 2008

If you're looking for flower and gift deliveries with impact and style in the Shinjuku Kabukicho area, the ONLY sane choice is LOVE'S CLOVER; in fact, as their slogan points out: "It is only one flower in the world."

LOVE'S CLOVER caters to the men and women so devoted to Japanese nightlife, they'll pay to hang out with the hosts and hostesses who will listen to your problems and encourage you to buy another drink. In addition to really fucking expensive bouquets and arrangements sure to impress a true Top Dandy, LOVE'S CLOVER also delivers festive champagne towers, holiday decorations, and floral columns and archways to the host club or hostess bar of your choice.

LOVE'S CLOVER can even create copyright-violating cartoon character arrangements, bouquets with encrypted messages, or representations of just about any animal in the *bestiarum vocabulum* (small dogs seem to be popular for some reason).

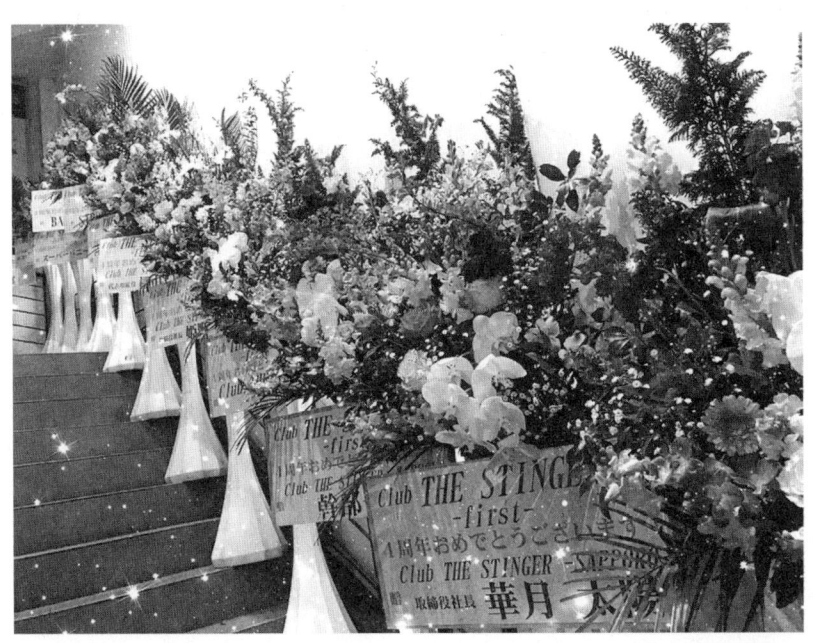
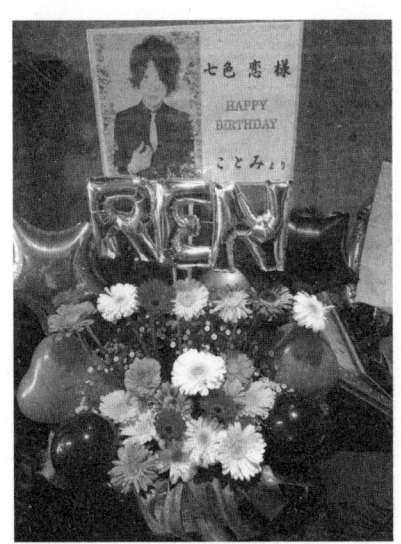
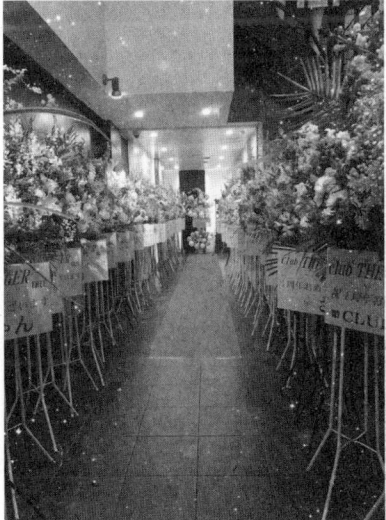

You can also order snacks for your favorite hosts and hostesses. While the snacks you can order for hostesses are limited to Sno-balls and Ding-Dongs, LOVE'S CLOVER offers a skull-fucking assortment of HOST CAKES made to order for special occasions. These cakes are topped with a gigantic edible photo of your most beloved host.

LOVE'S CLOVER appears to have closed around 2012.

Female Android at Tokyo Department Store Looks for Love

February 2012

Ah, Valentine's Day, when a young man's fancy turns *to finding a creepy inhuman female android to swear love and devotion to* . . .

Or at least, this is the basic idea behind a new promotion taking place at the Takashimaya department store in Tokyo's Shinjuku district.

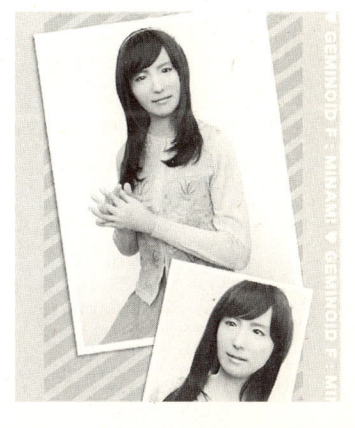

Behold, sitting in a see-through prison, Geminoid F, a mechanical marvel created by assorted Osaka University robot boffins. A slogan above her cage reads: "Android falls in love? She is waiting for you!"

Modeled after an actual flesh and blood woman in her early 20s, Geminoid F is equipped with a purse, a cell phone, and

Terminator-caliber data sensors that give her the ability to react to people around her with smiles and/or uninterested yawns . . . just like real women do when you bang on their glass cages with candy and flowers!

Call it weird or unnatural if you want, but this week we've also had reports of Hello Kitty working at Hooters and a study that shows one-third of Japanese youth have given up on sex and relationships. I think that romancing a Japanese fembot seems downright normal by comparison.

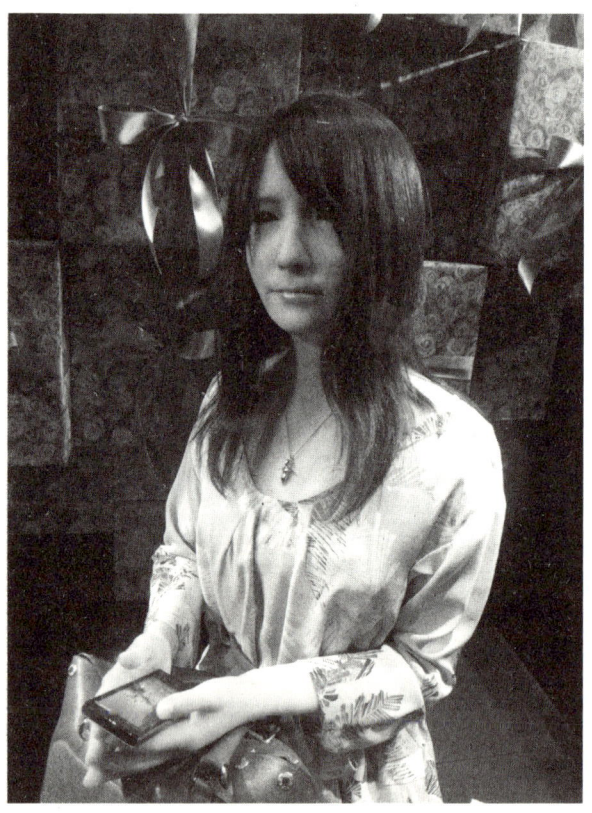

Eye-Popping Robot Girls Restaurant Opens in Tokyo!

July 2012

In Kabukicho's overheated hothouse environment, you need a serious gimmick to separate yourself from the competition. Enter the latest contender on the block: the Shinjuku Kabukicho Robot Restaurant.

Built at a cost of JPY 10 billion by some real "Good Fellas" (if you know what I mean), the Robot Restaurant shines garish lighting on female robots and flesh and blood cabaret girls for a hallucinatory experience that should do for the jaded, thrill-seeking salarymen of Japan what Chuck E. Cheese does for little kids.

For an entrance fee of around USD 37, patrons can stare slack-jawed as enormous robots roll around controlled by scantily clad female "pilots." Meanwhile, army girls patrol for enemy robots on armored vehicles that would shame anything in Disneyland's Main Street Electrical Parade.

There are even musical shows and revues performed by the girls, including traditional Japanese taiko drumming and a marching band.

And should any of this phantasmagorical spectacle fail to entertain, you can always lose your mind on cheap whiskey and chain-smoke like a chimney while taking in the otherworldly décor!

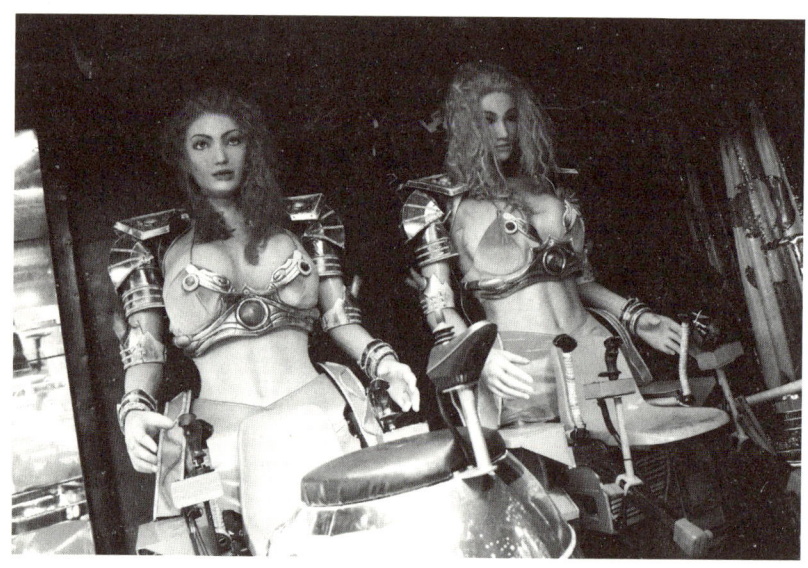

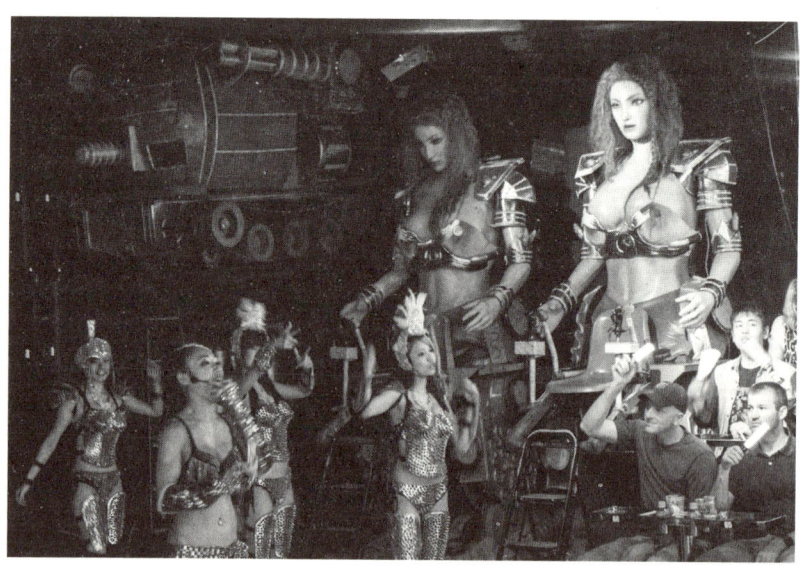

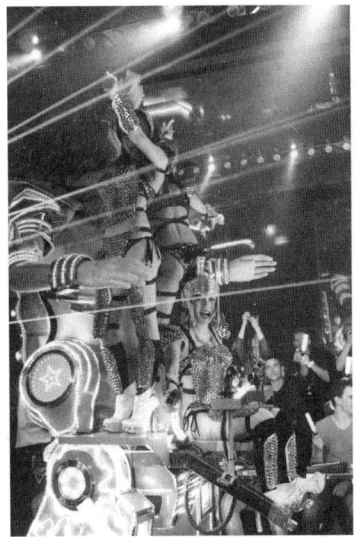 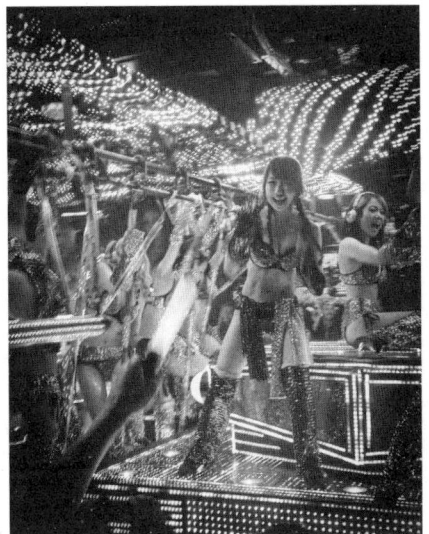

In truth, the joint is more like an old school *kyabakura*, or "cabaret club", than an actual honest to goodness restaurant. Three measly food items are all that's listed on the menu, a perfunctory measure probably because it's easier to get a license for food service than to apply for a "giant robots plus army girls and marching bands and motorcycles" license. Either way, here's wishing the Shinjuku Kabukicho Robot Restaurant the very best of luck, as it awkwardly rolls the human race one step closer to a well-deserved Robopocalypse.

The Robot Restaurant closed in 2020, another casualty of the pandemic, but their still active social media accounts threaten an inevitable comeback.

ICONS

Tower Records Shibuya: No Music, No Life

It's November 2021 and I am going to shop for vinyl at Tower Records in Shibuya, Tokyo.

There is a merciful but brief lull in the middle of a seemingly never-ending pandemic. COVID-19 cases are finally going down, people are starting to come out into the streets again. But it's a different world outside now. Foot traffic is down everywhere across Japan. Many old hangouts and tourist-friendly locations in Tokyo have closed for good.

It's not easy to have a good time.

Only one place in the entire Shibuya area seems to be defying the downwards trend in retail shopping and entertainment. Indeed, it uniquely seems to be doing better business than ever. You'll know you're close by when you see people in the area clutching familiar-looking orange and red shopping bags adorned with the company slogan: TOWER RECORDS—NO MUSIC, NO LIFE.

I'm on a hunt for old LPs, but today is (unbeknownst to me) also the launch date of a new single by Japanese boy band King & Prince. It looks like there's a riot going on. Hundreds of fans gather in front of Tower Records to take photos of the huge window displays. The dreamy members of King & Prince themselves are nowhere near this building, and yet fans are lining up to worship their images anyways: to take selfies with King & Prince posters and to buy tons of related merchandise inside.

The store lobby is crazy and crowded. People—mostly young women in ubiquitous masks—occupy nearly every square inch, from listening stations to store displays. It seems strange to see this mob at a time when popular music seems to have so little value (aside from providing "content" for streaming platforms). But here we are. To see a bricks-and-mortar music store this huge and vibrant in 2021 is nothing short of jaw dropping.

You might think that such a crowd would be an exception and that Tower Records only lights up like this during a launch event, but—aside from dead hours during weekday afternoons, when the core customers are at school or working—there is nearly always a constant stream of people riding up and down the Tower Records escalators to their various destinations.

Tower Records in Shibuya is a big place, spanning 84,000 feet across eight floors. Each floor is like a small store unto itself, dedicated to different tastes and genres: J-pop, Jazz/Classical, Western music (aka Rock), Anime songs, and Idol girl group music. But the killer app keeping Tower Records buzzing right now is K-pop. Japan is the second biggest market for K-pop outside of Korea, and fittingly, the K-pop floor at Tower Shibuya is the busiest, with tons of people (mostly girls) scanning the racks, taking pictures of the displays, and hanging out.

The latest addition to the floor plan, Tower Vinyl, opened in September 2021. This is what brought me back to Shibuya after months of self-imposed lockdown: the lure of used records, the chance to buy anime and movie soundtracks never released on digital formats, or just the excuse to waste time by flipping through stacks of old rock records, some of which I had when I was a kid.

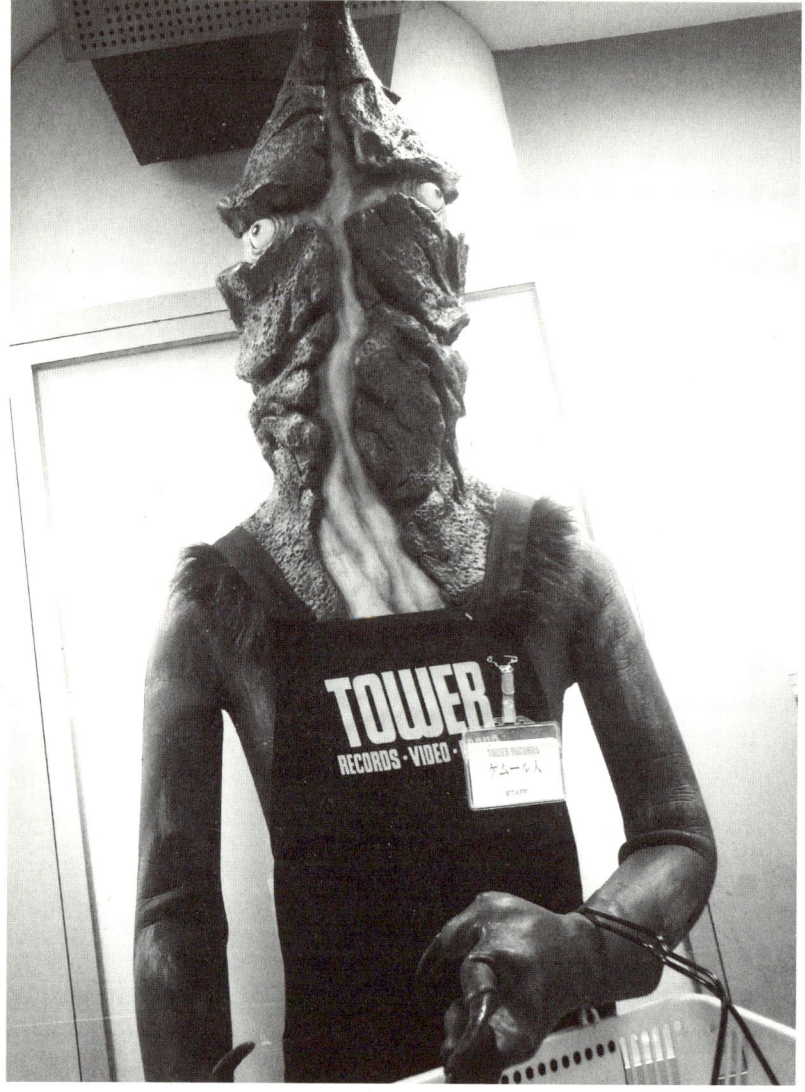

An Ultra kaiju working part time at Tower Records in Shibuya, Tokyo.

It's 1981 and I am buying vinyl LPs at Tower Records in Sacramento, California.

Going to Tower Records was nearly a weekend ritual for me growing up in the "totally awesome" 1980s. In a Northern California city that didn't seem like it had much to offer, Tower Records (along with Tower Books and Tower Video) was a vital connection to music and ideas from around the world, including Japan. On the Tower racks, you could sometimes (but not always) find copies of Japanese anime magazines like Animage, robot, and spaceship model-building bibles like Hobby Japan and import records.

Founded in my hometown of Sacramento, California, in 1960, Tower Records grew to become a pop culture empire, opening stores around the world, until mounting debt and other management problems led to massive closures and a complete dismantling of the brand in 2006, except in one nation on Earth.

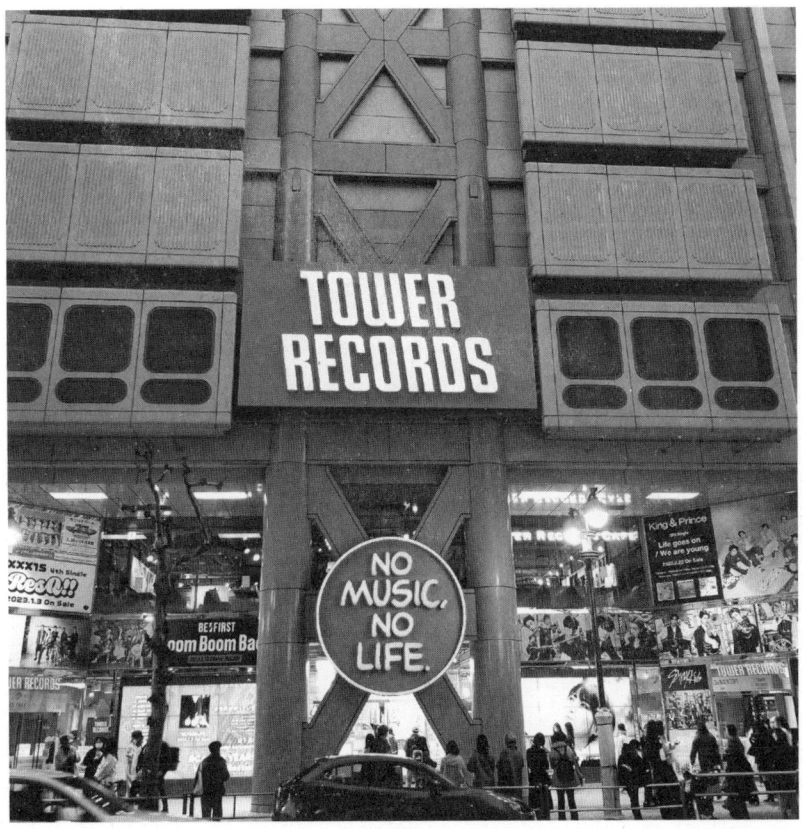

Japan.

Tower Records first opened in Japan in the early 1980s and still thrives here to this day, with 81 Japanese stores currently in operation.

Mark Viducich, a shipping clerk who became the CEO of Distribution for Tower, explains in the 2015 documentary *All Things Must Pass: The Rise and Fall of Tower Records* that the mania for American culture helped drive the rapid success of Tower in Japan. Japanese people didn't want rock and roll records pressed in Japan. They wanted the real thing from America.

Tower Records founder Russ Solomon, meanwhile, believed that Japan's love of Tower was grounded in what Tower had done all along: hiring authentic music fans and using their passion to light the way forward. The display racks of Tower Shibuya are filled with obsessively handwritten notes—part encyclopedia entry, part love letter—that store clerks have scrawled as recommendations or enhancements to artist bios. They look like memorials to missing persons.

All Things Must Pass concludes with Russ (who passed away in 2018) walking through the massive Shibuya location one last time to savor the dream.

At Tower Vinyl, there is a steady stream of middle-aged people like me, along with younger record collector types: the next generation of crate diggers. At the New Arrivals bin, I see a woman in her 50s snapping up a used copy of the *Flash Gordon* soundtrack by Queen (my Christmas present from 1980). I grab a US pressing of *Reckoning* by REM to compensate and head for the register.

I found out the hard way: if you actually want to buy something at Tower Records Shibuya on the weekends, good luck. There are long, long lines. No quick ins and outs. It's the revenge of retail shopping striking back, but I've got to admit that standing around and waiting to buy something feels vaguely nostalgic.

Over the next few weeks, I become a regular at Tower Vinyl Shibuya.

I buy a UK first pressing of Pink Floyd's *The Wall*.
The *Lensman* anime drama LP.
The *Trainspotting* soundtrack.
The all-analog remaster of *Loveless* by My Bloody Valentine.
Couples by Pizzicato Five.
The Peel Sessions by The Chameleons.
Substance by Joy Division.

I don't mind that most people at Tower Records are into music that I have precious little interest in. The K-pop and J-pop boy band fangirls keep the doors open and the lights on. And at this point in history, maybe that's all that matters.

NO MUSIC. NO LIFE.

Tower began closing some store locations across Japan in late 2021, but business at the Shibuya location remains strong.

SCENES FROM THE OTAKU-VERSE

Meet the otaku: Japan's secret rulers and nerdy underclass obsessed with life's minutiae—from anime, comics, and toys to trains, guns, and monster movies.

Life and Death in an Otaku Paradise

October 2007

When many tourists visit Japan, they want to see where the otaku lives.

Defining otaku as "passionate fans of Japanese animation, robot models and comic books" is easy, but it may not cover all the bases. There are as many different kinds of otaku as there are fans or obsessives about any number of niche interests: guns, laser discs, trains, stamps, mythological creatures, stereo cables, samurai swords, the stuff that dreams are made of . . . and the crap that makes up the background noise of everyday life.

Otaku culture is often deeply connected to people's childhoods or their younger selves. Very few become otaku late in life. Would I even be here in Tokyo if Japanese toys and monster movies hadn't possessed my soul when I was a toddler? Otaku are the people who never got the message to put away childish things.

The center of otaku activity in Japan used to be Akihabara, a Tokyo neighborhood famous for its used electronics stores and tucked-away hobby shops. It was a gathering spot for weirdo loners looking for anime goods and 2D girlfriends, wannabe music idols performing in the streets, and obsessives searching for parts to build their dream machines.

Right now, it's a humid and gray day in Akihabara, around high noon. The late summer is inviting lethargy and the Tokyo district's neon colors will also be muted until nightfall.

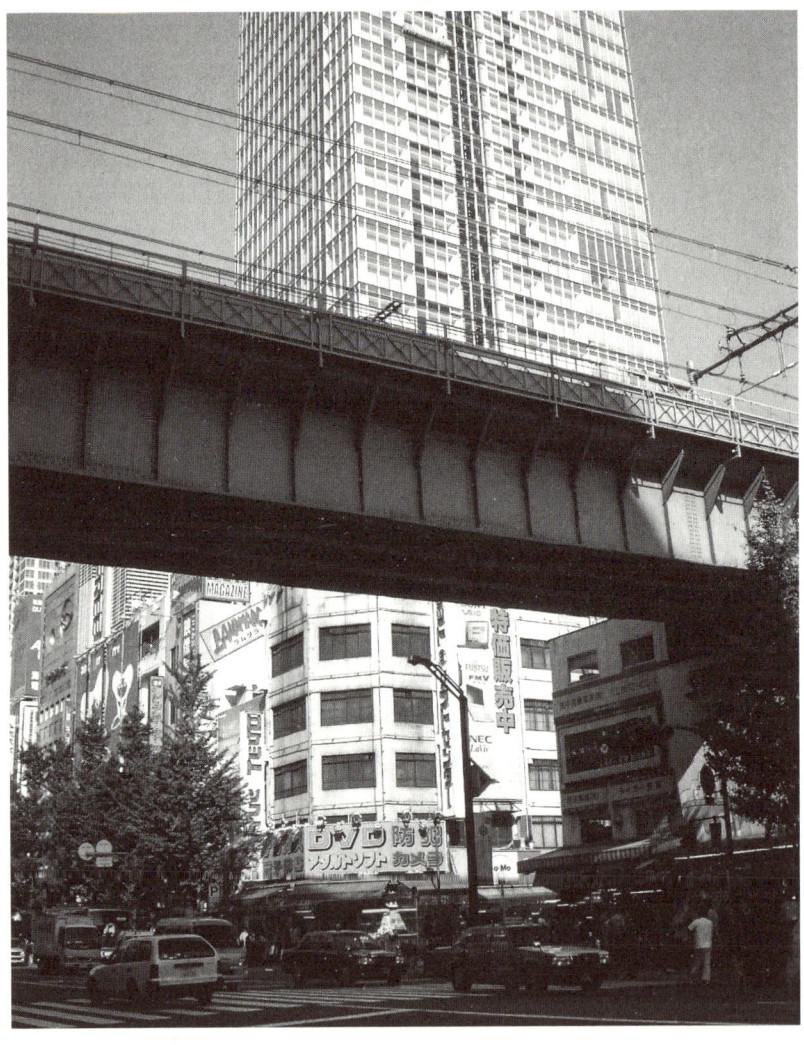

Akihabara, Tokyo, 2007.

SCENES FROM THE OTAKU-VERSE

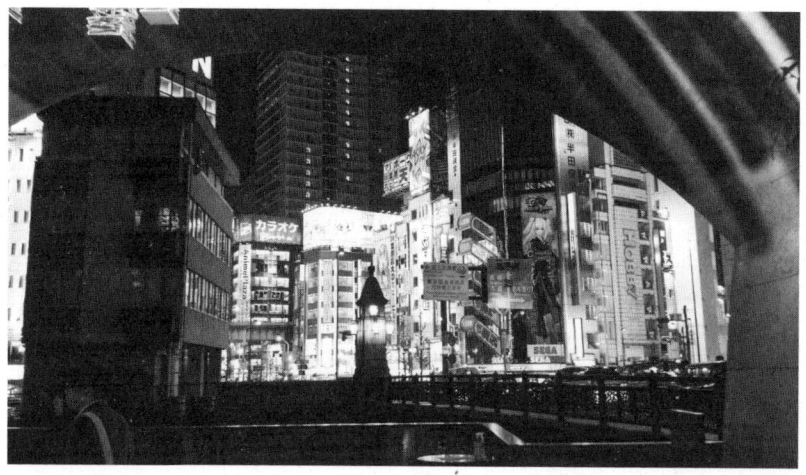

The girls have yet to arrive on "Maid Row" to hand out fliers for their increasingly famous maid cafes, and when they do, they'll be standing in front of the now-closed Akihabara Department Store, a former haven of cheap eats, which will soon (like much of the area) turn into yet another construction site.

Despite the best efforts of the government-affiliated Yokoso! Japan tourist campaign, which sought to promote an image of a vibrant and crackling Akihabara—the Liberal Democratic Party's Taro Aso, in a recent failed bid to become Japan's next prime minister, tried to tap into this idea by holding a campaign rally here—there's not a lot of excitement going on today.

Then Patrick W. Galbraith arrives at the station. He's dressed in a cosplay costume outfit, pretending to be Goku from the anime classic *Dragon Ball Z*. Clad in an orange karate uniform and a totally ridiculous spiky-haired blond wig, the 24-year-old Alaskan proves an irresistible sight to Japanese people just off the train. He's mobbed for pictures, posing with groups of girls, small children, and even tough-looking teenagers who engage in mock superpowered battles with him.

Galbraith, a student at Sophia University and an unashamed *otaku*, works part time for a multipurpose company called Akibanana that

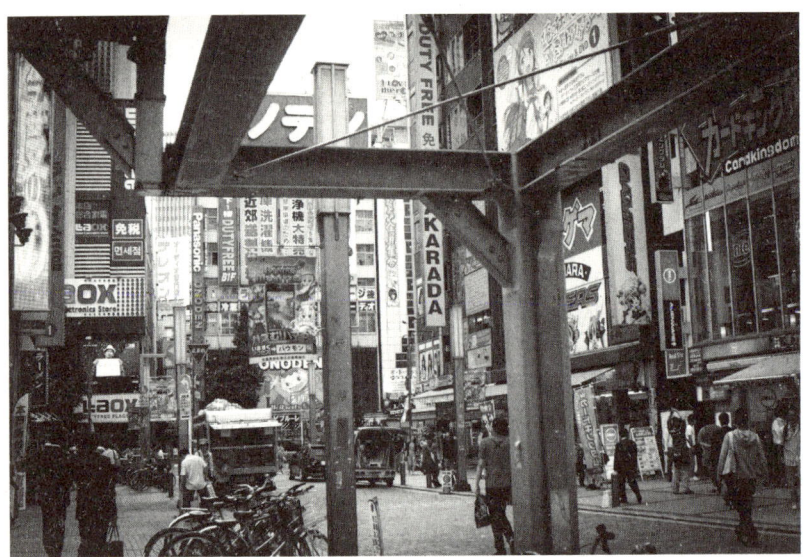

caters to the needs of every geek who wants to visit Japan. Today, he'll be a tour guide for a group of stylish employees from Paris Miki, makers of contact lenses and eyewear. The day before, the group studied traditional Japanese culture via temple visits and tea ceremonies. But now, this bemused assortment of German and French nationals will enter a maze of anime, manga, video games, and gadgets for the very first time, led by an American outrageously dressed like a manga superhero come to life.

"I feel in a way that I'm doing people a favor," Galbraith says of his choice of tour guide uniform. "They come out the station and think, 'Wow, this is a weird place,' and then they are really in the mood to enjoy Akihabara."

* * *

Akihabara was once a black-market locale for used electronics in the postwar era. In the years of economic miracle-building that followed, it became a haven for consumer electronics and home appliances. This is how it acquired the nickname "Electric Town." The area was further transformed by the PC boom of the 1990s, when otaku took over the neighborhood and built a striking, virtual living room writ large for themselves in the process, filling it up with their hobbies and objects of desire.

Throughout it all, Japanese mainstream society wrote off otaku as socially maladjusted misfits and deemed their hobbies an escape from reality. Funnily enough, though otaku hobbies were seen as a social deviance in Japan, these pursuits—anime, video games, monster movies, and underground Japanese culture—only continued to grow abroad. Now, it seems, by accident or design, all sorts of people are keen to enjoy Akihabara, to see otaku in their native environment, and to sip "Akiba Cola" in a maid cafe.

The big guys have been closing in ever since. The Yodobashi chain opened a massive Yodobashi Akiba superstore, offering electronics and otaku goods like robot model kits, Airsoft guns, and collectible toys at cutthroat prices that the smaller stores on the street couldn't hope to compete with.

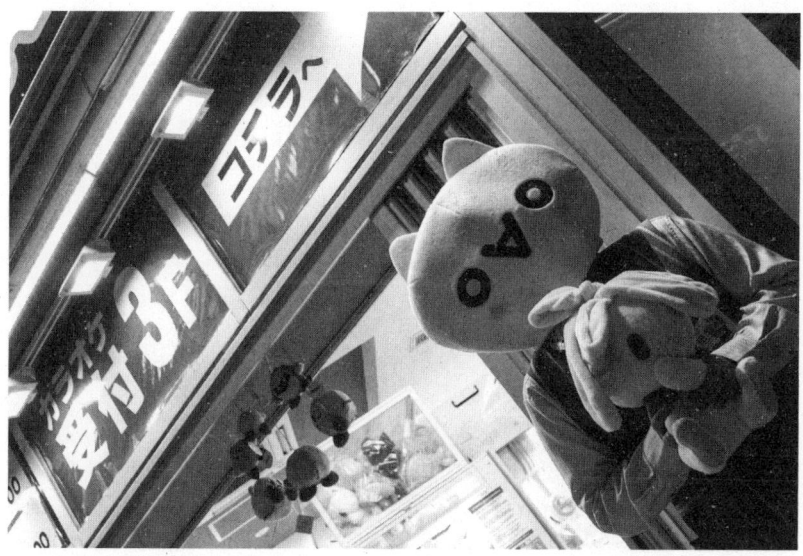

Then, communications giant NTT monopolized the area north of Akihabara Station with their Akihabara Cross Fields complex, which, according to their corporate spin, is a "global center for the IT Industry, providing office and conference space, convention halls and showrooms." A 2006 headline in the *Nikkei* weekly newspaper mapped out the future: "Otaku ceding domination of famous Electric

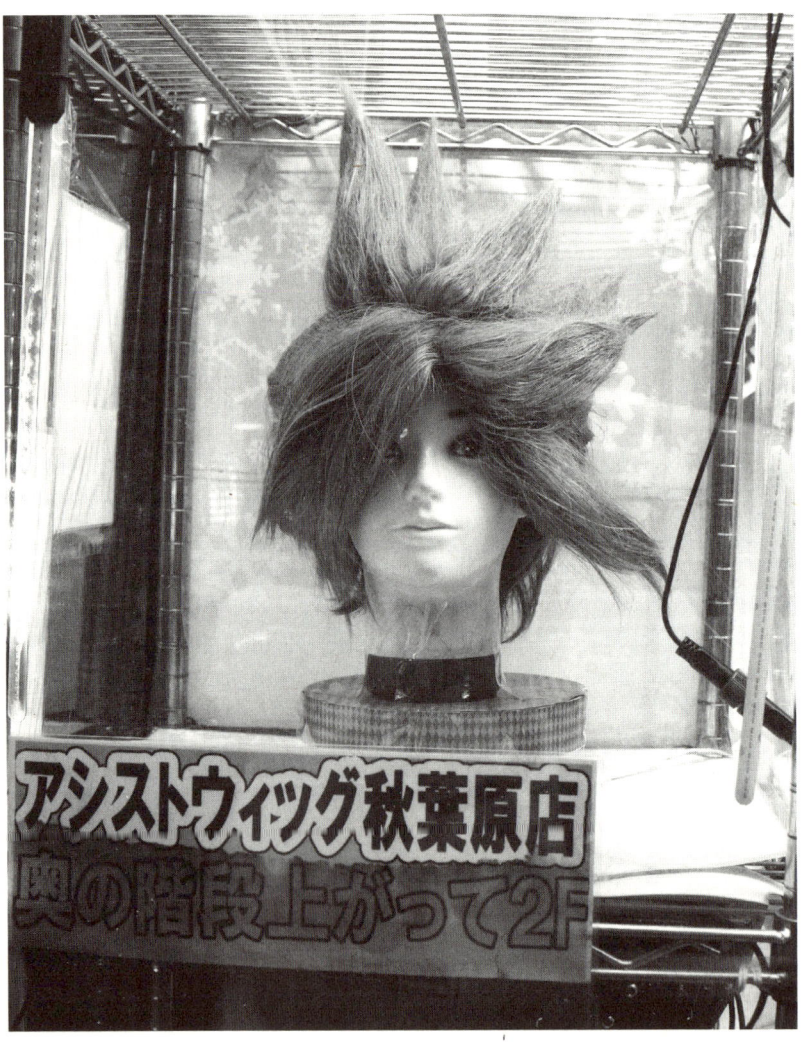

SCENES FROM THE OTAKU-VERSE

Town as development lures IT firms." While the paper was excited about the area's transformation into a massive "business center," Akihabara soon lost much of its local character and now resembles any other colorless metropolitan area (some recent store openings include a new Royal Host family restaurant, a Tully's Coffee, a McDonald's, and a Starbucks). The corporate-backed Akiba has even become downright hostile to the otaku who once called it home.

Patrick Galbraith leads his tour group to the Tokyo Anime Center, located inside the Akihabara Cross Fields center. Aside from a collection of vintage animation cells and statues of iconic characters like Astro Boy, there isn't much to see. Which is just as well, because the staff has told Galbraith that he's not allowed past the door.

"Apparently, being dressed like an anime character inside creates some kind of copyright problem," he explains.

Galbraith takes it all in stride, but I can't believe what I'm hearing. It's as if someone has twisted that old line from *Dr. Strangelove*: "Gentlemen, you can't pretend to be an anime character in here! This is the Anime Center!"

There is little relief on the streets outside. Akihabara in 2007 was rife with tales of the police bothering otaku for gathering in large groups. Otaku also used to be known for staging impromptu sang-ing-and-dancing mobs to cheer on the pop idol girls who sing in the neighborhood's underground theaters, but that's all been cracked down on and shut out. In short, The Man doesn't want otaku in Akihabara any longer, which seems a bit strange; after all, a featured article on the Japan National Tourist Organization website calls the area an "Otaku Mecca."

An organized backlash came on June 30, when the "Akihabara Liberation" protest was held. More than 400 otaku turned out for the police-escorted march, many of them dressed as anime and manga characters, others sporting the look of the classic Japanese student protester from the 1960s: hard hat, gauze mask, sunglasses, white gloves—and all of them voicing various complaints about the path Akihabara has taken.

In my dreams, a genuine counterculture movement would arise out of such sentiments, complete with radical manifestos, street fighting, and maids tossing Molotov cocktails.

But it isn't likely to happen. A surprising number of otaku are starting to simply avoid Akihabara in lieu of other options. One of my friends, a manga artist named Denki Watanabe, says, "Akiba is a little too noisy for me recently. I now go to Nakano instead." He's referring to Nakano Broadway, an indoor shopping mall, with nary a non-otaku chain store, full of vintage toys and anime goods. The catch is, unless you are a fan of such things or a rabid collector yourself, there really isn't much else to see and do. Still, Denki says, "It has the same decadent charm that Akiba used to have."

* * *

What Watanabe means is that Nakano Broadway has allowed the nerdy spirit of Japanese otaku to pursue whatever weird, maladjusted path it wants to, safe from the prying eyes of the straight world.

This is just as well, because not every aspect of otaku culture is ready for prime time.

Galbraith guides his foreign tourist brigade past the mouth of an inferno: a back alley where the deadly Aum Shinrikyo cult used to have an office. He briefly mentions that "We won't be going this way" before pointing out a row of vending machines selling canned *oden* (slowly simmered radish, hard-boiled eggs, and other ingredients) for the tourists to check out instead.

There's a good reason for this well-timed diversion. A few steps further down this alleyway, just across from the gleaming Cross Fields building, is the awful truth about Akihabara. If you peek

SCENES FROM THE OTAKU-VERSE

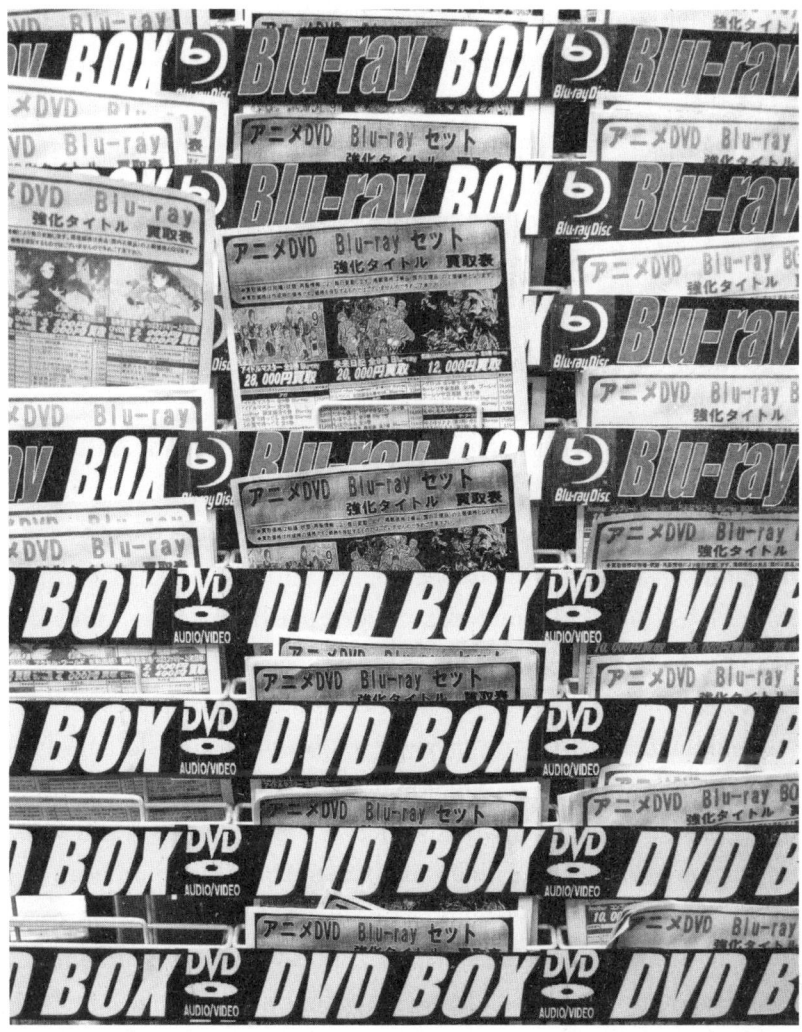

behind the curtain, the neighborhood is actually a hotbed of pornography (both animated and otherwise), adult toys, triple X-rated manga, and sleazy photo books of underaged girl idols that would burn a sane person's eyeballs right in their sockets.

How long can politicians, tourist organizations, and even the Ministry of Economy, Trade, and Industry (which is sponsoring the Akihabara Entamatsuri 2007 festival next month) afford to simply pretend that this stuff doesn't exist? And what will happen when they start paying attention? If they think that otaku hobbies are unpalatable now, wait until they get a load of some of the stuff on these shelves.

But even if Akihabara's "dark end of the street" is razed to the ground, the lonely otaku in search of virtual company will still have plenty of other options. After all, you can find similar hardcore material around just about any transportation hub in Tokyo—or even in the country's local convenience stores.

What will be harder to recapture is the spirit that made Akihabara buzz in the first place. Akihabara wasn't just about anime, manga, video games, and titillation. It was the side effect of collective fantasy and private desire that was desperate enough to find expression through technology, commerce, molded plastic, pixel, and drawing paper.

Some people want to police the limits of the human imagination, but otaku want to push the envelope. Otaku *need* to push that envelope, because they are looking for alternatives from the reality they inhabit and a world that would otherwise box them in. Their wild, unhinged, expansive imagination is the only escape route from the institutions that make life tough—finding a mate, getting a job, marriage, family, the day-to-day grind—things you are told are normal but that you often find are the most dysfunctional of all. Akihabara was a fragile and secluded place to explore their dreams in an otaku paradise.

Now, those dreams are threatened by a dull and dreary reality.

Akihabara and Nakano Broadway still remain top destinations for otaku from around the world, but old-school otaku maintain things changed for the worse around 2006–2007.

The Shokotan Tapes: An Interview with Shoko Nakagawa

June 2008

Although she's a manga artist and a fashion model with a quartet of photo books to her name, Japanese celebrity Shoko Nakagawa aka Shokotan is most often positioned as a pop singer.

But what truly defines her is her willingness to embrace and share with the public her love for a wide gamut of geeky hobbies. It's impossible to imagine another female star of Nakagawa's stature who would say, "I like stuff like anime, comics, blogging, cosplay, and drawing manga. After I get home, I sit in front of the computer for five or six hours straight. I play video games and enjoy anime until the early morning."

Having seen fan culture from both sides, as spectator and spectacle, she has a unique take on the otaku world, starting with:

How do you personally define the word "otaku?"
Shoko Nakagawa: The word otaku can cover so much territory. There are many different types of otaku, including people who love anime,

manga, trains, or idol singers. It's hard to reduce it all to just one word. It's so wide . . . Even though I can call myself an otaku, some people might actually say that I'm not extreme or obsessive enough to be an otaku. Sometimes I wonder what divides the line between otaku and not-otaku. The only thing I can say about otaku for sure is that they are people who live with a greedy passion for something.

What about the words "fan" and "maniac"? You hear these words a lot in place of the word "otaku" in Japan.
"Fan" is a little lighter than "otaku." But "maniac" seems even more hardcore than "otaku."

It seems like the number of female otaku have really increased over the last few years, both in Japan and the United States.
I feel like the Internet has something to do with that. Just speaking from my own experience, before I even acknowledged myself as an otaku, I didn't have any female friends that I could share my

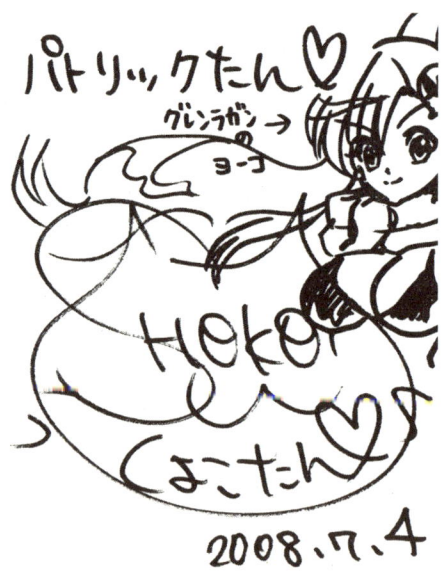

SCENES FROM THE OTAKU-VERSE

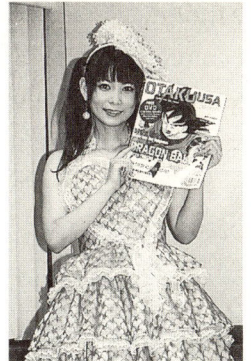 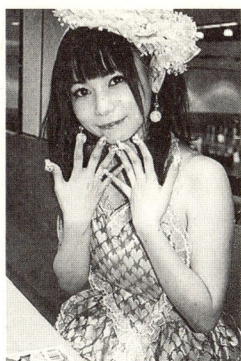

interests with. But eventually, using the PC, I was able to find other girls who had the same interests as me. Maybe there were always female otaku out there, but they only began to become visible on the Internet. Some female members of my fan club are coming to my concert tomorrow, and about half of them are dressing up in cosplay. I'm really happy to have female fans.

Don't you think that you might have had some sort of impact on the number of female otaku out there?
No, I'm just one of them. Although, to be honest, I do get many letters that begin "Because of you, I was able to . . ." and I feel really happy to hear that. After I came out and said that I was an otaku, my life became more enjoyable. I can't live without my hobby; it's the source of my energy. I feel like we are living in a time where girls can be proud to be otaku.

Do you think that recent events in Akihabara will have any significant impact on otaku culture? *(On June 8, 2008, seven people died and ten others were injured after a man hit pedestrians with a truck and then stabbed people in the neighborhood)*
What happened in Akiba was a very sad incident. If a criminal is found to be a fan of a particular anime or otaku hobby, then people

will bash that anime or hobby. But the crime is the person's responsibility, not the otaku world. Otaku culture is not evil. The person's behavior was evil. People may be afraid to come to Akihabara right now, but I think that the otaku love for their hobby won't change. The industry is only growing stronger. I think and hope that this event will not have much influence on the otaku world.

The World's Oldest Living Otaku: 25 Years of Fred Patten

August 2010

I've spent a lot of time staring at the cover of Fred Patten's 2004 book *Watching Anime, Reading Manga: 25 Years of Essays and Reviews* ... and it sometimes feels like it stares back.

On the cover is an illustration of an old man (a stand-in for Fred himself) seated in a La-Z-Boy reclining chair, surrounded by towering piles of books and magazines. There's lots of junk on the floor: robot toys, laser discs, and video cassette boxes. The disheveled figure is focused on a TV set planted directly in front of him. On the screen is the serene face of a female anime character, seemingly beaming in from another, more colorful world. The overall vibe is dusty, dingy, *too real*. For anyone who has spent a lot of time watching and writing about media, it seems like a glimpse of an all too probable future: isolated, surrounded by tapes and comics, kept alive (barely) by soft drinks and instant ramen. I am going to guess that the cover is no joke. This is likely an accurate depiction of how anime historian Fred Patten really rolled.

MONDO TOKYO

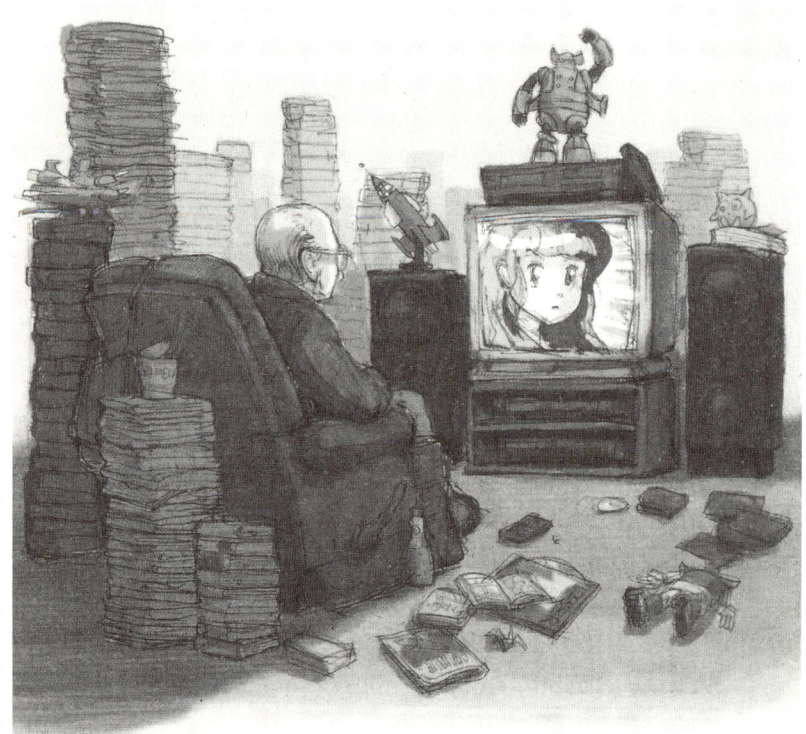

WATCHING ANIME, READING MANGA
25 Years of Essays and Reviews

Fred Patten
Foreword by Carl Macek

Fred was passionate about many things; anime was only one of his niche interests. He had roots going back to the very dawn of comic and sci-fi conventions in the US. You can find pictures of Fred, young, strapping, and dressed as the Golden Age Flash at the 1962 World Science Fiction Convention in Chicago. It was hard to reconcile that image with the Fred you might run across decades later at a more recent Anime Expo. At these events, filled with much younger fans, Fred definitely seemed like what he was: a retired librarian of technical documents who spoke in an emotionless "just the facts" style of patter. He was also a "furry"—part of the fetish subculture whose members enjoy imagining themselves as anthropomorphic animals. He'd been a writer, editor, and event organizer in the furry scene since it first got started in the 1970s. In other words, Fred seemed to be the living embodiment of pre-Internet geek culture when "fandom" was nearly invisible, very strange, and anything but cool.

I once interviewed Fred—before he retired from the writing game—for my 2006 book *Otaku in USA*. After reading the piece, my Japanese editor decided to bill Fred as "The World's Oldest Living Otaku." And why not? After all, Fred Patten had been active in anime fan culture since the early 1960s, even before many Japanese otaku had been born!

By day, Fred was a librarian at the Hughes Aircraft Company's Technical Document Center, a gig that lasted until the end of the Cold War in 1990. But in his off-hours, he wrote about comics and animation for a handful of 'zines. Leafing through his nearly 400-page book, which spans from 1979 to 2004, it seemed that 1980 was a big year for Fred Patten, a pioneering anime journalist. February 1980 marked his debut as professional writer after years of toil in the amateur press. Issue 4 of *Fangoria* (yup, the horror movie magazine) contained Fred's article "Dawn of the Warrior Robots: The Beginning of a New Breed of Action Hero!" which introduced US readers to the likes of Mazinger Z, Getter Robo, and other Super Robots of the era.

Fred's early efforts at promoting anime to overseas audiences did not go unnoticed in Japan. From 1978 to 1981, he was tapped by Toei Doga and Tokyo Movie Shinsha to help test-market their productions at American sci-fi and comic book conventions. And not all the feedback was positive. Fred told me: "One convention in the early 1980s listed the anime room in its program book as 'the Fred Patten conspiracy to make you watch cartoons in a language you can't understand.'"

But Fred had some pretty major conspirators in his corner, starting with the "God of Manga" himself, Osamu Tezuka. After briefly meeting each other in 1977, Tezuka would come to rely on Fred and the small circle of fans that he belonged to (the LA branch of the Cartoon/Fantasy Organization aka the C/FO) to show him around the SoCal area and to supply him with information about the burgeoning popularity of anime and manga outside of Japan. Says Patten in his book, "(Tezuka) was bewildered but flattered that so many Americans, who did not understand the Japanese language, had taken the trouble to figure out the plots of his manga from the pictures alone."

The editors at *Variety* magazine, America's showbiz bible, had a sense that Japanese cartoons could have foreign appeal. They didn't know about Fred and the small groups of foreign fans who were already promoting and spreading the gospel of Japanese animation around the globe, but they noted anime's growing mainstream success in Japan—"the animation industry is well over a trade volume of $500,000,00"—and they could see the opportunity for international investment and distribution.

Variety peered into its crystal ball and estimated that Japanese animation might someday become a "$1-billion entertainment activity." They even anticipated that a "breakthrough" of some kind

SCENES FROM THE OTAKU-VERSE

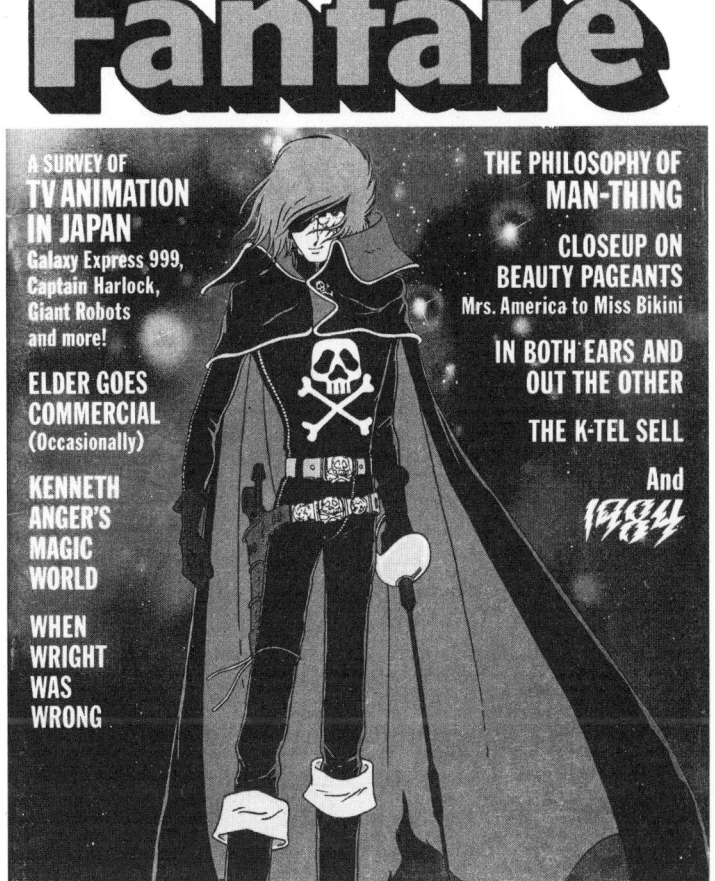

Fanfare magazine from 1980 featuring Fred Patten's writing on anime inside.

"might materialize in the U.S. through co-production agreements or direct acquisitions." This report probably gave some incentive to any number of guys in Hollywood to buy a ticket to Japan to see if they could get a piece of the action.

Fred was already on the case and trying to make *Variety*'s breakthrough happen. On the strength of Fred's tireless efforts, the great manga god Tezuka "convinced numerous Japanese cartoonists such as Go Nagai, Monkey Punch, and Yumiko Igarashi that they ought to come to the 1980 San Diego Comic Con to see for themselves that they had so many fans."

Fred and his buddy Robin Leyden were asked to act as liaisons to 30 visiting Japanese guests in all. And as Tezuka's 1980 film *Phoenix 2772* screened to a rapturous response at Comic Con, it seemed to some a breakthrough between the Japanese anime industry and American audiences could—or should—soon follow suit. But as Fred writes: "contact between American fans and the Japanese animation industry faded after 1981 when it failed to lead to any significant commercial results."

What happened? Was *Variety* wrong about anime's foreign potential? Did Fred's energy go to waste? The breakthrough *would* happen . . . it would just happen many years later. Time would eventually validate all that Fred had worked so hard for: *Demon Slayer: The Infinity Train*, an anime fantasy epic, was the highest-grossing movie worldwide in 2020. In the early 1980s, however, Japanese creators like Tezuka and American fans like Fred had to play the waiting game.

Fred would become a player behind the scenes at US distributor Streamline Pictures, helping to bring the likes of Hayao Miyazaki's *The Castle of Cagliostro* and *Golgo 13: The Professional* to our shores. He would also continue to write about anime and manga for a number of publications.

In *Watching Anime, Reading Manga: 25 Years of Essays and Reviews*, Fred looks back on the class of 1980 and notes that "fans were performing an important cultural service by helping to introduce Japanese animation to Americans" and that this would have "a significant effect" on popular culture. Someone reading his words in 2004, when the book was released, might think he was being hyperbolic or overstating his case. But today, as anime only gets bigger and bigger, we know that he was right. Sometimes, all you need is a ragged room full of DVDs, robot toys, and a reclining chair to see the future.

Fred Patten died in 2018 at the age of 77. Before his death, he donated 900 boxes of "fliers, posters, programs, progress reports, press clippings, audio/video recordings, toys, clothing, and other material" to the library collection at UC Riverside in California. I want to jump in those boxes someday and see what treasures are inside.

The Death of a Producer: Arrivederci, Yoshinobu Nishizaki

November 2010

"Galaxies collide! An empire crumbles! An entire planet is flooded!"

Sunday, I woke up to read the news that *Space Battleship Yamato* producer and cocreator Yoshinobu Nishizaki—a towering figure in the anime industry if ever there was one—had fallen into the sea from his new boat (a research vessel named *Yamato*) and drowned. He was 75 years old.

Nishizaki's death occurred in the middle of a full-blown *Space Battleship Yamato* revival in Japan. *Yamato* had always been big, of course; in Japan, the success of the *Space Battleship Yamato* TV series and the movies that followed changed the anime industry, the music industry, heck, even the entertainment industry. It's no exaggeration to say that *Yamato* was to Japan what *Star Wars* was to the Western world: a massive sci-fi epic that defined the era's pop culture. When *Yamato* was distributed abroad under the title *Star Blazers*, it changed many lives—including my own. But *Yamato* was

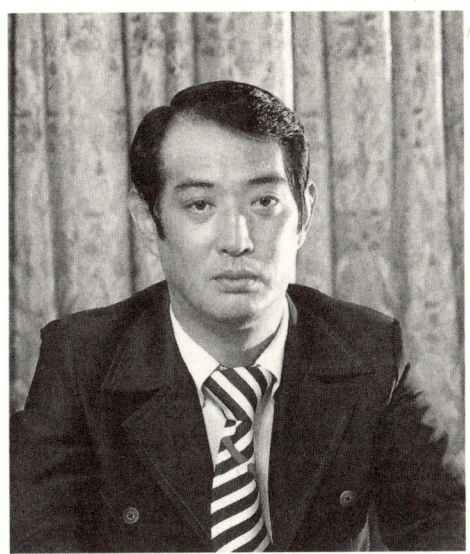

Yoshinobu Nishizaki, aka "The Nish."

now suddenly bigger than ever, spurred on by the release of a new live-action film.

The bad news came close on the heels of another major blow to the anime world. Summer 2010 ended with the sudden and unexpected death of celebrated director Satoshi Kon (director of *Perfect Blue* and *Paprika*). Admittedly, things were different this time. Kon was only 47 years old. Perhaps his greatest works were still ahead of him. Nishizaki, however, had already made his impact.

But who was the man who had shepherded *Yamato* since its origins in the 1970s? The old books I had collected over the years revealed two sides. Pictures of Nishizaki (and there were always pictures of Nishizaki) showed either a severe unsmiling businessman—the sort of guy you would not want to work for—or a grinning benevolent Walt Disney-like figure, shaking hands with legions of young *Yamato* fans at movie premieres.

No matter how one wanted to think of him, Nishizaki's legacy came with lots of baggage. As the news of Nishizaki's death spread throughout the internet, all the rumors and old war stories came back to light.

There was mention of the "Nishizaki Incident" in which he crafted a contract that denied manga god Osamu Tezuka any income from several anime he had created. It was a cutthroat move that effectively destroyed Tezuka's studio, Mushi Productions. Nishizaki had also been sued by manga artist Leiji Matsumoto over the copyrights to *Yamato*.

Most notoriously, Nishizaki had recently spent years in jail on drug and gun charges.

Nishizaki's questionable past meant that fans were quick to jump to conspiracy theories about his death. The elderly Nishizaki had been seen in a wheelchair of late, so why would he suddenly take up swimming? Why did it take a full 20 minutes for a rescue team to reach him after he plunged over the side of his boat? His assets included the rights to a massive entertainment franchise that had now made the leap to a live-action film. Could it be that somebody thought he was worth more dead than alive?

Even in death, Nishizaki was creating controversy and making headlines. It was a fitting end for a master showman. Nishizaki was an independent outside the studio system, and he had a vision that Japanese animation—which up to that point was only made for television or marketed in kiddie matinees—could be a huge theatrical event. He created gimmicks for every *Yamato* movie release, much like William Castle did back in the 1950s; unlike Castle's cheesy gimmicks (such as his Percepto electrified movie seats), Nishizaki's were always state-of-the-art. The Yamato films, which dominated the Japanese box office from the late 1970s to the early 1980s, had six channel surround sound, widescreen aspect ratios that suddenly changed in the middle of the movie and multiple endings. It's the kind of stuff we might take for granted today, but back then, it was downright revolutionary.

As Gainax studio founder and former Otaking ("King of the Otaku") Toshio Okada points out in his new tell-all book, Nishizaki had studied and modeled his persona on the moguls of old school Hollywood. With epic movies came a lot of bad habits: substance abuse, greed, abuse of power, womanizing, and shady business deals.

Okada likens Nishizaki to a dinosaur, the last of his kind; someone who was out of step with the way that the entertainment world—and anime industry—was headed. God-like producers would be increasingly eclipsed by superstar directors and creator-run studios like Gainax and Ghibli.

Although his subsequent anime productions, such as *Blue Noah* (1979) and *Odin* (1986) were destined to fail and become jokes, Nishizaki would insist on playing the role of the big shot tycoon to the hilt. But for every failure, when Nishizaki's ideas did manage to connect with an entire country's imagination, the result was... well, YAMATO.

And although it was the work of many hands, Nishizaki was to the *Yamato* franchise what Gene Roddenberry was to *Star Trek* or

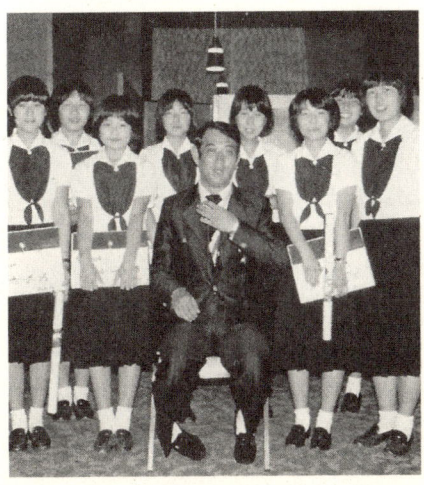

George Lucas to *Star Wars*. The cultural phenomenon couldn't have happened without him ... or without us demanding more.

With Nishizaki's strange and oddly timed passing, a great age passed on as well. *Space Battleship Yamato* is fated to live on, but I don't think it will ever be the same.

The original Yamato anime series began the remake process starting in 2013 with Space Battleship Yamato 2199. *Some fans swear by them, but I can't say a Yamato saga without Nishizaki has done much for me.*

The Wild Frontier

January 2011

There's a million different ways to get your kicks in Tokyo. Alas, many of them are certain to drain your wallet dry, especially now that the US dollar is worth about as much as Monopoly money (maybe even less by the time you read this).

So here's a tip: go low-budget. Get as far away from the crowded, trend-driven parts of town as you can. Pass up Shibuya, Harajuku, Roppongi, and the rest of them and head north to Akabane.

A humble place in Kita-ku—gateway to suburban Saitama—Akabane is regarded by some snobbish locals as being a flat-out slum. Compared to an actual slum in the United States, though, it starts to look positively utopian. The low cost of living means that fun there comes cheap, especially when it comes to playing with GUNS!

Well, Airsoft guns, not real ones—but hey, Japan has to keep that crime and murder rate low somehow.

Located near Akabane JR station, Frontier is an Airsoft gun range where anyone can pop in, grab a firearm off the rack, and happily blast away at a variety of targets at the rock-bottom price of JPY 200

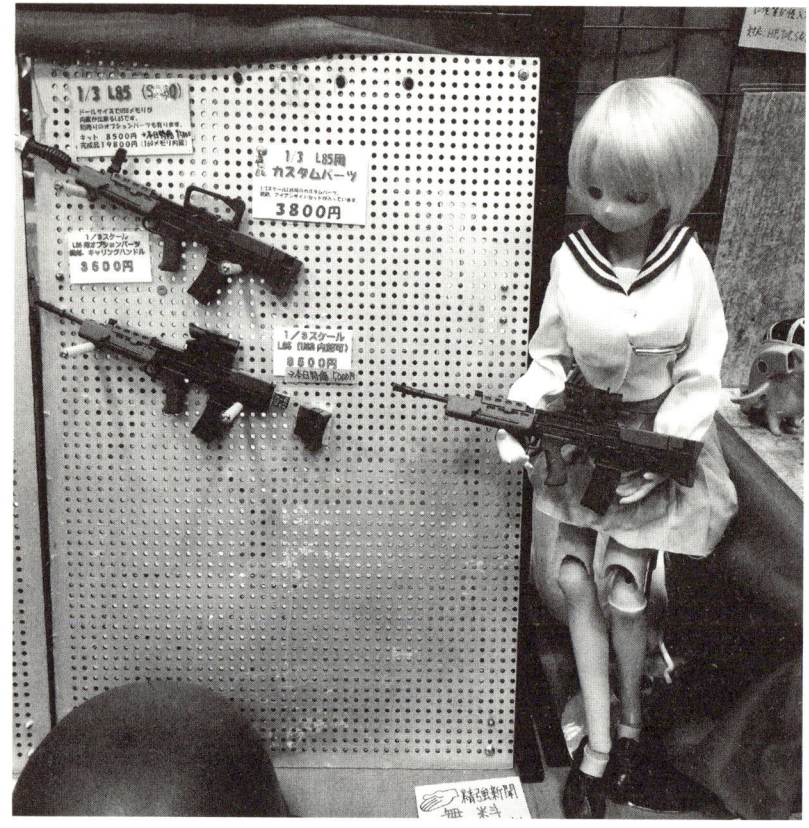

for 30 minutes of adrenal gland-bursting action. That's about USD 2.50 at today's exchange rates.

The lack of accessibility to actual firearms has helped to create a species of fake gun aficionados in Japan, who covet and collect replicas that look and feel as much like the real thing as possible. Akabane must be full of such folks, because this shooting range is only part of the Frontier empire in Akabane. There's a nearby Frontier hobby shop which stocks basic goods that every growing boy needs, like Gundam robot model kits and Tamiya model paints. Then there's Frontier Gun Gun, which specializes in selling new and used replica weaponry and military surplus clothing.

SCENES FROM THE OTAKU-VERSE

The two-story Frontier shooting range facility opened in July 2010, so everything inside looks and feels new. Fluorescent lighting and white stucco walls give off a general sense of an office building taken over by gun-crazy nuts. You'll always find a textbook military otaku guy sipping a Coke behind a desk while surrounded by imitation implements of death and destruction. He's your new best friend as you choose your poison: assault rifle, automatic handgun, sniper rifle—even shotguns!

Most of what I know about modern warfare comes from (you guessed it) the *Call of Duty: Modern Warfare* video game. Which is probably why I reached for two old standards to rent on the range: the Glock 19 handgun and the M4 automatic rifle. The helpful guy on staff showed me everything I needed to know about inserting little plastic BBs and what to do if the guns jammed, and then he left me alone to vent my frustrations. Heavy blue drapes kept the outside world from ever knowing what a crack shot I am when it comes to Frontier's myriad of targets. They range from the standard bull's eye to a set of metal plates that make pleasingly loud DING noises when struck. The mood was kept jovial throughout by decorations on the wall, which included a "combat target" of a dirty crook pointin' his gun at you and a poster advertising the recent *A-Team* movie.

* * *

But why?

Try as you might, it is impossible to ignore military otaku in Japan. Go to a neighborhood hobby shop in Tokyo, and right next to the Pokémon cards, Ultraman figures, and robot model kits, you'll find racks of Scarface-ready Airsoft assault rifles and shotguns. Go to a Godzilla film festival, and guys in camouflage and army boots will inevitably be sitting next to you crunching on popcorn. And, of course, such folk can regularly be found at seasonal events like Comic Market and Wonder Fest, sometimes clad in *verboten* Imperial Army or Nazi regalia.

It seems that military worship and gun fetishization are just part of the menu in otaku hot spots, adjacent to the anime goods, maid cafes, and other tourist-happy markers of Cool Japan. I asked my friend Slasher for some insights into how this came to be, and he passed my questions along to Toshi Tada and Taryan Takahashi, a pair of contributors from *Movie Treasures* magazine. Here's what they came up with.

What is the stereotypical image of a military otaku in Japan? For example, if a military otaku type was going to be parodied on *South Park*, what would his character be like?
Broadly speaking, there are two types of military otaku in Japan. First, there are Airsoft gun lovers. Then there are the traditional

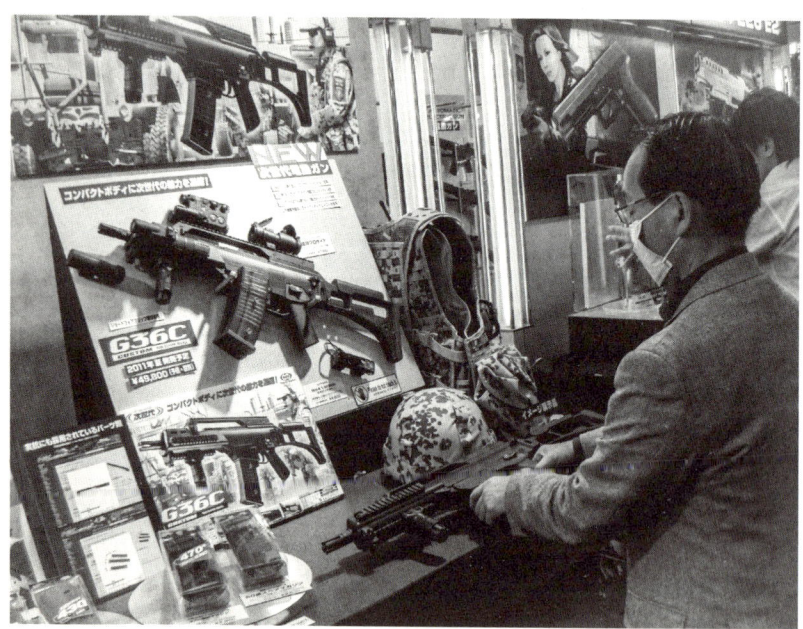

Military otaku at the Japan Hobby Show, 2022.

military otaku types, who tend to be a bit older. They are all driven by a thirst for knowledge and data. The older ones are interested in history while the younger types tend to be attracted by military things in anime and games. If a Japanese military otaku were to be parodied on *South Park*, it would probably be a crazy guy who covers himself up in a military-type uniform and plays Airsoft games in the woods.

To some foreigners, Japanese military otaku might look like a right-wing militia. Are they political animals or is this just a form of cosplay?
There are two different kinds. The military otaku you might find at Comiket tend to be on the liberal side, but the socially withdrawn *hikikomori* types (withdrawn shut-ins who never leave their apartment) tend to have right-wing beliefs. Although there are many layers in-between, it's not likely that any of these guys would actually arm themselves to fight an "invading army," so there's not really a militia kind of thinking involved.

Japanese people can't own real guns, although they can buy super-realistic replicas. Is that one of the main reasons why Japan has such a pronounced military otaku culture?
Probably, although most of them are content with alternatives such as model guns and Airsoft weapons and don't really want to own real weapons. Japan hasn't fought a war for 70 years and most people lack the passion for fighting. (Although there have been some cases where people have modified their model guns to function like real guns. It hasn't happened in a few decades, though.)

In many countries, if you are the sort of person who loves guns and military culture, it's possible to become a cop, join the army, or become a security guard and get a real weapon that way. Is this something military otaku in Japan sometimes do?

The rules for police to handle weapons in Japan are extremely strict and not something to aspire to. For example, if you are a cop in Japan who draws your gun in the line of duty, then that's going to be extremely problematic. Meanwhile, the Japan Self-Defense Forces' biggest job is NOT TO fight. So, it is unlikely that a military otaku would become a cop or join the JSDF in order to shoot a real gun.

I'm always surprised at how much crossover there is between anime otaku and military otaku in Japan. Does otaku culture itself help to create military otaku?
It depends on what generation they belong to. Japanese anime used to have a lot of war stories like *Space Battleship Yamato*, *Gundam*, and all those anime that followed. I suspect that Japanese World War II trauma was dramatically reduced during the late 1960s to the early 1970s, and that war related fiction finally came to be accepted as a form of entertainment. This led to a fever for military plastic model kits and stuff like that. War is now completely normalized in anime, and it isn't unusual to see an anime scene with even underage girls in a war setting, shooting guns and driving tanks. So yeah, there must be some sort of connection between these cultures.

Is there a social stigma to being a military otaku in Japan? Will the neighbors think you are weird if you go around the block in military camo?
In general, Japanese cops are trained to suspect people in camouflage, along with beards and backpacks, so you are likely to be stopped by the police if you wear military gear. However, casual clothing from Uniqlo and other brands offer "light" military fashion, and it is OK to wear them as long as it's not excessive, and you won't be stigmatized. (Akihabara is known as the worst place to walk around in military gear because of the 2008 massacre there.)

SCENES FROM THE OTAKU-VERSE

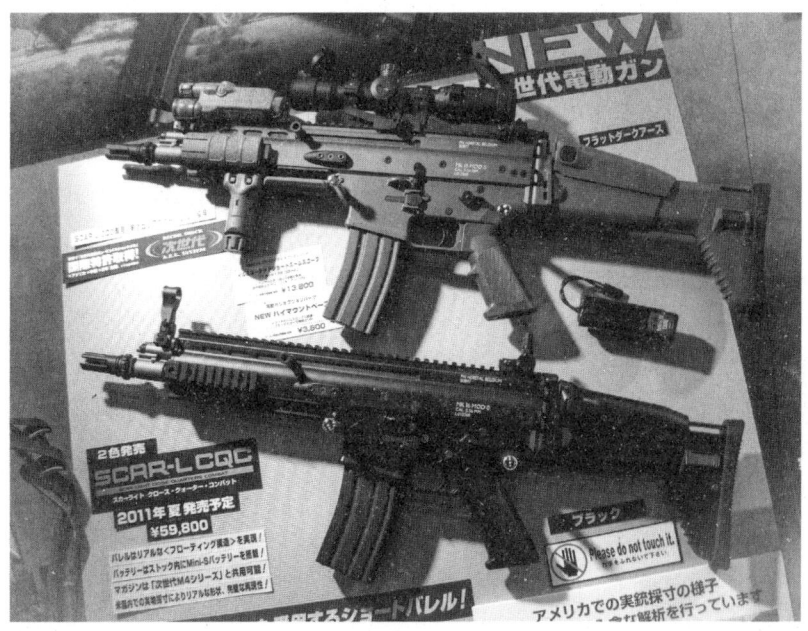

Foreigners get freaked out (and rightfully so) when they see Japanese people wearing Nazi costumes, even if it's clearly just a costume. How do the Nazis fit into military otaku culture?
Basically, otaku who dress in Nazi cosplay don't actually sympathize with Nazi philosophy and beliefs. From their perspective, they simply like the Nazi aesthetic for its style of "efficiency over quantity." Also, even though they know what the Nazis did and what they represent, the attitude is "It happened far away in Europe a long time ago," so they don't take it seriously or consider the implications. This mentality has roots in the position that some Japanese people took after World War II; they considered themselves victims and wanted to stop thinking that they were "the bad guys" or that there was anything to apologize for.

* * *

Bring your own gear, and that's all you'll ever need spend beyond the JPY 200 cover. The store can also hook you up with additional kit to transform you into a budget commando, including gun rentals, ammunition, and the ever-present cans of compressed air. Total cost at Frontier for two people to enjoy an hour of target practice: JPY 1500 (about USD 18.00, cheaper than a movie ticket for one person in Japan). Now *that's* entertainment!

A Bonkura Life

November 2011

What does it mean to be "bonkura"?

Since the word has its roots in Japanese gambling circles as a term for "a guy who can't make money," let's say that *bonkura* is analogous to "loser" in English. The bonkura guy is an otaku subspecies that you'll find roaming through the alleys, bars, and record shops of urban Japan.

He has a specific look: a T-shirt, probably a black one, with either a band logo or a cult movie character on it (there's even a fashion label called BON-KURA that sells these); blue jeans; sneakers. He daydreams about double cheeseburgers and greasy pizza pies.

You can be successful, drop the uniform, and still be deeply bonkura. Kevin Smith is probably one. Quentin Tarantino is definitely another. Unlike most otaku nerds, bonkura guys are not anti-social. They will seek out and bond with others who share the same wild enthusiasm for trash culture that they do. A bonkura is not a hipster and doesn't care much about being cool or showing off. All they want out of life is raw stimulation and to satisfy the unsophisticated desires of the eternal teenage boy within.

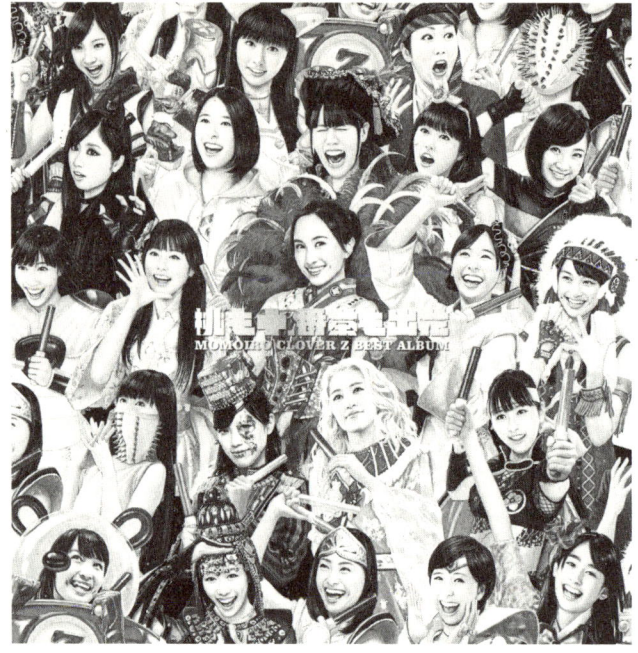

Momoiro Clover Z CD cover.

By the same token, a bonkura guy will always suspect on some fundamental level that he is a loser. Despite his impressive comic or movie collection, maybe he's bad with women, lacks a proper education, doesn't have any discernible skills, or just can't get ahead in the big crazy world. And like the song "Loser" by Beck, he can then take a kind of masochistic perverse pride in being called bonkura by others or undermine outside judgment altogether by calling himself a loser before anyone else can.

As with many Japanese subcultures, you can find a rallying point for bonkura on the magazine racks. Debuting in 1999, *Eiga Hiho* (*Movie Treasures*) became the monthly publication for Japanese bonkura guys (I am unaware of any bonkura women; as in the gambling dens of old, they aren't really allowed inside the clubhouse... probably because the specter of a nagging mom or

SCENES FROM THE OTAKU-VERSE

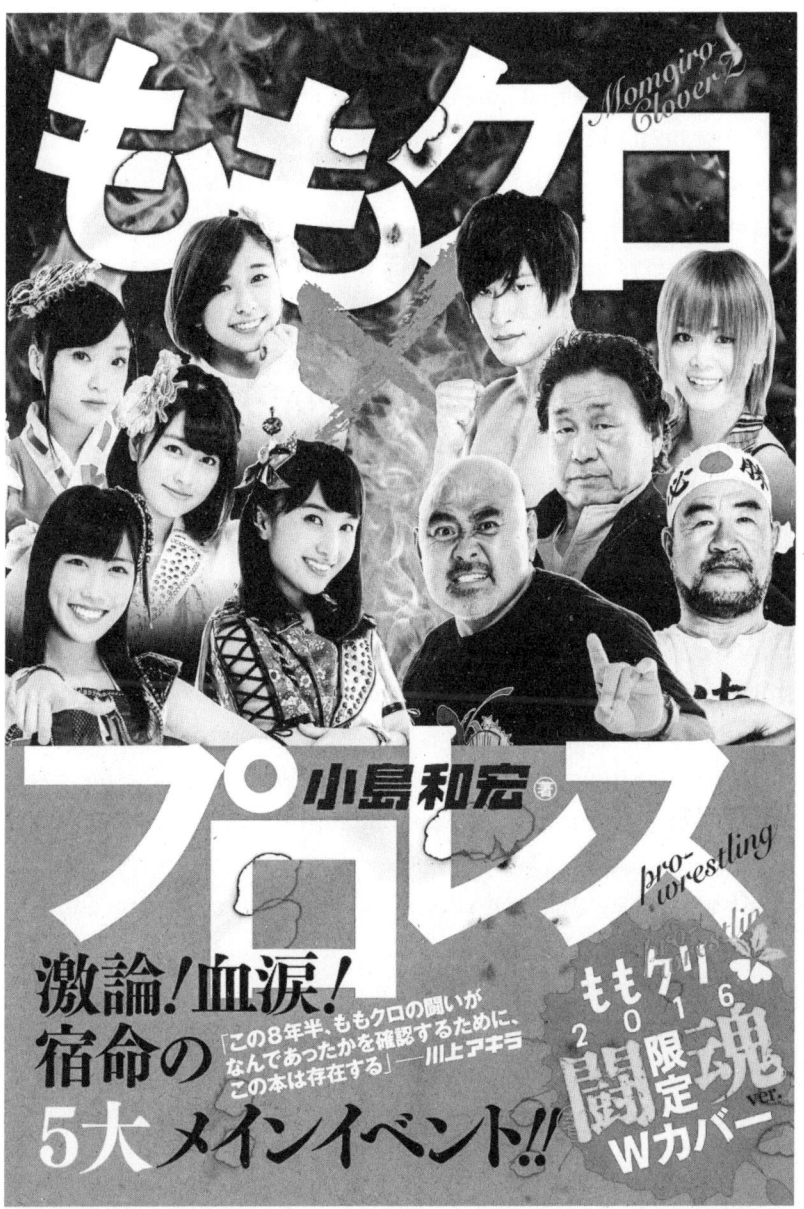

Poster for a Momoiro Clover Z x Pro-Wrestling event, 2016.

annoying sister looms large). Look inside an issue of *Eiga Hiho* and you'll find a litany of classical bonkura iconography: monster movies, action figures, karate killers, spaceships, explosions, splatter, rock and roll, guns, hot chicks, violent video games.

Some bonkura guys are fans of a Japanese pop idol group called Momoiro Clover Z. The group's entire presentation style is founded on two key bonkura genres: pro wrestling and TV superheroes of the Power Rangers variety. Now, here's the thing: Japanese pop groups are usually all about making their fans happy. Momoiro Clover Z does things a little differently.

In August 2011, Momoiro Clover Z gave a concert at the Yomiuri Land amusement park in Tokyo, home of countless superhero stage shows for little kids. Pop groups like Momoiro Clover Z, in which all the members are teenaged girls, tend to attract adult male fans (*okina tomodachi* or "big friends"), and they've shown up in force. A bunch of them are bonkura guys, and they've donned bright, color-coordinated clothing in the style of Momoiro Clover Z's singing heroines. Bonkura guys aren't above debasing themselves in name of the things they love.

But before the music starts, a giant evil panda takes to the stage, escorted by evil minions. The panda taunts the audience: "Who are you no-good adults? Why are you wearing such colorful T-shirts? Don't you know that real adults are supposed to wear black and white? And what about work? Don't tell me you took the day off to come here!"

Of course, Momoiro Clover Z soon comes to the rescue, and the girls defeat this alarming figure before starting to sing and dance. However, they cheerfully admit that all is not right with their audience: "It's okay to be an adult who is a little strange . . ."

Some kind of implicit rule between spectator and spectacle has been broken. But Momoiro Clover Z's act both affirms the bonkura's cherished outsider status and calls them out on it. It's an important part of the bonkura ritual: call yourself a hero even as you call yourself a loser.

As for me, I get where bonkura are coming from. My own collection of faded monster movie T-shirts can attest to that. So, I say: it's okay to be an adult who is a little strange.

The Best Otaku Shops in Tokyo

February 2012

Japan is a paradise for otaku obsessives, but where do they go to buy their collectible goods and other assorted treasures? There are countless otaku shops all over the country, and many of the best are in Tokyo, where Japan's otaku elite gather to buy and trade monster toys, games, old records, and other otaku paraphernalia.

These are the otaku haunts to check out if you want to get a glimpse of the otaku lifestyle and maybe even pick up a few treasures of your own.

Commit

Before digital animation took over, Japanese anime was made the old-fashioned way: using paint on sheets of celluloid to create "cels." Over the years, countless cels leaked out of the anime studios into the collector's market, and thousands of them can now be found at this store within the Nakano Broadway shopping mall. The walls are lined with binders bulging with one-of-a-kind cels, and smaller bins are outside for casual browsing. Bad news: cels featuring popular

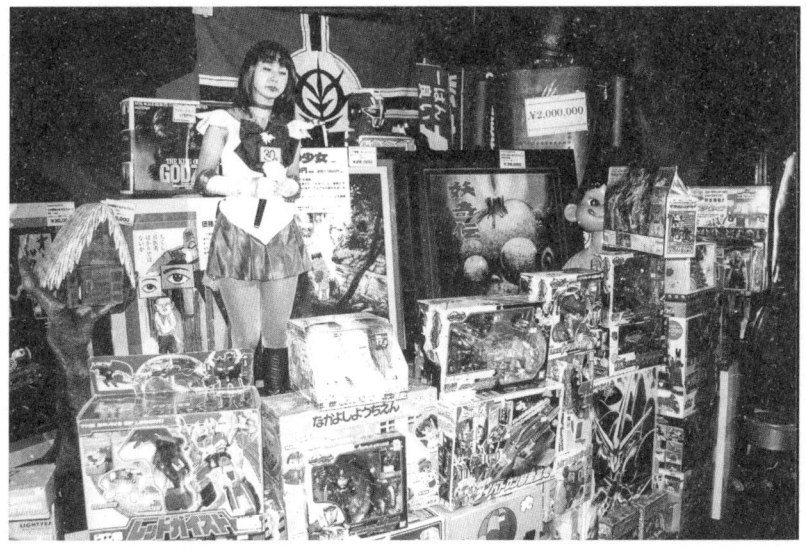

Mandarake, Shibuya, Tokyo, 2002.

characters, such as those from Hayao Miyazaki's anime movies or the *Evangelion* series, often go for art gallery prices. Good news: equally striking cels, from less high-profile works, can be had for the price of a fast food meal.

Gachapon Kaikan

Japan's gachapon prize vending machines (the name comes from the sound that the vending machine makes: "gacha" when a dial is cranked and "pon" when the prize drops) dole out brilliantly detailed toys and figures ranging from anime and manga characters to animals and tiny bowls of replica ramen. Gachapon machines are found all over Japan, but the motherlode is at Akihabara's Gachapon Kaikan, where more than 450 machines fill a warehouse-like space. Blaring rock and J-pop heightens the confusion. It's like playing the slots at a rundown otaku casino, but at JPY 100–JPY 500 a pop (around USD 1–5), you can afford to lose a bit until you score the prize that you really want.

Mandarake

Created by a CEO who said that his "mission is to take over the world using manga and otaku things," Mandarake is Japan's number one chain of secondhand anime and manga superstores. Locations can be found throughout the country, but the 16 original stores, each specializing in a different otaku obsession, are inside the Nakano Broadway shopping mall and are still the best. Over a million items line the shelves, and some 45,000 manga titles, anime DVDs and toys are bought and sold each week. Be sure to check out the surreal spectacle of the buy/sell counter, where otaku line up to trade in treasures for cash, only to go right back into Mandarake's black-lined corridors to reinvest.

Gojira-ya

Meaning Godzilla Store, this humble shop showcases vintage merchandise from the king of the monsters' cinematic reign of terror, including figures and movie posters. As one of Tokyo's oldest toy collector's shops, it also has a range of other anime and manga-related goods from Japan's golden era of character merchandising (including Astro Boy, Gigantor, Ultraman, etc.). Glass cases overflow with rare die-cast toys and colorful vinyl figures, and model kits and action figures are stacked on the floor, making the place feel like a messy nerd's bedroom. The indisputable highlight is the Godzilla-themed bar downstairs, where you can sip cocktails and eat snacks while watching men in rubber suits pulverizing miniature buildings on a big screen.

Animate

Animate is located in Ikebukuro's Otome-dori (Princess Road) district: an area filled with shops specifically catering to female nerds, tucked away from the bustle of male-dominated Akihabara. Eight floors are mostly populated by teens and young adults, and filled with the requisite anime goods and merchandise, but the real selling point here is the large selection of homoerotic-themed manga and novels from the "boys' love" genre; it's a popular and influential subculture within a subculture that is aimed at women customers.

Cospa Gee Store

Cosplay ("costume play") is one of the most popular activities for otaku to indulge in: dressing up like anime and manga characters for conventions and photo sessions. While hardcore cosplayers often create their wardrobes from scratch, plenty of off-the-rack costumes, ranging from Sailor Moon to Final Fantasy fare, along with accessories and wigs, are available for sale—or just to try on— at Cospa Gee in Akihabara. Every square inch of the store is lined

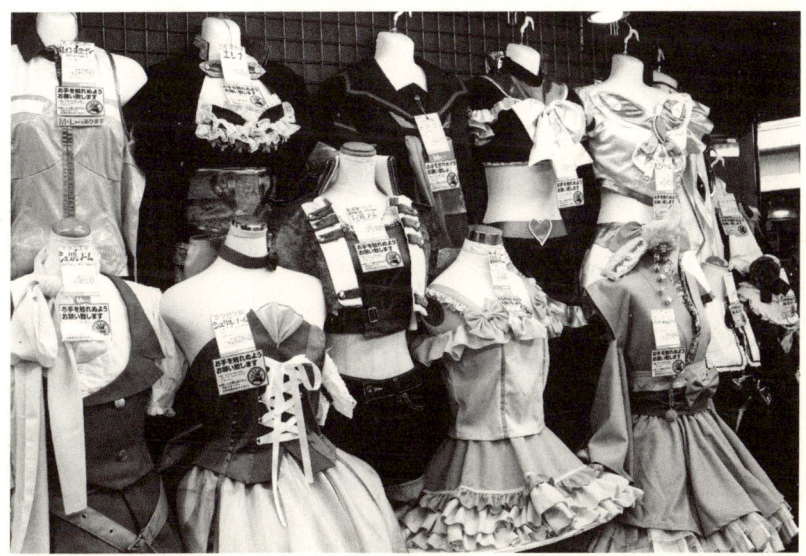

with ads hawking the latest arrivals, and the store also carries a wide selection of sharp and well-designed anime T-shirts for people who want to show their otaku colors without going the whole nine yards.

As of this writing, all of the above stores remain open and in operation. May it ever be so!

More Anime, More Problems: An Interview with Terumi Nishii

November 2019

Terumi Nishii is an animation director and character designer who has had a long career in Japan working on such hits as *One Piece*, *Pokémon*, and *JoJo's Bizarre Adventure: Diamond Is Unbreakable*.

In April 2019, Terumi made headlines when she tweeted in English about difficult working conditions in the anime industry, flat out telling her audience of mostly foreigners: "No matter how much you like anime, it is not advisable to come to Japan and participate in anime work. Because the animation industry is usually overworked."

In this interview with Terumi, we zero in on some of the biggest problems facing animators in Japan today, before considering some possible solutions and rays of hope.

What were the conditions like when you first entered the industry?
Terumi Nishii: It was really fun. I moved from Osaka to Tokyo to work at a studio. It was the best time in my career and in my life.

I was in sort of a training program in an anime studio called Cockpit. I could do the thing I loved and get some money for it. It wasn't enough to live on—I was only getting paid JPY 2,800 a month (about USD 25) during the testing period—because I was just doing tracings of other people's drawing. A few months later, I was offered a job there for around JPY 50,000 a month (about USD 450) doing phone operator work, sales, and some project management.

What made you want to speak out recently about the negative side of the anime industry?
Around 2014, I was working on the *Mushishi* anime, but the show was taken off the air because we couldn't meet the production schedule and we had to delay things a whole season just to catch up. I felt really bad about that. Then I started looking around the industry and saw that things like that were happening more and more. Shows were not able to meet their deadlines. And that's when I started to realize there was a problem.

JoJo's Bizarre Adventure began having similar issues as well, and around 2015 or 2016, it just felt like there weren't enough people who could do the work sufficiently. The industry was getting into a situation where no one could even make storyboards correctly and the big studios could no longer find outside vendors who could do the work. That wasn't an issue in the old days.

What do you think are the root causes of these staffing problems?
There's a situation now where there are more and more anime series than there used to be, and you are not allowed to reduce the quality of the animation, so there's a lot of overwork. There didn't used to be so much outsourcing in the industry, but now there is a lot of it. And that has increased the number of people that have to work on each project. In the past, it might take two months to complete a job,

but these days you have double the number of people working to try and complete the same kind of project in one month.

Instead of an anime project being made in one studio, it is outsourced to ten different studios and everyone is working on multiple projects at the same time. And if you have to keep the quality high while trying to shrink the timeline down to finish off projects, then that just makes the job tougher and tougher. The project managers really can't sleep. They are working hard 24/7. It requires better management and everything just becomes more complicated.

You tweeted that ". . . with the increase of the number of works in recent years, some people have broken minds and bodies." Do you have more specific examples?
Two of my *sempai* (senior colleagues) died in their 40s and I definitely think it was because of overwork. A lot of people have had aneurysms or heart attacks because of overwork. Lots of people need to pause their work because of doctor's orders telling them they need to rest. I know someone who was working as a project line manager who had an issue with a blood clot in his leg. He couldn't walk any longer and had to take time off. There are cases where people die, and those often make the news, but there are a lot of cases that you don't hear about where people are overworked and have to take a break for medical reasons.

Is the anime industry looking for any solutions to these problems?
Most people are resigned to the situation as it is now, and I don't really see a lot of people trying to fix things. The studios actually only have a few employees and are outsourcing and using contractors for everything, so it's a problem that can't be fixed by just one company alone. Everybody has to do it together. It's really hard to fix the problem because it's not all in one place.

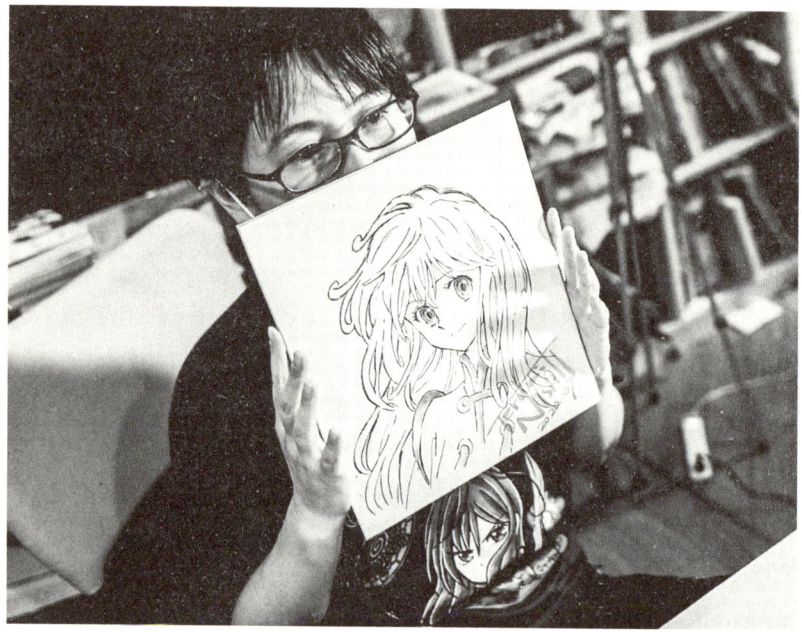

Terumi Nishii and a character from her Crown of Ouroboros *manga.*

Twenty years ago, the situation was different. There wasn't as much work, so the industry could be more choosy about staffing. These days, there's way too much work and there's not enough people. So, if you have some level of talent, then you can find a place in the industry, one way or another. That doesn't mean you will make a lot of money or make a living, but you can participate in it.

Retention is also really bad in Japan. There's lots of great artists in Japan and lots of young people who want to get into the anime industry, but back when I started in the late 1990s, ten people would enter an anime studio and within three years, 80% of them would be gone. This has only gotten worse. There are no good statistics for exactly how many animators there are in the industry today and how long they actually stay, but from my experience, a lot of artists leave. I only know a few people from my student days who are still working in the industry right now.

We've talked a lot about the problems facing the anime industry. What are some things that can be done to help it?
Currently, I am working at a company that is trying to hire talented artists as actual employees (not contractors) and is teaching them digital methods to make Japanese-style anime using tech.

We're starting to see some anime come out now that was made using CGI, but it looks like the old hand-drawn 2D style, so I believe there could be a solution using both methods to create a hybrid.

There are advantages and disadvantages for making anime with either CGI or 2D, but I think there are more advantages if we move toward a digital process. There is a lot of waste when you make anime using the old analog method. So I'm trying to figure out how to merge the two styles together so that viewers can still enjoy Japanese-style anime while taking advantage of technology to make it a more efficient process.

Another big advantage of going digital is that we can work with overseas vendors easily and they can participate in the process as well.

What can anime fans do to help people working in the industry?
I get this question a lot from anime fans in Japan. They say things like, "We buy lots of anime goods, but the money never gets to the creators and they are still struggling. What can we do?"

The easiest and most popular solution now is to go to a fan event like Comiket and buy *doujinshi* (self-published books) directly from an animator working on your favorite show. When you do that, your money goes right to them.

Then there are things like Pixiv FANBOX, which is a bit like Patreon. I have a Patreon account too, but it's a little bit hard for me to manage because I have to do everything in English and I don't know how to communicate so well with foreign fans. But I think that things like Patreon are a good way for international fans to support the animators who are working on their favorite shows.

Do you have anything else you'd like to say to foreign anime fans?
Every time I go overseas to an anime event, there are always fans that come to me and say, "I want to be an animator too. How can I become part of the industry?" At these events, I'm usually pretty polite and soft on these issues. But I think that if these young people really want to enter the anime industry, they can try, but they need to understand the conditions: there's no union for workers and there's not a lot of protection.

I feel bad that I've said things that would discourage aspiring animators from other countries. I didn't really intend to do that. I just wanted artists who want to enter this industry to understand that the conditions are pretty severe right now. They should understand that before they try to enter this world. I actually want foreigners to enter this industry to help to change it for the better.

Taking It to the Streets: The Otaku Reclaim Akihabara

November 2020

Tokyo's Akihabara neighborhood—also known as Akiba or AKB—has changed a lot over the years. It used to be a grungy and aloof hideaway for otaku supernerds, until gentrification and real estate development came for the area in the early 2000s.

Mass media interest in the otaku lifestyle followed with the release of *Train Man* in 2004, a hit otaku love story that started out as a series of online message board posts and eventually became a successful book and movie. The area's reputation darkened in 2008 after a crazed 25-year-old killed seven people in the middle of a street decorated with anime and video game characters. Finally, the travel boom of the 2010s opened up the tourist floodgates, and millions of people started to add Akihabara sightseeing to their Tokyo trip itinerary.

By 2020, Akiba had become crowded and exhausted: part Disneyland, part dingy tourist trap.

Even so, I decided to go and walk around Akihabara today. That's right, in the middle of a global pandemic. I had to do it because the word had gone out: one of the massive, multistory Sega video arcades that had been a landmark in the area for over 17 years was closing down for good.

I put on my mask, refilled my hand sanitizer, and headed out. Like so many other places in Japan that have been affected by COVID-19, hard times have befallen Akihabara. The weekday afternoon crowds were sparse. Yet, I was not the only one who wanted one last peek at the iconic red and blue six-story Sega arcade before it shuffled off to oblivion. In front of the arcade and on every floor were makeshift memorials: handwritten messages scribbled on Post-It notes saying *sayonara* and thanks to the building and its staff for the memories.

I used to love coming out to Akihabara, even when it started getting Disneyfied. There was always a thrill in the back of my mind when leaving the subway station and taking the Electric Town exit for the main drag of Chuo-dori and the Vegas-like strip of anime

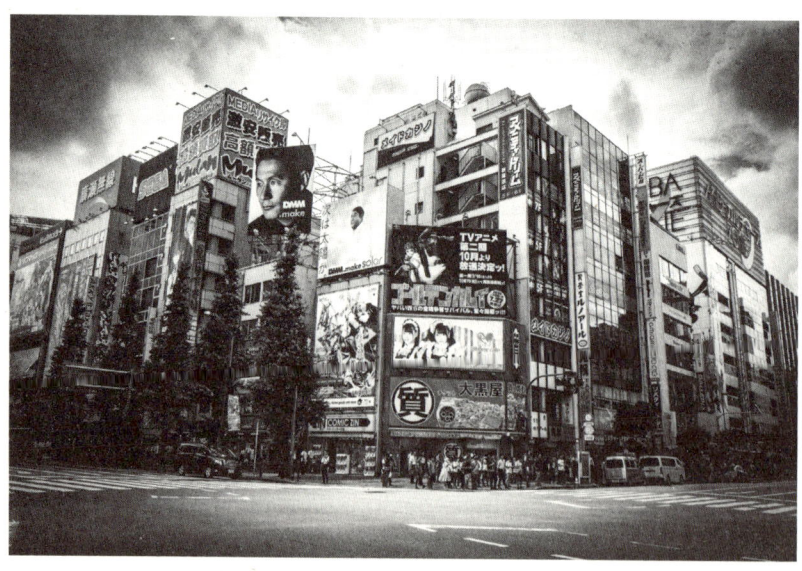

SCENES FROM THE OTAKU-VERSE

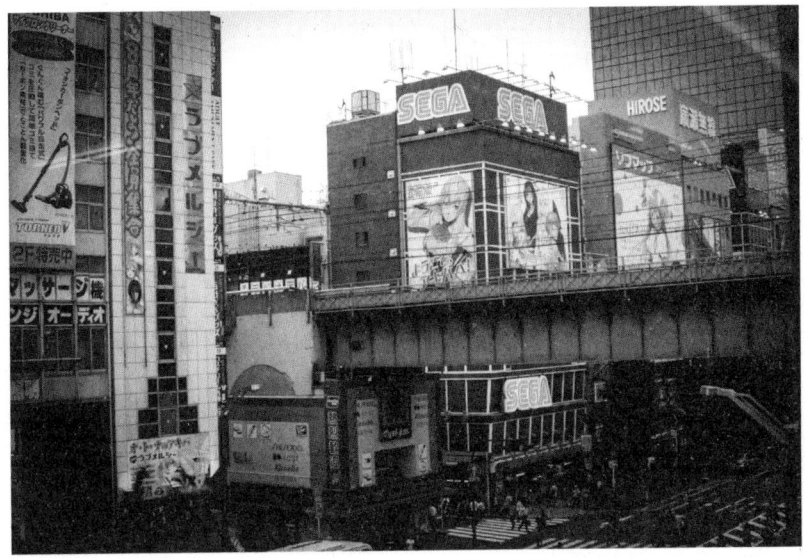

and manga characters plastered on huge buildings there. *What will I see this time?*

Sometimes that gamble would pay out: a vintage toy score, a rare animation cel in a bin marked "junk," or even a parade of *itasha* sports cars covered in anime characters. Adventures in Akihabara were a game of chance, not unlike the crane games in the Sega building. But lately, there hadn't been a whole lot of prizes. As I walked around the arcade for the last time, a few people used the giant robot simulator machines, but the staff were already beginning to pack up.

Honestly, many of us didn't expect Akihabara to last even this long. Once the touristification started, then that seemed to be it. As far back as the early 2000s, many pundits (guilty as charged) were declaring the death of good old Akihabara. But somehow the deep otaku heart of this place and locations like the Sega arcade had endured well past any number of would-be extinction level events.

Strolling through this neighborhood during the pandemic, it looked like Akihabara had momentarily shrugged off its glossy coat and returned to its roots. Time seemed to have slipped back by years, if not decades.

There were no tourists . . . at all. I was the only visible foreigner for blocks at a time. The men hanging around were either salarymen in their button-down shirts and black slacks or young people (both male and female), decidedly nerdy and not cool, sometimes alone or occasionally travelling in packs. Anime pin badges covered their backpacks. Shopping bags from stores like Animate and the Kaiyodo Hobby Lobby hung in their hands.

It was a genuine miracle: the otaku had taken back Akihabara. Nature is healing, as they say. But was this just a brief pause in the heat death of the universe or a genuine New Normal? Even if Akihabara blows apart into a billion pieces, it is clear that the otaku themselves will remain the Most Valuable Players in Japanese pop culture, for both good and bad.

So . . . am I an otaku? Well, I've been called "an American Otaku" and even founded a magazine called *Otaku USA*, so I guess I have no choice but to wear the label. But what are my otaku obsessions? Godzilla movies must be my thing, although I've known people far more hardcore about giant monsters and miniature buildings. Maybe I'm into anime and manga? I guess, but only up to a point. I have to confess that the 2D entertainment of the 21st century hasn't quite entranced me in the same way that the old stuff did.

I think I am an otaku *about* otaku: the culture and the spaces they inhabit. But in a pandemic world of social distancing, shut-ins, and lives lived almost entirely online, with webcams and endless streams of content to consume, where will the otaku go? When the tourists finally start coming to Japan again, what spaces will they visit to get a glimpse of how the otaku live?

ICONS

Leiji Matsumoto: Time Never Betrays a Dream

December 2010

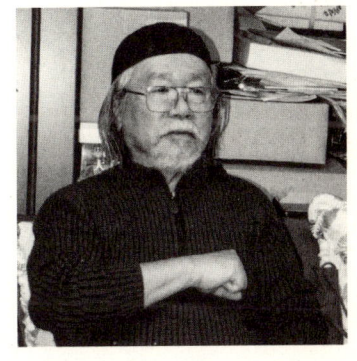

A perfectly ordinary suburban Tokyo neighborhood, somewhere in Nerima.

Nothing stuck out much in the cold winter night—just rows and rows of unremarkable houses—until I spotted a battleship lookout tower in someone's front yard.

That's how I knew we'd found where Leiji Matsumoto lived. Who else but the creator of Space Battleship Yamato *and* Space Pirate Captain Harlock *would have a huge naval reconnaissance platform sticking out of his driveway?*

You ever hear of the folks with *My Neighbor Totoro* tattoos who hang around the Ghibli Museum and idolize Hayao Miyazaki? That's how I feel about manga artist Leiji Matsumoto.

Watching *Space Battleship Yamato*, the revolutionary early 1970s animated series that Matsumoto helped to design and develop, threw me into the deep end when it aired on American TV in the 1980s (renamed *Star Blazers*). As a preteen, I rummaged around the bookstores in San Francisco's Japan Town for Matsumoto manga and sent away for untranslated VHS tapes of the *Yamato* movies. The first time I ever wrote about Japanese animation, it was for a Leiji Matsumoto zine that was circulated among fewer than ten like-minded fans.

I had managed to sneak my way into a small group of anime dorks who had travelled over from America to interview Leiji Matsumoto at his home in Tokyo.

Through a series of mishaps, our translator had helped to arrange a home invasion. The resulting Q&A would be published in Otaku USA *magazine, of which I was the editor-in-chief. The long game was finally paying out; perhaps this was the only reason I worked for an anime magazine in the first place . . . to be in the right place at the right time to bum-rush this interview!*

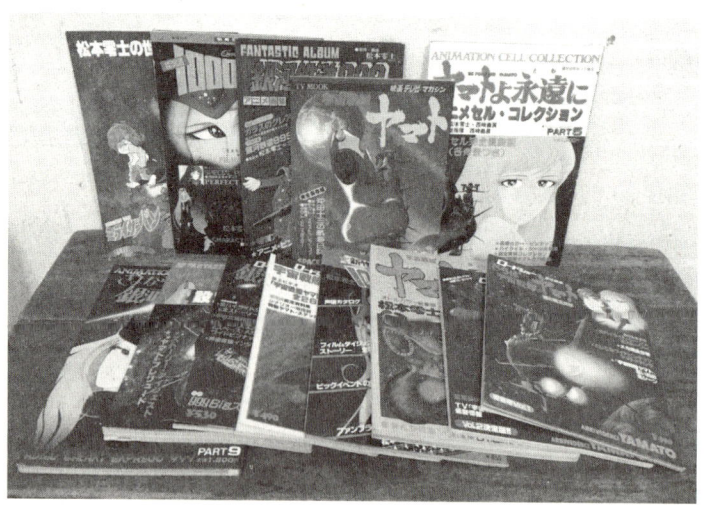

What was the appeal of Matsumoto's work in comics and animation? At first glance, there was outer space. And for any kid who had grown up under the spell of *a long time ago, in a galaxy far, far, away*, Matsumoto was more than happy to hand out starships and laser guns. In truth, his "World War II in space" aesthetic predated Star Wars by several years—a fact I will never let anyone forget: *Yamato* debuted in 1974, *Star Wars* in 1977!

But it wasn't just about outer space action; the more you dug into Matsumoto's output, the more complex it became. Individual works, like *Captain Harlock* and *Queen Millennia*, all seemed to take place in the same universe, with relationships and events crisscrossing each other on a cosmic timescale. If you spent enough time connecting the dots, it became clear that the connections were more than a mere "crossover event"—it was someone's personal mythology forming page by page, panel by panel, across a dozen manga serials.

I stood at Leiji Matsumoto's front door, feeling a bit like Dorothy at the gates of the Emerald City. Seconds later, I discovered what lies just beyond his doorway: a taxidermized gazelle (a souvenir from an African safari in the 1970s) standing watch over a hallway stuffed with empty cardboard boxes.

This was not a normal person's home.

Matsumoto contained multitudes. His stories could range from simple tales for young girls, to intensely researched military adventures, to sex comedies, funny animal capers, outer space fantasies, and beyond. Other manga artists of his generation, like Osamu Tezuka and Shotaro Ishinomori, had similar artistic ranges. But Matsumoto had his own unique escapist vibe, a sort of melancholy cross between daydreaming and stargazing, which was baked into everything he made.

An assistant got us settled into a sofa and chairs in a front room. Tea and coffee were served. The walls were decorated to look like the surface of the moon, complete with stars and a big blue planet Earth. FAR OUT!

The cosmic view might have been meant to distract from the rest of the room, where stacks of books, pages of original art, animation cels, and background paintings were strewn about haphazardly.

This is what happens when reality leaks into your imagination . . . or maybe it's the other way around?

In the 1970s and 1980s, Leiji Matsumoto envisioned a romantic space-age future. As time marched on, his style fell out of favor with newer anime fans who wrote him off as hopelessly dated. But to older otaku like myself, he was one of the prime visualists of not just anime and manga, but science fiction to boot. When Daft Punk made their retro dance record *Discovery* in 2001, it made perfect sense to tap Matsumoto to provide the accompanying music videos. Daft Punk wanted to resurrect a fantastic old sound that deserved new attention, and Matsumoto's work deserved the same treatment. Great stuff never really goes out of style. I'm reminded of a line from *Galaxy Express 999*, Matsumoto's iconic space opera story: "time never betrays a dream."

Leiji Matsumoto entered the room where I was sitting. He looked every bit his 73 years of age, a bit small and frail compared to his publicity photos of yore, but there he was.

There were three types of heroes in Matsumoto's stories. First, you had the stunted losers haunted by beautiful—usually lanky blonde—women. Matsumoto drew these guys with unkempt hair, big glasses, and comic strip facial expressions. American fans called them "potato heads." In many ways, they were similar to the nerdy

SCENES FROM THE OTAKU-VERSE

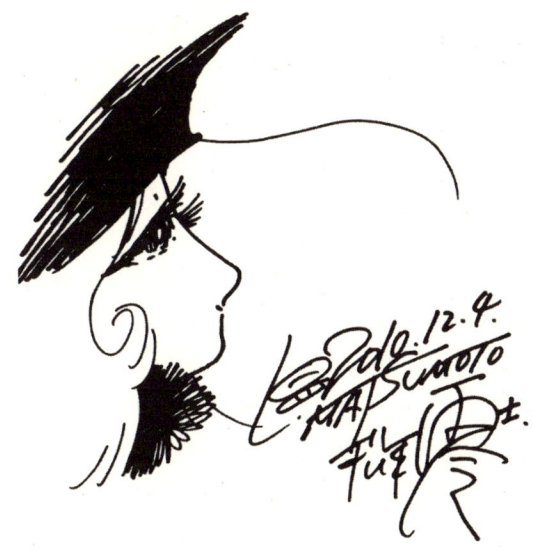

young men who feverishly consumed Matsumoto's work (and perhaps mirror reflections of Matsumoto himself, because he drew his self-portraits in the same style).

Next up were the hot-blooded young dudes with one finger on their laser pistols, such as Kodai in *Space Battleship Yamato*. They had to learn to control their anger and passion, usually at the behest of stern father figures.

Finally, there were the Matsumoto characters that everyone remembers best: the iron-willed iconoclasts like Captain Harlock and Eternal Wanderer Emeraldas, tall and rock star skinny, living their lives to the highest standards afforded to outsized Nietzschean archetypes. Characters like Captain Harlock could get away with saying stuff like: "We will not pray for anything. Nor will we seek help from anyone. Never again will we fight under another's flag. We will keep on fighting only for what we believe in, under only OUR flag, as long as we live! Under MY flag!"

You could tell Leiji probably had some self-esteem issues, but he also possessed a powerful imagination cobbled together from the ghosts of the Pacific War, the American occupation, and countless hours spent alone drawing. By doing so, he had mapped out his own id, ego, and superego in the form of sci-fi comics and animation projects.

I let my compatriot Tim Eldred handle the bulk of the Q&A interview. He was the biggest *Yamato* fan out of all of us as well the guy who had arranged to make the interview possible in the first place. For the most part, I was content to just sit there and ask myself, "Well, how did I get here?"

Only toward the end was I able to get in one question of my own. I asked Matsumoto what he remembered about the making of 1981's *Adieu Galaxy Express 999*, the epic sequel to *Galaxy Express 999* and my favorite anime film of all time, which I remain convinced is an underrated masterpiece of mood, pacing, and emotion.

He simply said, without giving it a second thought, "The first movie made a lot of money, so we made another one."

There was no mystical insight, no breakthrough epiphany, in meeting my favorite anime and manga creator.

He was there.

I was there.

And maybe that was what he had been trying to show me all along: who needs reality when you can make up your own story?

My Top Five Favorite Leiji Matsumoto titles

1. The Battlefield
2. Space Battleship Yamato
3. Space Pirate Captain Harlock
4. Adieu Galaxy Express 999
5. Queen Millennia

Leiji Matsumoto passed away on 2/13/2023. May we meet again someday in the Seas of Stars.

THREADS

Chronicles of extreme fashion from the big-haired men of Host Knuckle *to Harajuku kawaii style.*

The Men of *Host Knuckle*

February 2008

And then God created... *HOST KNUCKLE* (full name: "Hard Core Men's Nobility and Guynes Host Knuckle"), a one-shot special "mook" magazine from Million Shuppan, publishers of that perennial favorite *Men's Knuckle* magazine. Sharing the same resources and models as its parent publication, *Host Knuckle* assumes that you're a "host": a male model with flashy clothes and big hair who caters to female customers' requests in Tokyo's popular "host clubs." The *Men's Knuckle* magazine concludes with ten pages of job recruitment ads for host clubs, but *Host Knuckle* assumes you're either already in the running for a coveted "King of Dandy" bouquet from your fans or you just need that subtle push over the edge, led on by visions of hot women and wads of cash.

Host Knuckle kicks off with a spread of dudes modeling clothes at Shinjuku hotspots, all of which are across the street from each other: the Taito game center, the gateway to Sakura-dori, and, of course, the outside of the Don Quijote discount store. How the photogs managed to put this together without even a single *dasai gaijin* tourist bumbling into the frame is something of a minor miracle.

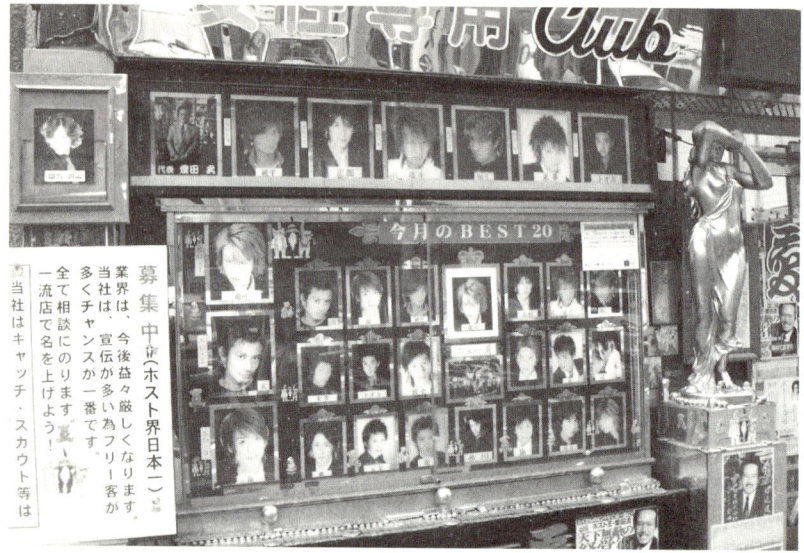

Hosts are ranked by popularity at club in Shinjuku, Tokyo.

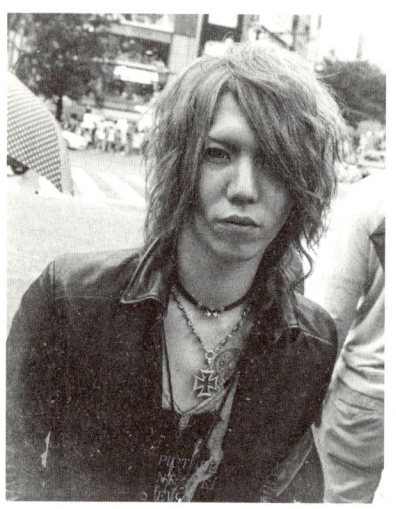
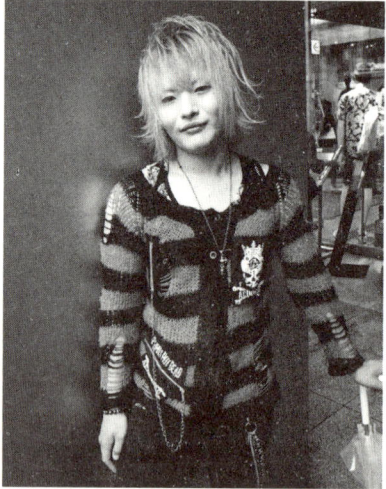

It's hard to believe these habitual street rats even HAVE places to live, but the "Host's Room" feature adds a touch of reality, even as it builds up the dream to greater heights. Tiny, single room apartments are decorated in monochromatic color schemes. Big ass TVs are common, as are miniature dogs and house cats. Conversation pieces include drawers full of nothing but instant food, fridges full of booze and stamina drinks (you better believe these dudes are chugging lots of Ukon no Chikara turmeric beverages), books about host clubs and entrepreneurship, a complete set of collectible *Final Fantasy* soda cans, assorted video game systems, and in one guy's case, an "Electric Personal Body Massager" (read: vibrator).

The "Host and Money" feature gives you some idea of how many JPY 10,000 bills you'll be able to stick in your oversized Vuitton wallet once you get on-board the "one month, two paydays" system. There's also a guide to where your money needs to go if you want to maintain the lifestyle: car payments, food, accessories, phone bills, suits from Shibuya 109-2, and more. The article claims: "Love is the triumph of the imagination over intelligence. MONEY IS LIFE."

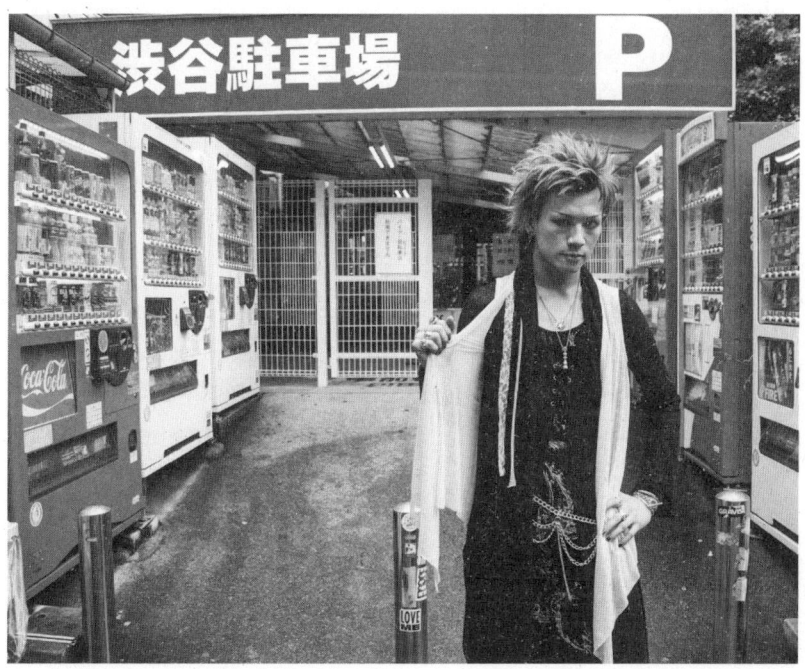

But, of course, there's more to life than just counting cash. Hosts need love, too! Which is why there's a guide to romancing gals during off-hours. Before revealing your masterplan to take them to the "rabuho" (aka Love Hotel, specifically intended for sexcapades), *Host Knuckle* first recommends buttering up your partner with one of the following activities: dinner, karaoke (aim for subliminal message hidden in song lyrics), shopping, going to a movie, driving, and, last but not least . . . reading manga stories together! There's also a handful of "no goods" to be avoided, like offering the girl money straight up or "grabbin' them cakes," Junkyard Dog style, in public. Good to know! Thanks, *Host Knuckle*!

"How to Host" is a fascinating verité day-in-the-life look at the inner workings of the clubs AI$ and AAA. Starting at 7 pm, employees prepare by mopping the floor, unpacking crates of booze, and polishing up the tables and ashtrays. At 8 pm, the doors open and the nightly regimen begins of welcoming the female customers, lighting their cigarettes, handing them glasses, filling them up again, and emptying ashtrays.

The next event on the schedule could happen at any time: a customer bravely orders the "Champagne Course," which can cost her thousands of dollars in one fell swoop. Her reward is having all hosts gather around her table, where they yell into a microphone and everyone guzzles some of the good shit.

At 12:30 am, it's time to get lost. Occupational hazard warning: a few of your fellow host employees will be totally shit-faced and piss-drunk at closing time, if not earlier. Give them some water or something. The same goes for the customers, who also need to be shown the door and escorted to the elevators. Make sure they don't leave their Louis V. bag behind!

And then? World is yours, baby. Find an open spot near the entrance of Kabuki-cho and just stand around looking cool. Maybe someone will take your picture for a *Men's Knuckle* "street style"

feature. Perhaps you can whistle while the girls pass by or ruthlessly try to pick them up using assorted "nampa" seduction techniques.
Repeat till fade or the first train home . . .

Little Devil Swallowtail Butterflies: The Girls of *Koakuma Ageha*

February 2008

Koakuma Ageha magazine's top "charisma model" is Mika Kagoshima, age 21. She occupies an exclusive position in *Koakuma Ageha* known as an "Agejyo": a sort of queen of the *mizu shobai* or night entertainment business. She may not be a classic beauty, but Mika is probably popular because she's a little different from the other girls in *Koakuma Ageha*. For starters, she races sports cars for fun and profit (!!), and puts as much pride into her banana yellow automobile as she does her hair, make-up, nails, and jewel-encrusted cell phone.

But aside from getting her hair done at a place called 'Natural Control Jesus Loves Me,' what is she *REALLY* like? Along with the rest of the magazine's Agejyo elite, Mika's consumer habits are carefully scrutinized in every issue. In January, I learned that Mika likes Contact cold medicine, Vermont instant curry, and doesn't play video games. Her hobbies include "having fun at night" and she likes guys who are "tall, who don't have a flat face, and who will let me be selfish."

Koakuma Ageha has inspired imitators such as *Celeb-ich* (sounded out as Celebrity Bitch), but the production quality in these is lower and several notches trashier. The fashion is less about projecting "I'm a pretty princess" and more like something out of a 1980s Italian postapocalyptic movie. Overall, there's little comparison. I asked my friend, Jay, to shed some light on what makes *Koakuma Ageha* special.

Patrick: Why does the magazine *Koakuma Ageha* (founded in 2005) feel like something new? It's considered the bible for girls in the "hostess" industry, filled with pages of gals covered in caked-on make-up, false lashes, and fake tans, but there shouldn't be anything fresh about all this; after all, hostess club culture itself and the Japanese sex industry have been around forever...

Jay: Maybe the fun of it is that the magazine pretends these girls are actually innocent. There are no recruitment ads asking for readers to become hostess girls at their local clubs, such as you'd find in the back pages of a magazine like *Men's Knuckle* (*Koakuma Ageha*'s equivalent for male hosts). When the models list their occupation in the magazine, they say things like "office lady," "event coordinator," even "day trader."

Nobody wants to tell or hear the truth in Japan. I could say, "Hey everyone! *Koakuma Ageha* is full of nothing but sex workers, and they don't really look that great without all that makeup," but it's so lame to say that. It's more fun to say, "Oh my god, they're so gorgeous! They look like princesses!" You have to join in on the game to really enjoy Japanese culture.

Patrick: The clothes and styling found in *Koakuma Ageha* borrow a lot from Gothic and Lolita fashion (spanning the dark and gloomy at one extreme and the cute and innocent at the other), and also leans heavily on the *Hime* ("Princess") Gal look. Fairytale imagery is a huge part of the magazine. There clearly is some deep-seated childhood fantasy playing out here about being a princess, marrying a prince, and living happily ever after. And yet, when you think about the reality of what these girls do for money, it seems like such a contradiction.

Jay: Gothic and Lolita culture and style should never have merged in the first place. But in spite of that, people in Japan mixed them anyway. That's really the strength of Japanese culture: you can combine whatever you want, even two things that are extremely different. And the more different the extremes are, the more interesting the resulting mash-up culture is.

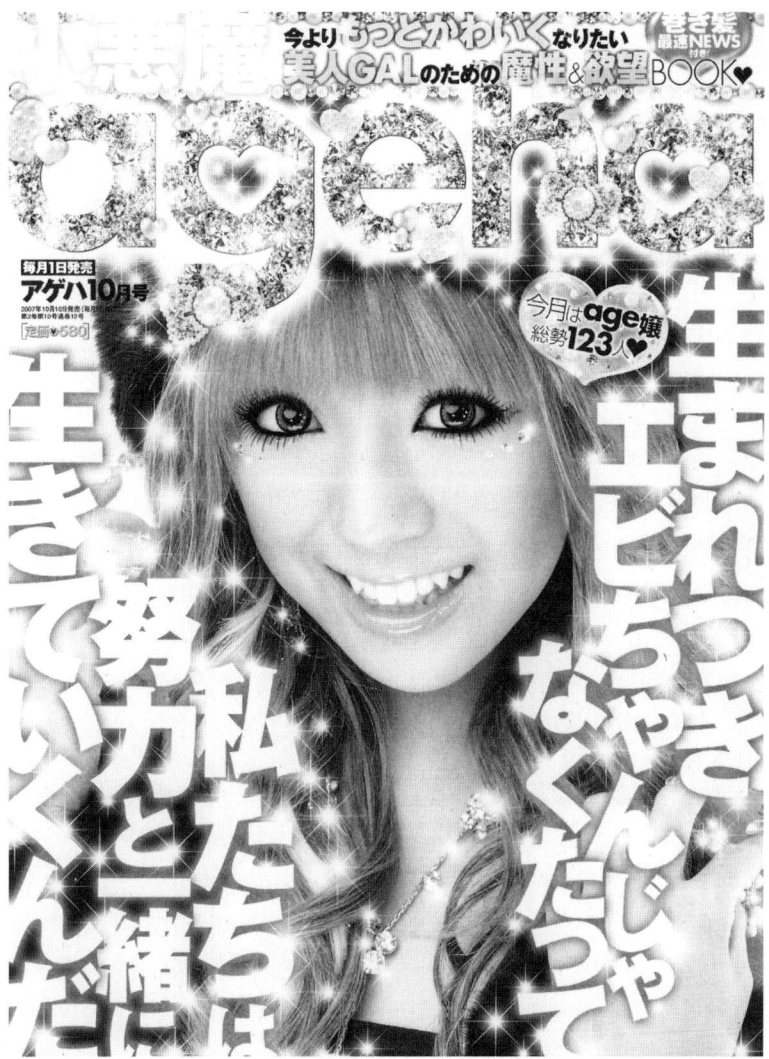

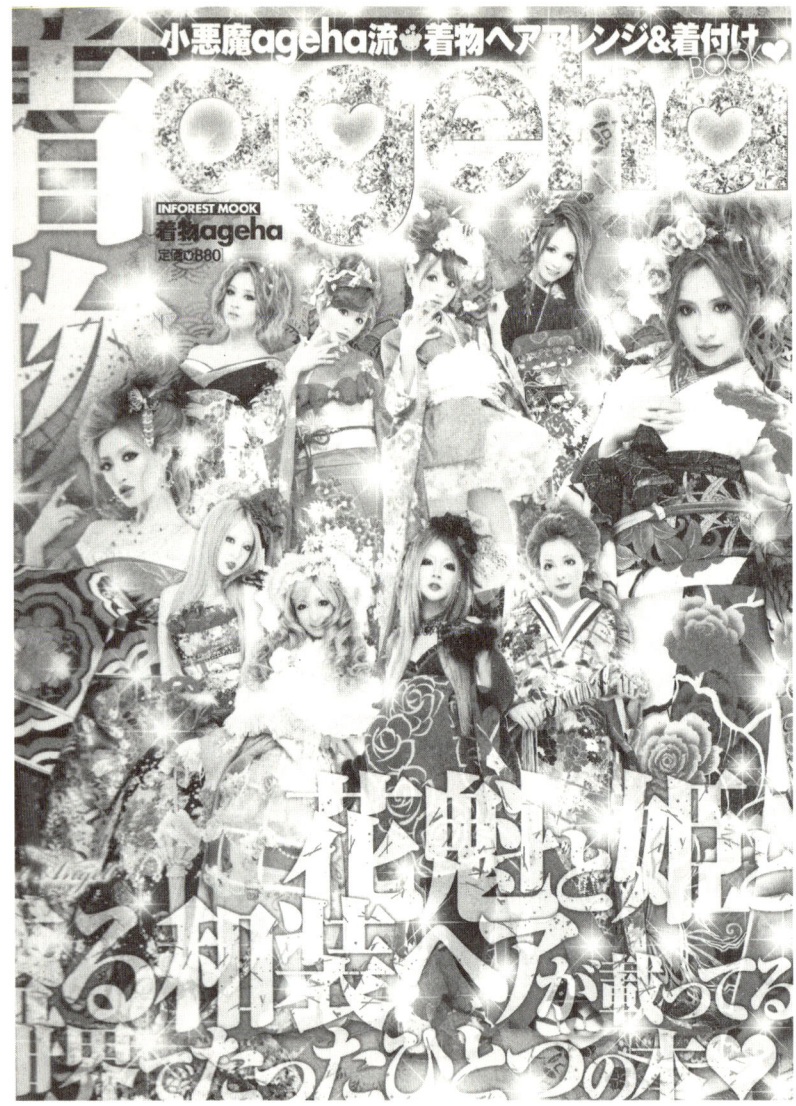

Patrick: When you read fashion magazines for young women in America, you'll find a lot of content about volunteering in third world countries and helping people in need. But you look at any magazine for a similar demographic in Japan, and it's just bald-faced consumerism all the way.

Jay: Japanese society has made some women numb about their own value. Young women aren't often encouraged to create or find meaning in their lives or to develop an ethical foundation of their own.

This is the stage that Japanese youth culture has been at since the beginning of the 1970s. The failure of counterculture and the student movement was a huge disappointment to the older generation, and they raised their children to believe that ideology cannot change anything. So, in the short run, why not just try and be financially successful? Be a winner! Get a good job, then meet a good guy, get married, and have some security.

Koakuma Ageha *has gone through several publishing hiatuses over the years, but it is currently still publishing its print magazine.* Men's Knuckle *and* Host Knuckle *have been downgraded to a few online social media accounts. Thousands of host clubs and hostess clubs are still operated across Japan.*

Shibuya 109-2 Elegy

October 2010

Dig if you will packs of dandified men roaming the streets in absurd distressed jeans, limited edition T-shirts emblazoned with naked women, all manner of taste-defying metal accessories, and pointy shoes only suitable for killing cockroaches. The glittering images conjured by their brand names alone will tell you most of what you need to know about the look: JACKROSE, Mayhem, Black Flame, Wild Party, Lick Riot, and yes, Vice Fairy (ask for it by name).

Since opening its Oniikei ("Big Brother Style") men's floors in 2006, the Shibuya 109-2 building in Shibuya became ground zero for those loveable, big-haired roustabouts known as Gyaruo ("Male Gals") and Center Guys as well as other purveyors of some of the most extreme fashions to be found anywhere on Earth.

The logic behind the lifestyle was pure Evolutionary Psychology: some young Japanese men were willing to dress really silly because—like nature's peacock or bird of paradise—resembling one's own object of desire can sometimes be the best way to attract a mate. In short, in order to get in bed with a Gyaru, it often helps to look like a Gyaru.

THREADS

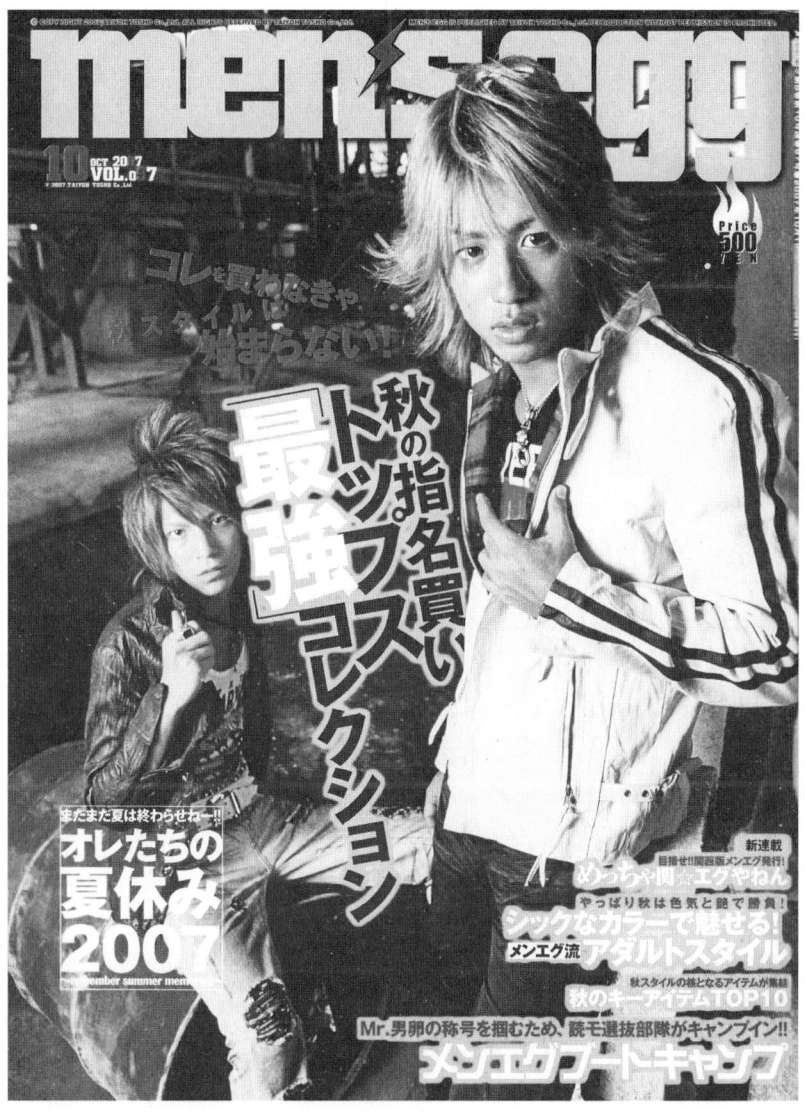

Since no one was marketing men's clothes for such a highly specialized purpose, early adopter Gyaruo were said to wear their girlfriends'—or latest conquests'—clothes in a pinch. Reacting with typical speed to a burgeoning market, the Japanese fashion industry soon gave these bold men a Kingdom of Their Own.

Originally, the 109-2 building existed merely as an afterthought to the main 109 shopping complex just down the street. In addition to housing a Hello Kitty store, it mainly dealt in mega cheap girls' accessories. The typical customers were female middle school students. But in the wake of the new Gyaruo boom and the instant success of the 109-2 men's floors, a new empire was forged.

National demand for VANQUISH "Sex is Heaven" jumbo towels and Buffalo Bob's Coffee and Donuts underwear became so high that Mini-Men's floors began popping up at other 109 stores across Japan, including Machida, Shizuoka, and Ichikawa. Competing retailer Marui even got in on the act by transforming one of the floors inside their Marui Men building (originally set up to compete with high fashion retailer Isetan Men's) into a "Gorgeous" and tacky shopping arena populated by the same brands that had become synonymous with 109-2.

Of course, I also got caught up in the madness and mania surrounding the 109-2. After I'd written my book *Japanese Schoolgirl Inferno: Tokyo Teen Fashion Subculture Handbook*, I'd become invested and curious about where the energy in trashy, low-rent youth culture was headed next. Trips to the 109-2 store soon became mandatory to follow the trail to the new frontier, although the reception to my presence there—indeed, to any gaijin who dared to venture inside—was chilly at best. The quizzical and mildly offended expressions from the staff and customers gave off a none-too-subliminal message: THIS IS OUR SCENE, YOU DON'T BELONG, GET OUT AND GO HOME. After a lifetime of not belonging and being out of place no matter where I went, the last thing I was going to do was take this personally. They had a point, so how could I complain?

Fast forward to Fall 2010, and the classic Gyaruo has now become an endangered species. It is as if they've already followed the mythic Gonguro and Manba into the dusty pages of history. Clearly, some of

THREADS

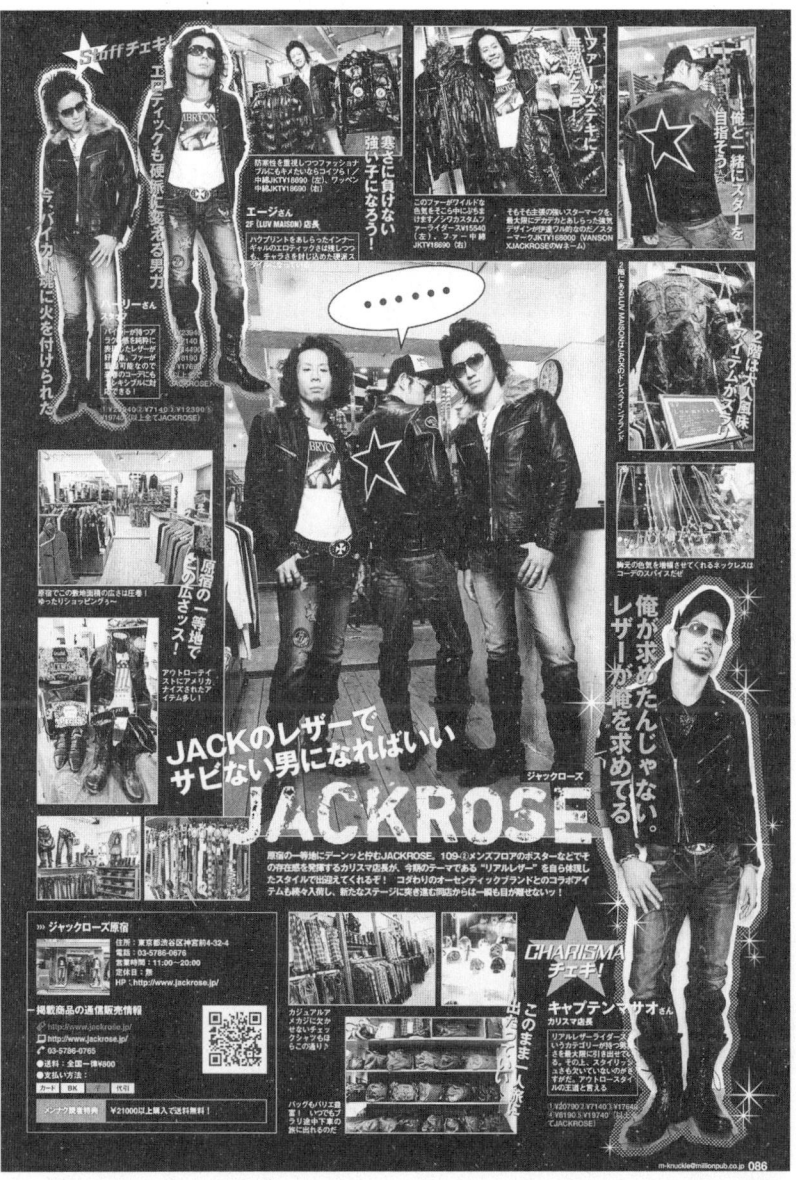

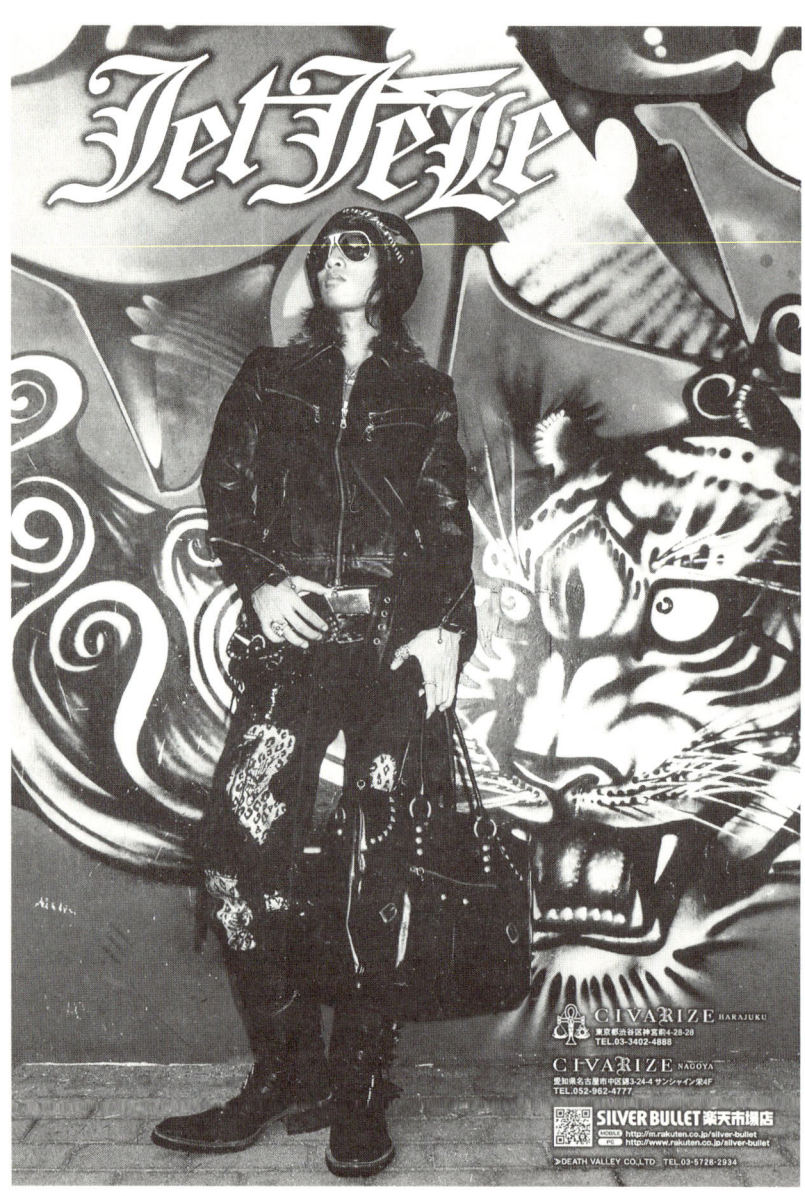

the original kids graduated or leveled up to the more complete host clubs look and lifestyle; a trip to Shinjuku, Kabukicho on any given night will turn up hundreds of big-haired dudes in cheap suits desperately trying to make a buck however they can. But something deep and fundamental has changed at the base of operations. And all is not quite right at the Shibuya 109-2.

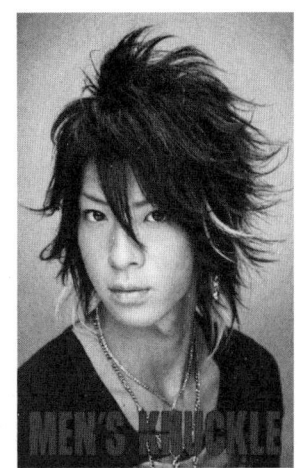

Wednesday night, around 6 pm, scene of the crime: the fifth floor of 109-2. The second I step into the JACKROSE store, a sales clerk begins chasing me around the show floor with a sales catalog in his hand, until I break down and let him give me the hard sell. He leads me to a stack of JACKROSE/ROLLING STONES/AC/DC collaboration shirts—a product line about as fresh and exciting as senior citizens Mick Jagger and Angus Young themselves nowadays.

I pass by the remains of the CASVA store, which once sold "gorgeous" purple zebra jackets and imitation snakeskin trousers suitable for a 1970s Times Square pimp or a duke of Dogenzaka Street. Now, all that once glittered is gone, replaced by drab American Casual gear. The VANQUISH store, formerly the bestselling brand at 109-2, looks like a neutron bomb had gone off inside. A single, sad black and gold Adidas tracksuit under a fake crystal chandelier surveys the scene like the Ghost of Christmas Past.

I have to get out. I make for the escalator and have nearly passed the threshold of safety when someone grabs my arm and began to pull. It's the clerk from the S.I2.C. store. "*Okyakusan! Okyakusan!*" ("Customer! Customer!") he screeches, like one of those man-starved hillbilly women in an old Popeye cartoon. In America, this is where you reach for the pepper spray, but in Japan, all you can do

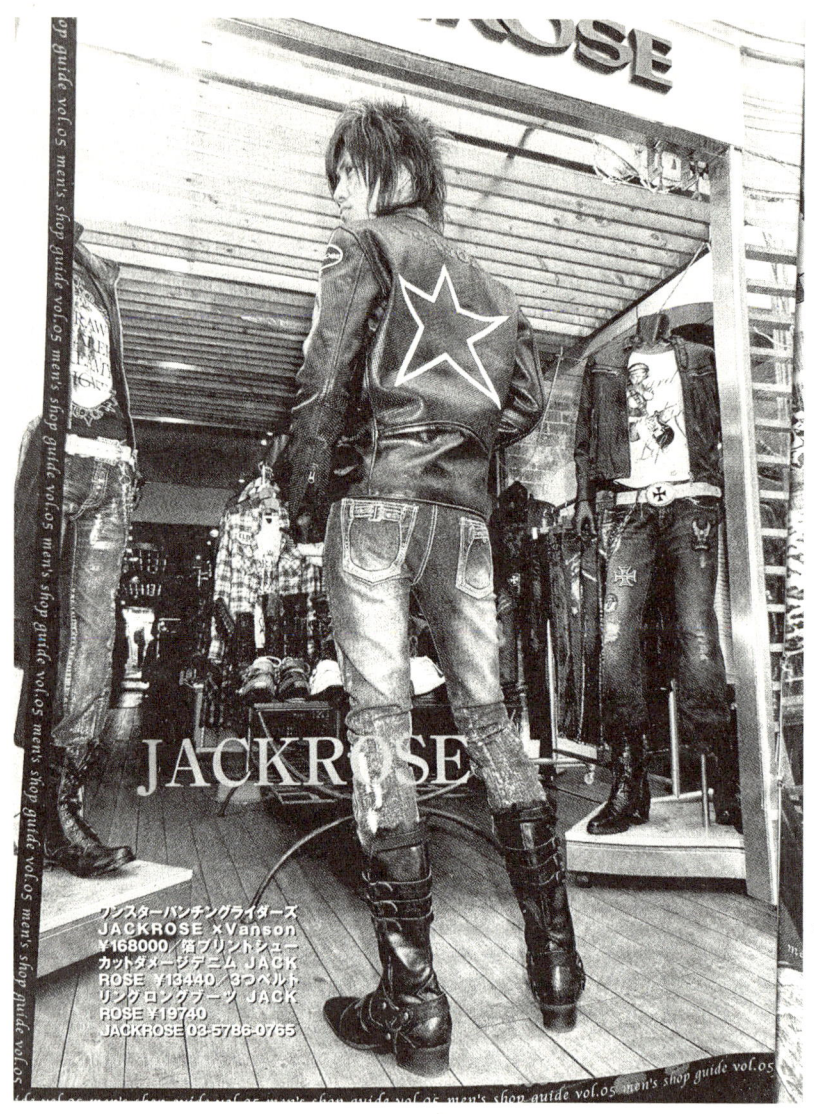

is meekly say *"Sumimasen, sumimasen"* and try and run away fast. And thus does the 109-2 rid itself of me.

After spilling out on the street, I struggle to find some answers for what had happened. How had 109-2 gone on the skids so fast? Why did everyone inside suddenly want to be my best friend when before they were laughing behind my back? An insider, who chooses to remain anonymous, speculates: "It's sad. No one can afford to wear and enjoy stupid clothes anymore. I think most of those guys are just shopping at (low-budget and largely suburban bad-taste retailer) Shimamura now." Hey, at least it's not H&M or Forever 21, but still . . .

I'm on my way out of the 109-2 building, perhaps for good, just as another customer makes his arrival. He's surrounded by a group of three or four girls who take his picture as he grins, reveling in the sheer joy of JUST BEING THERE in Shibuya, at the *actual* 109-2, loving the "all new, all different" shopping experience as much as I disdain it. The clothes he's wearing are nothing special, but that could easily be changed so long as he pays by cash, credit, or debit. I try to pick up on what he is saying to his adoring flock of females, but I can't figure out a word of it. He's speaking Chinese. If Japan can't sell its "gorgeous" fashions to its own citizens, it might be able to export this expired sense of cool to other countries.

109-2 rebranded itself as MAGNET by SHIBUYA 109 in 2018 in the hopes of really going after those tourist bucks. A few of the legacy Gyaruo brands like VANQUISH held on for a while, but were eventually phased out for good. The most popular store there now sells One Piece anime goods. So it goes.

Made in Japan: Harajuku Fashion Brands

November 2011

A PR puff piece ran in the *Washington Post* with the headline "Gwen Stefani designs Harajuku kids' clothes for Target." It seems that Stefani, the lead singer of group No Doubt, will be expanding upon her "Harajuku Lovers" brand to include "Harajuku Mini," a collection of children's clothing inspired by the street styles found in Tokyo's Harajuku district.

Bit of a flashback here: Stefani first began associating herself with Japanese fashion in a big way back in 2004 with her song "Harajuku Girls." The next step was the creation of a "Harajuku Lovers" lifestyle brand overseen by Stefani that included apparel and fragrances.

The problem was that all of these projects merely seemed to be out to exploit the buzz that surrounded Tokyo's Harajuku fashion district in the wake of 2001's internationally bestselling book *FRUiTS: Tokyo street style*. But for all the work that Stefani and her brand did to associate themselves with Harajuku, there was never any actual connection with Japan.

According to the owners of a local store in Harajuku, hype only raises the price of real estate and pushes out independent businesses. Over the last few years, Harajuku has been invaded by international brands like H&M and Forever 21 who have opened mammoth stores hoping to ride the buzz. I think it's fine for people to be interested in this stuff, but some of the money has to go back to keeping the foundation firm.

Why should I care? After all, I'm an adult male, with zero need for Harajuku-inspired apparel in my wardrobe. I guess I care because fashion is such a major part of Japanese pop culture that it simply can't be avoided. Even if you only focus on anime and manga, clothing and style are bound to pop up on the radar. And when it comes to Japanese pop culture, I think we all want things that are authentic, not watered-down Americanized versions thereof.

If you like Gwen Stefani and her Harajuku-inspired brands, then that's cool. Even Kyary Pamyu Pamyu of PONPONPON fame admits in interviews that early exposure to the Harajuku Girls brand was a life-changing experience. But for the sake of those of you who want the real thing, I've rounded up a list of five cutting-edge brands that are actually from Japan. No, you won't find any of their goods at your local Target store, but maybe that's for the best?

6%DOKIDOKI

6%DOKIDOKI first opened its doors in Harajuku during the dawn of the contemporary street fashion scene in 1995. Since then, the brand has evolved into a wild and colorful look that owner Sebastian Masuda calls "Sensational Kawaii" and "Happy Anarchy." 6%DOKIDOKI's tiered skirts and baby doll dresses have been widely copied by others seeking to emulate Harajuku style, and while the extreme end of their fashion may not be suitable for all, 6% also sells a wide range of low-priced accessories much loved by celebrities and locals alike. And, of course, mention must be made of 6%DOKIDOKI famed model "shopgirls" Vani and Yuka, who are without doubt the real "Harajuku Girls" *par excellence*.

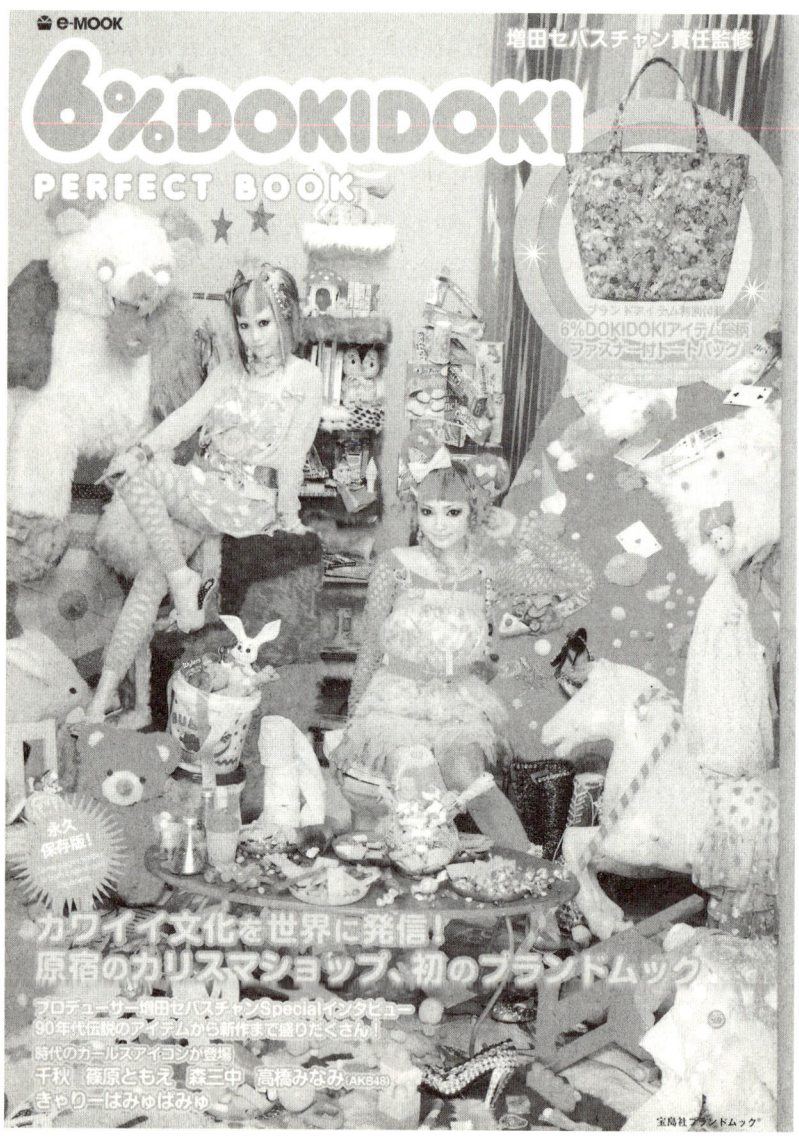

SPINNS

Since opening their flagship store in Harajuku in 2010, SPINNS has become enormously influential in the world of Harajuku fashion. For starters, Kyary Pamyu Pamyu often models for them and their club-ready clothes and accessories are featured in magazines like *KERA* and *Zipper*. There is no single SPINNS style. Shoppers are encouraged to mix and match to create their own "fashion coordinates," but lots of pastel colors, animal prints, and zany cartoon imagery figure prominently. SPINNS does not do international shipping . . . yet. But a visit to their "head shop" in Harajuku is a must.

Super Lovers

A staple of Japanese fashion since 1988, Super Lovers caters to the rock and punk crowd. Design motifs—such as skulls and crossbones, Union Jack flags, and metal studs—take their cues from classic UK punk style but are served up with neon colors and a sense of playfulness that's pure Harajuku. The similarities between their name and Gwen's "Harajuku Lovers" seem too close to be a mere coincidence.

Spank!

Spank! started off in 2004 as a store that worshipped at the altar of the 1980s with style icons, including the likes of Strawberry Shortcake, the Care Bears, and Jem and the Holograms. Now, Spank! also produces their own clothing and accessories which follow a similar pastel-colored path somewhere between trash culture and fancy goods.

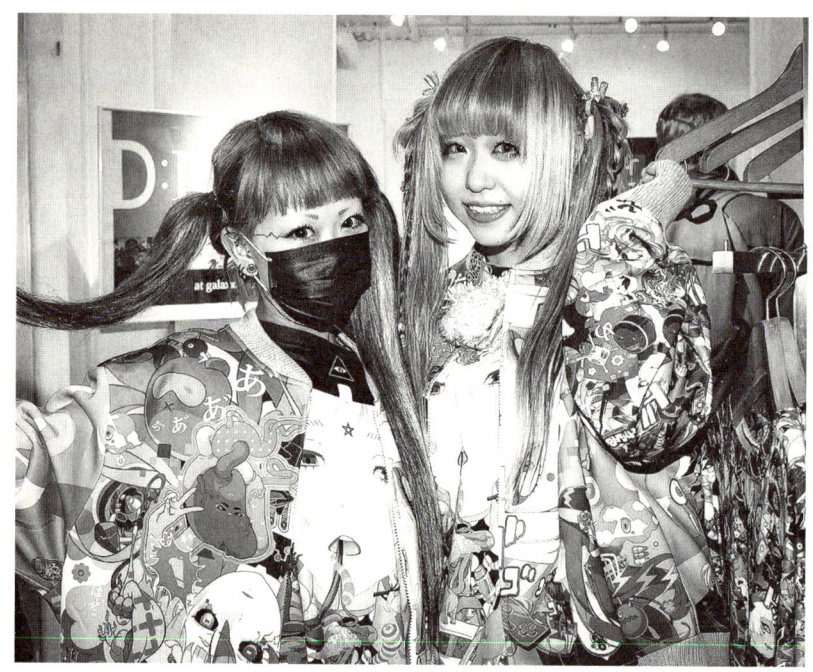

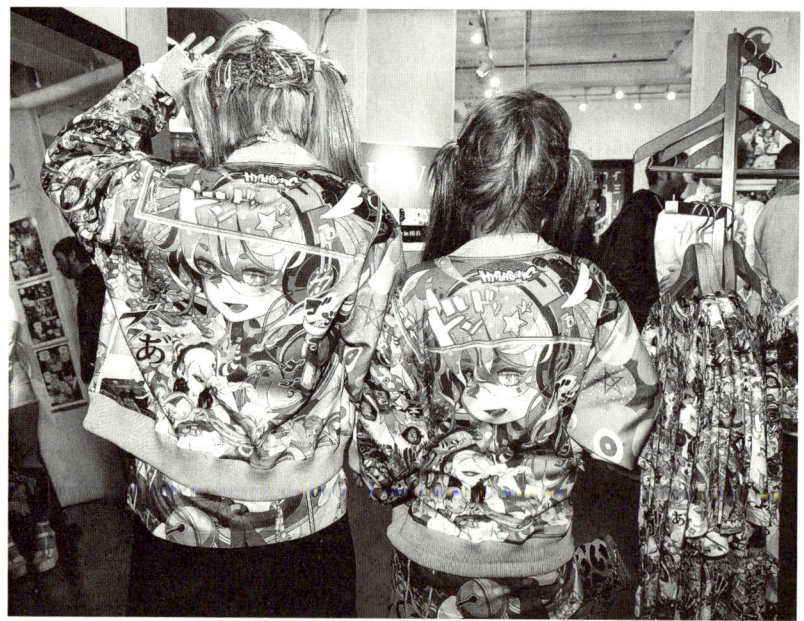

Fashion party at galaxxxy, 2015.

galaxxxy

The galaxxxy store is located in Shibuya, just around the corner from some of Tokyo's most popular dance clubs. Just like a DJ manning the turntables, galaxxxy remixes the past and present to create an energetic new style that, as their English promotional materials put it, "combine neon cracks and exploding of galaxxxy." While casual looks can be mined from their apparel, this is really state-of-the art clothing for clubgoers and party animals.

I'm happy to report that all of these brands and stores are still alive in various forms, COVID-19 be damned.

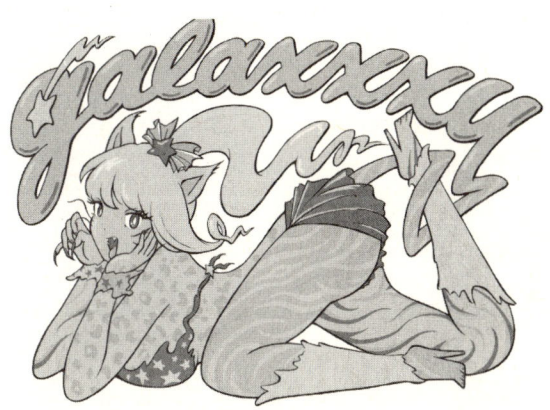

On "Aymmy in the batty girls" and the Retro Adventures of Ayumi Seto

October 2013

"Aymmy in the batty girls" is a new lifestyle and apparel line featuring ASOBISYSTEM model Ayumi Seto as the brand's director and "image character" mascot Aymmy.

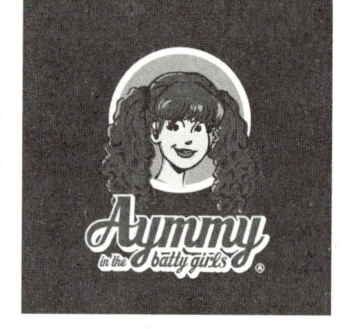

According to the official website, "It is a brand that projects a lifestyle fashion of 'Aymmy' a 17-year-old girl from California" who apparently lives the American Dream and is "working in a diner."

Based on the accompanying illustration, Aymmy looks like a long-lost background character from an Archie comic book and appears to have been raised in some kind of hermetically shielded fallout shelter where the 21st century never happened.

Aymmy's fictitious bio (which overlaps with Ayumi Seto's own catalog of interests) claims her favorite foods are hamburgers and Cherry Cokes. Her favorite movies are *Ghostbusters*, *E.T.*, and

The Return of the Living Dead. Her favorite musical groups are The Ramones, The Damned, The Sex Pistols, and The Dead Boys (featuring dreamy Stiv Bators).

Built on these foundations, the brand is promising clothing and goods in the following fashion genres: Kidz, SK8 (skate), School, and Rock. Coordinates like this have long been the stuff of countless photo spreads in Harajuku-kei magazines like KERA and Zipper, which regularly feature the tomboyish 20-year-old Seto. Even more, the caps and sports jerseys "Kidz" aesthetic that batty girls will be rolling out has been a cornerstone for Harajuku and Shibuya style since the "cutie" 1990s.

The lookbook for "Aymmy in the batty girls" shows Seto stalking the streets of LA with soda pop in hand, paying homage to Dr. Pepper in a Melrose antique store, posing in front of a juke box, and contemplating a milkshake. Some of the photos and clothes do make overtures to punk and surfer looks, but it's clear that the real target of this sentimental journey is a nostalgic nonspecific past: the post-Elvis 1950s or the pre-Beatles 1960s. Pure *American Graffiti* territory.

Of course, this is nothing new. Retro junk culture has long been inseparable from girls' fashion in Japan. For decades now, magazines from egg to Koakuma Ageha and all points in-between have shown us models in both cheap and expensive garb gorging themselves on greasy foods surrounded by trash pop iconography: hot dogs, soda pop, supermarkets, 1950s diners, old comic books; all of it emblematic of the hyper-consumerism that America hotwired into the DNA of postwar Japan.

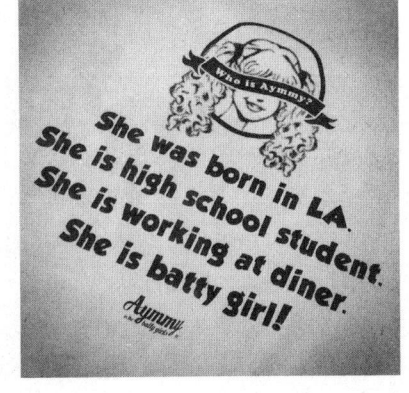

But the models in the spreads are usually just stand-ins for the real work of stylists and designers: human mannequins. Ayumi Seto, however, appears to be the real deal. Way before "Aymmy in the batty girls" was announced late in September, Seto's Instagram had dedicated itself to cataloging pop art, old movies, and comic book covers. Even now, copious plates of hamburgers tend to outnumber the selfies.

Indeed, Seto is practically a character from Phil Dick's *The Man in the High Castle*, an emissary from an alternate Japan that won the war and now collects symbols of vanishing Americana. Notably absent from the "batty girls" fantasy is any evidence at all of the digital world we now inhabit. While writing this piece, I took a break and walked down a city block for a coffee. Literally everyone was looking at their phone or interfacing with some kind of device, be it iPhone or MP3 player. But by gosh, here is Seto's alluringly old-fashioned world of colorful physical objects, and you have to admit, it looks like fun. And I don't care what you're selling: fun is the ultimate commodity.

You gotta wonder: will there ever be a "new" nostalgia? Will modern strip malls and boring Starbucks mugs ever inspire Japanese fashion the way junk food and antique shops do? Will the Westward-gazing batty girls find an audience overseas, let alone in

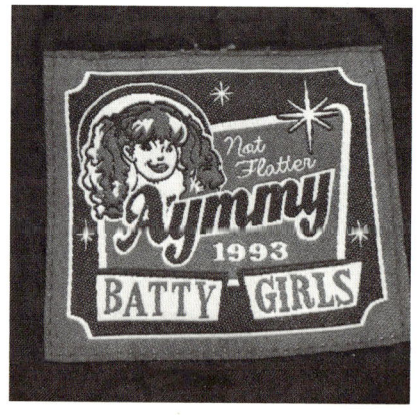

their own "Harajuku kawaii!!" backyard? Will girls who look like Aymmy ever sling hash from 9 to 5 at diners again? Did they ever in the first place? Can a 20-year-old Japanese girl get away with pretending to be a teenager from California, and is that any crazier than 30-somethings playing teenagers in *Grease*?

    I can't say for sure, except that stranger things have happened before, and hamburgers are always delicious.

Harajuku Burger Queen: An Interview with Ayumi Seto

April 2014

Japanese fashion model Ayumi Seto loves America. Signed to the ASOBISYSTEM agency (home of Kyary Pamyu Pamyu) and master of the "Kidz" style coordinate, Seto recently launched her lifestyle brand "Aymmy in the batty girls": a startling mix of pop art, punk, junk food, and good old-fashioned US trash culture. Mid-April found Seto in San Francisco appearing at the NEW PEOPLE building during the Cherry Blossom Festival. It seemed as good a time as any to ask her some questions about her obsessions and her daily life. Occasionally breaking for swigs from a glass Coca-Cola bottle and dipping into multiple oversized bags of candy, Seto seemed right at home, even though she was half a world away from her usual Harajuku haunts. Here's how our conversation went.

Hi! Please introduce yourself and tell us what you do.
Hi, I'm Ayumi Seto. I'm 21 years old. I'm a model and a designer and I love America.

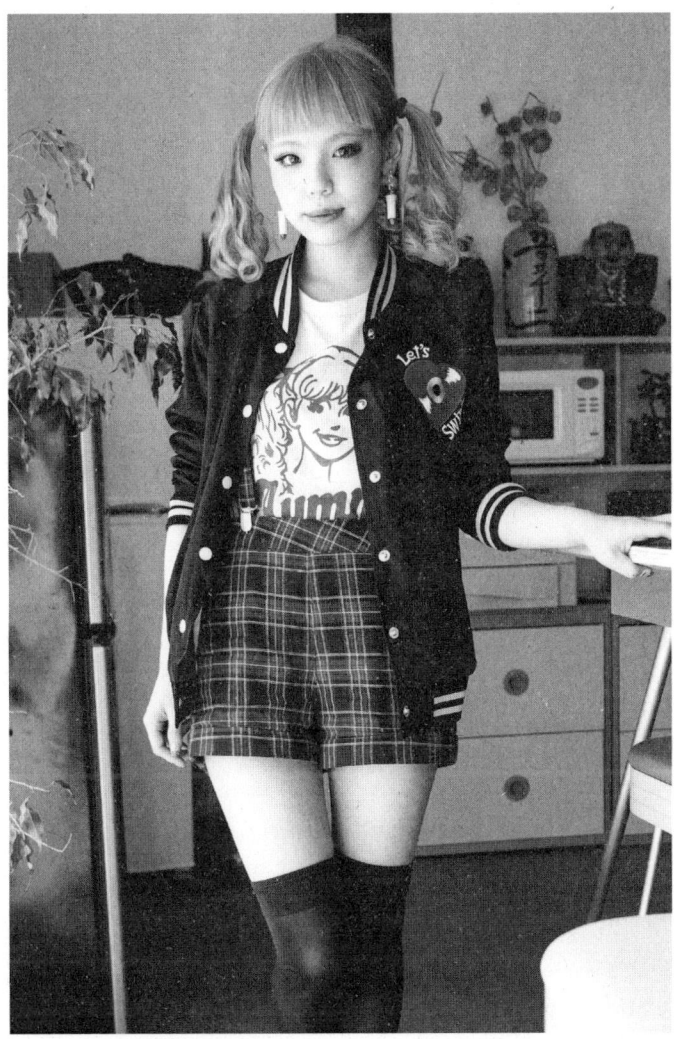

What exactly is your level of involvement with the BATTY GIRLS apparel line? Do you design the clothes and accessories yourself?
I start by illustrating the outfits. Next, I focus on each item and then draw each one of them. Then I take photos of the fabric I want to use, and have someone make a mock-up. So I pretty much work on the initial designs.

What are some of your favorite items in the BATTY GIRLS line?
There is an American varsity jacket made out of shiny satin with yellow, red, and blue colors. It also has a tiger and a hamburger on it.

What kind of people are attracted to the BATTY GIRLS style in Japan?
Girls in Harajuku who read fashion magazines like *Zipper*.

We don't really have the "Kidz" style in the USA. Can you explain what the appeal is?
I feel like girls are more attractive when they look childish or childlike. If you mix innocent things, like pop colors and childish hair (like twin ponytails), with grown-up items, then that becomes fashionable. I'm still thinking about what the appeal is.

A lot of kids around the world are now looking to Asia for style inspiration, especially in places like Japan and Korea, but the BATTY GIRLS line seems deeply inspired by American pop culture. Why is that?
First of all, I love American culture. I love the time period when America was becoming more economically powerful and everything had pop colors, things that people think of as "All-American." I feel that maybe they don't look for it consciously, but Asian girls love American culture and pop culture deep inside. That's why they are attracted to BATTY GIRLS and that's where the influence comes from.

I get a deep nostalgic feeling from the BATTY GIRLS clothing and the photo shoots you do. They're filled with vintage things like the 1950s-style diners and vinyl LPs. What kind of inspiration does the past give you?
When I started modeling, I had to put together my own outfits to be photographed. I had to train myself to know what I liked in

order to style myself. While doing that, I realized that I love a lot of old American clothes, and from there, I started to branch out. I already loved American movies, and then I started to get into classic American pop culture. I can't really explain what it does to me, but I'm just totally obsessed with the design and fashion of that time period.

You mentioned liking American films. Which ones are some of your favorites?
Grease, American Graffiti, Cry Baby, and *Rock 'n Roll High School*. And one more, although it's not really a fashion inspiration for me, *Back to the Future*.

I guess we should talk about Japan, too. How would you describe Harajuku these days?
The scene in Harajuku these days is driven more by individuality instead of fashion rules. Girls there dress up not to be evaluated by others—like being popular among boys—but because they want to wear what they like. So there's no genre right now. There's no single style that can describe everything available there now, and that's a positive thing.

You seem super busy these days. Can you describe what a typical day is like for you?
I wake up in the morning (laughs). I usually go to the press room at my agency's office and take pictures of what I'm wearing that day or go over the clothes that are available that day. I'll put together a coordinated outfit and take pictures and post them on SNS sites like Twitter, Instagram, and my website. In the evening, there's a lot of meetings about things like merchandising for BATTY GIRLS, or if there's an upcoming event, we hold meetings about it. Other times, I'll work on my own stuff, like designs for my brand or putting

together coordinated outfit sets. I usually don't finish working until about 11 at night.

You've spent quite a bit of time in California and the USA now. What are your impressions?
I love it here so much! I really want to live here!

What are some things you like to do here that you can't do in Japan?
I can eat pancakes all the time (laughs)! I love food . . . If I'm living in the USA, I can go to flea markets and find vintage American furniture and toys that would be a lot more expensive in Japan, and I can collect all of them.

And people?
I feel like when I am in Japan, it can feel small and kind of suffocating. A lot of people are uptight, always in a rush and under stress. But I feel like American people have a lot more freedom and they have space to stretch out, mentally as well as physically. There's more freedom compared to Japan and I'd rather have that.

Often, there's a lot of food in your photo shoots—like burgers, pizza, and soda pop. What is it like working under those conditions?
The image character for my brand is named Aymmy. She is a fictional character, she's not associated with me at all, and this girl is basically carefree. She doesn't care about dieting or getting beauty sleep, so she is always hanging out in bed eating junk food, playing video games, and then falling asleep like that. I want to convey that kind of free-spirited image with my brand, so I tend to bring a lot of food to the photo shoots and . . . I eat them too!

There's countless hamburger pictures on your Instagram . . . how do Japanese burgers compare to US ones?
I think the beef in the USA is definitely different than in Japan. It's meatier and it tastes better. Sometimes the Japanese burgers will have more fancy things, like better vegetables or a gourmet bun, but the patty in a US burger definitely tastes better.

Can you recommend a good burger in Japan?
There's an old-fashioned American-style diner called AS Classics Diner in Komazawa and the interior is very retro and classic. I used their burgers to cater my brand exhibition event. Can you recommend a place for me to get a burger in San Francisco?

It's Tops on Market Street. It's a diner that has been in business in San Francisco since 1935 and the burgers are really good . . . simple, but good. Finally, do you have a special message for our readers?
If you love Japan, Akihabara is always fun to visit, but please visit Harajuku. Please take some interest in the Harajuku style, because Japan has a lot of unique fashion styles.

"Aymmy in the batty girls" ceased operations in March 2019, but Seto is now overseeing a new brand called Dear Sisterhood. It's Tops in San Francisco closed for good in 2020, which is a damn shame because that was a tasty burger.

GODAO:
Fashion in the Dark

July 2021

The Japanese national news media has reported the arrest of a man who illegally obtained COVID-19 relief funds. The offender was the owner of eight different bars and clothing stores in Tokyo, but, because they were operating without proper health licenses, they fell into the category of *yami eigyō* or "dark businesses." That didn't stop this business owner from applying for relief money, though. He forged his own health licenses, claimed his company needed COVID-19 relief, and pocketed as much as USD 70,000 in government cash. His company's name wasn't mentioned in the press, but it didn't take long for word to get around Harajuku, and soon everybody knew: the owner of the shadowy octopus-like subculture and fashion empire that we will (for legal reasons) call GODAO was going behind bars.

GODAO was an Illuminati-esque pyramid of web stores, physical shops, bars, and hookah lounges dotted across Tokyo and Osaka.

Trying to figure out what the GODAO network actually *was* and how it managed to operate so many branches at once had always

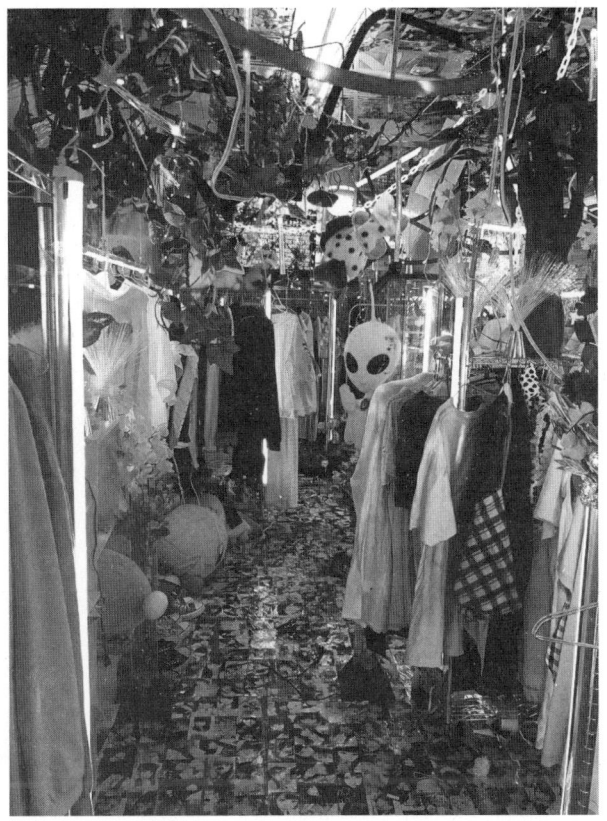

been like navigating a maze. That feeling of being lost in a labyrinth extended to the layout of their shops, too.

Going into the GODAO store in Harajuku was an intense experience on par with a funhouse or a hoarder's paradise. Thrift store-quality clothing hung from the ceiling. Black lights and random fluorescence on the floor provided the only illumination. Piles of broken Nintendo 64 video game consoles were stacked up in front of a register manned by a gang of teenage shopgirls in twin tail hairdos. Every inch of the walls and ceilings was plastered with tiny photographs of underground pop idol singers and GODAO employees, past and present. The air was heavy with the smell of

MONDO TOKYO

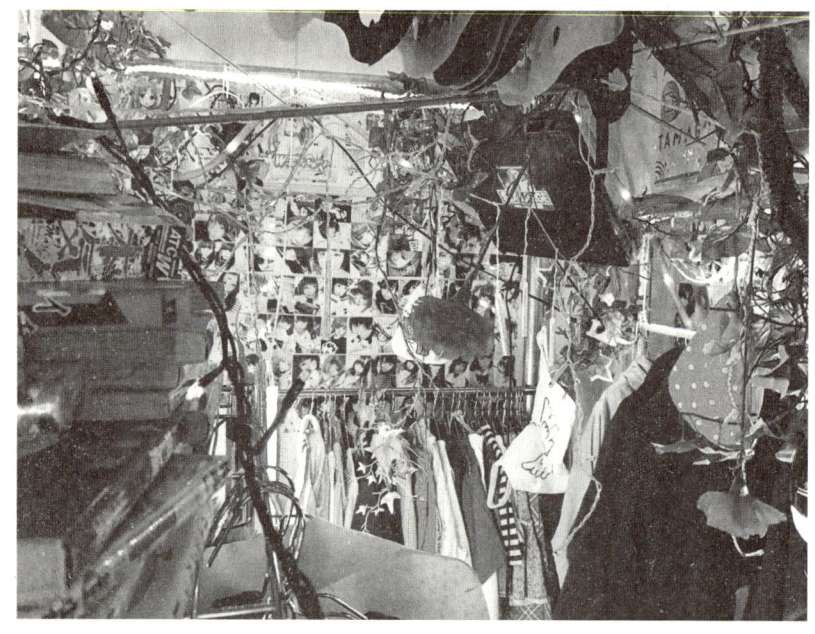

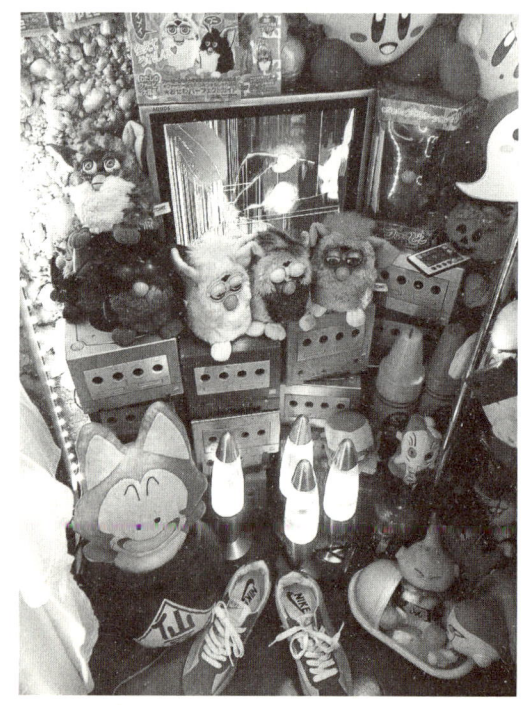

THREADS

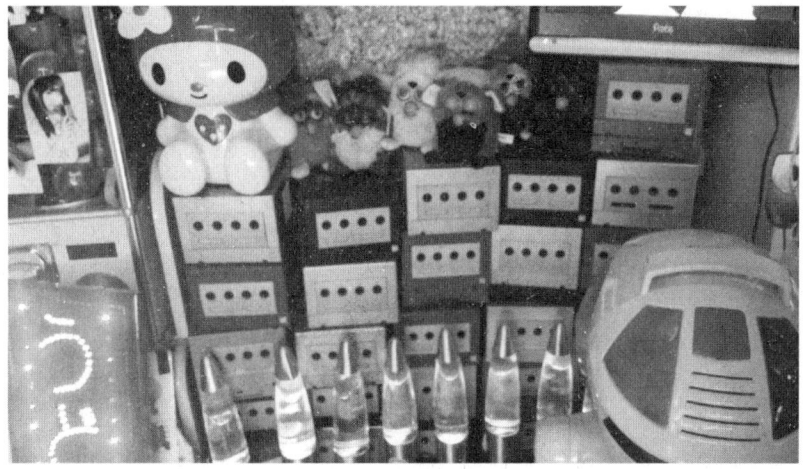

cheap incense. The store's iconography included plastic Jesus statues, inflatable aliens, and black magic conjuring circles, which decorated the shelves alongside tattered plushies of video game characters like Pikachu and Kirby. It looked like the headquarters of a strange cult that worshipped the 1990s trash culture. The only concession to the passage of time was that the store had its own Wi-Fi signal.

In addition to offering second-hand vintage clothes that had seemingly been pulled at random from a dumpster, GODAO stores offered their own original apparel creations. The fashion coordinates were a mix of otaku signifiers, internet jokes, and copyright violations. The GODAO logo itself was a knowing rip-off of the Nike emblem, right down to the trademark swoosh. The Psychic Shop logo was the Sony PlayStation logo, all warped and dripping as though it had been left out in the sun too long.

GODAO had one of the strongest aesthetics in all of Japanese fashion: nerdy, cute, conspiratorial, insular, fueled by junk food, anime, and the Internet. There were oversized hoodies on which someone had written *Nemui* ("sleepy") in what looked like Wite-Out liquid paper. There were laser-printed T-shirts featuring pictures of idol singers, unlicensed anime and game characters, marijuana leaves, and Internet Explorer-era computer graphics of the Vaporwave variety. It wasn't so much the clothes and designs themselves that were unique; it was the way the shopgirls could coordinate these items that collectively put them into a category *beyond cool.*

Despite the dirt-cheap quality, these shirts, hoodies, and accessories were all priced around USD 60 and even upwards into triple digits. You could say that it was a rip-off, but it was more like a tip-off. *Something was very weird about GODAO.*

The big problem, first and foremost, was that there never seemed to be any customers. The interchangeable, cult-like shopgirls

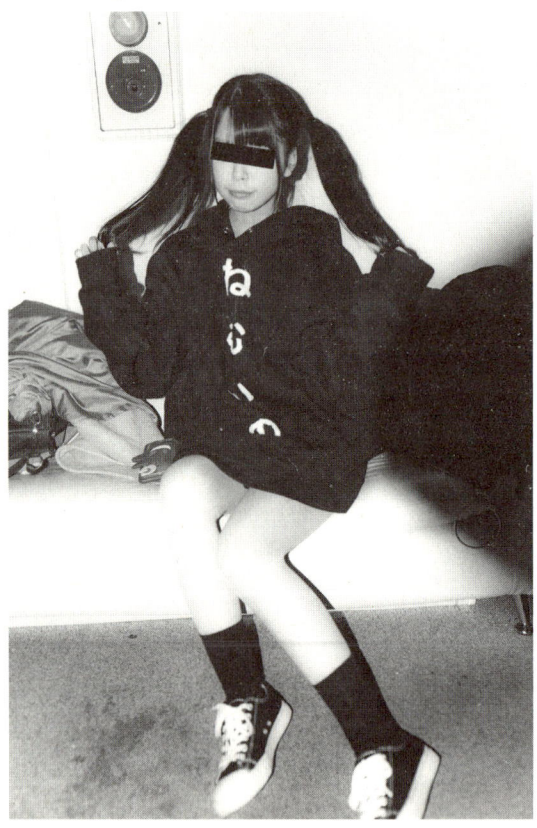

themselves were pretty much the only ones seen wearing GODAO clothes. They worked in empty stores by day and hung out in the GODAO bars and hookah lounges at night. And yet, there were more than half a dozen GODAO-related businesses open in Tokyo and Osaka. How did they manage to pay the bills and keep the lights on?

GODAO's owner was rumored to have burned down one of his stores to collect insurance money in the past. Yakuza members were sometimes seen hanging out at GODAO-owned bars. If you bought something with a credit card, one of the shopgirls would take a snapshot of the card and send the picture *somewhere* to *someone* to process the transaction.

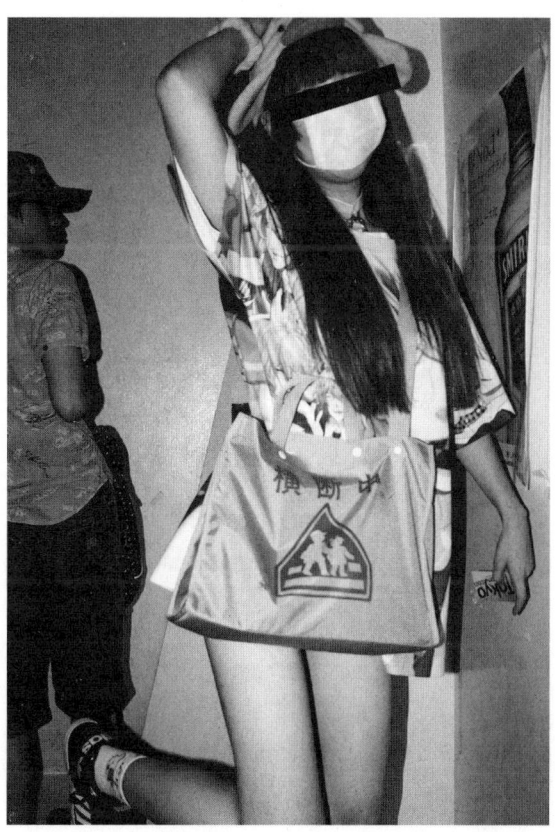

There always seemed to be something shady going on in the background. And yet, the GODAO crew themselves were down for anything. They would let visiting *gaijin* tourists play DJ sets at their clubs just for fun. A local foreigner (not me!) would sometimes ask the shopgirls to step on his face, which they did obligingly. GODAO did things differently from the rest of Japan, where everything is about boundaries and keeping up polite appearances. But you wouldn't want to trust them too far. Someone I knew ordered a GODAO New Year's "lucky bag" for about USD 150. She got her package in the mail a few months later: just an old Hawaiian shirt and a pair of jean shorts with the butt ripped out.

I have my own GODAO stories to tell. I was introduced to their head shopgirl through a mutual friend, and she let me use their stores and staff for a couple of photo shoots. You couldn't build a movie set that had better atmosphere and weirder lighting than those shops. I asked one of the shopgirls what it was like working there, and she just kind of shook her head and rolled her eyes. Another former employee told me the GODAO gang was "fun to hang out with, but not to work with," and that seemed fair and ultimately prophetic.

When the top brass was arrested for illegally taking that COVID-19 relief money, an empire crashed all at once. All the GODAO-related stores and businesses in Tokyo and Osaka shuttered one after another. Dozens of SNS accounts on Twitter and Instagram were either scrubbed of content or suspended outright. I imagined shopgirls getting whacked one after the other, like at the end of *Goodfellas*, so they couldn't testify in court. Although that hasn't happened, I don't think I would be surprised if it did.

So many weird, fun places in Tokyo closed down over the course of the pandemic—the Robot Restaurant, the Kawaii Monster Café—but the self-destruction of the entire GODAO subculture universe hurt the most. Crime doesn't pay (especially when you get caught forging business licenses), but GODAO had something more precious than stolen loot: genuine style.

And what's a fashion subculture without a few dark businesses having fun in the shadows?

Some, but not all, of the GODAO businesses and SNS accounts have been reactivated since this piece was written. It's not clear yet if anyone learned any lessons (particularly that crime doesn't pay), but hope springs eternal.

ICONS

Sebastian Masuda and 6%DOKIDOKI: Colorful Anarchy

6%DOKIDOKI was the very first shop that I ever visited in Harajuku in 1999. Back then, it was just a small store up a flight of stairs filled with accessories for quirky young women: Mexican wrestling masks, *Powerpuff Girls* toys, assorted items of psychedelic kitsch. The vibe was crazy and colorful, but these were merely the seeds of what was to come. In short order, the burgeoning *kawaii* (cute) art and fashion aesthetic would leave Japan and influence pop stars and fashionistas around the world.

    A few years later, 6%DOKIDOKI moved to another location in Harajuku and began selling their own original apparel, designed by the one and only Sebastian Masuda. This is where 6% cemented its reputation and where it still resides to this day. Filled with eye-popping colors and surreal touches like a merry-go-round erupting from a wall, 6%DOKIDOKI moved beyond its 1990s *kawaii* roots and evolved into a brand all its own: embodying the one-of-a-kind quality that has made Harajuku a global destination.

THREADS

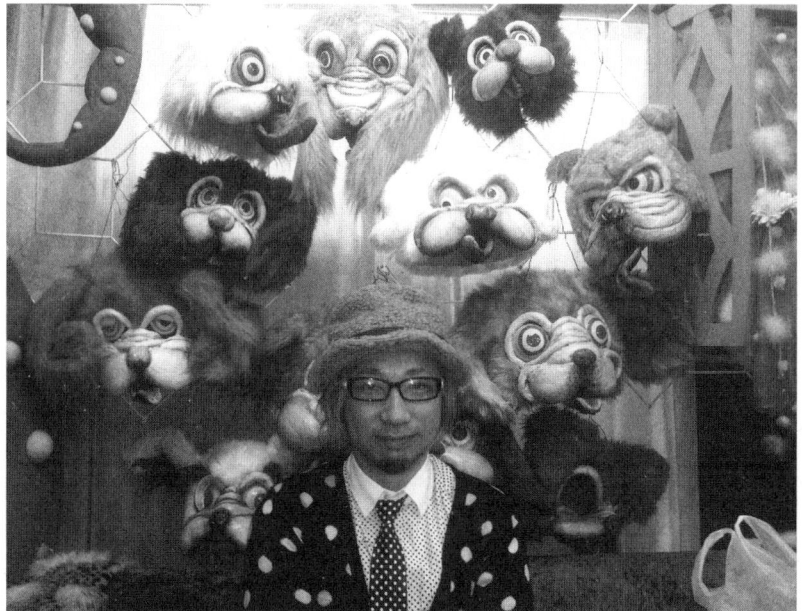

Sebastian Masuda at his studio in Tokyo.

I finally met Sebastian, the cofounder and public face of 6%DOKIDOKI, in 2008 and we became friends, although we seldom spent time one-on-one. Then, as now, Sebastian was nearly always accompanied by at least two 6%DOKIDOKI shopgirls: catwalk-ready staff members who looked like Barbie dolls after a night of debauched clubbing.

Sebastian was born in Chiba Prefecture in 1970. Interested in art and literature as a teen, he later moved to Tokyo and got involved with the experimental theater scene, spending time with Tenjō Sajiki, the famed troupe founded by underground icon Shuji Terayama. But theater productions were ephemeral: worlds built up and then were abandoned in a few weeks or even days. Sebastian wanted a more permanent base of operations to work his magic.

Matsuda opened 6%DOKIDOKI in 1995, a pivotal time for youth culture in Harajuku. As he told me about those heady days,

"In Harajuku, Omotesando Street and Takeshita Street were always very mainstream and upscale areas. They had all the brand names. The back alleys of Harajuku, on the other hand, were just for the locals. The rent was cheap and young people who weren't satisfied with current fashion trends could open their own stores there. These kids started to gather in the area to show off their original creations and to sell handmade goods and accessories in the street. It was the time of the so-called 'Harajuku Kids' and because of them, Harajuku became bigger and bigger."

For Sebastian and his followers, *kawaii* style was a kind of "colorful rebellion" against the gray normalcy of everyday life. Listening to loud music can damage your hearing. Looking at blinding day-glo colors can hurt your eyes. But sometimes, this is the best way to hear and see life to its fullest.

6%DOKIDOKI became a hub for the candy-coated extreme look of *kawaii* fashion and helped to generate buzz for the area. But

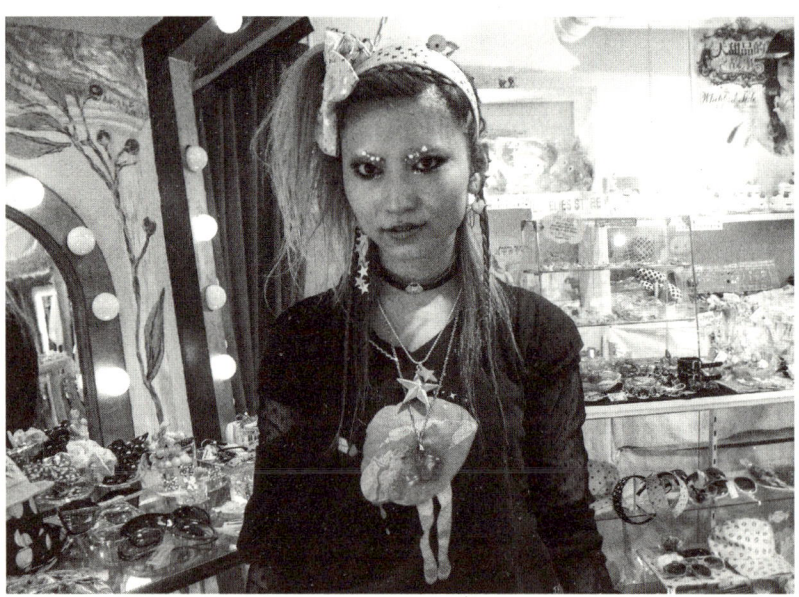

6%DOKIDOKI shopgirl Reiko, 2008.

eventually, globalization came knocking when mega chains like H&M and Forever 21 started opening flagship stores mere blocks away.

Said Sebastian in 2008: "It's getting harder and harder to exist in this area. The price of real estate in Harajuku continues to increase even during this current economic recession. Many big companies are investing in the area and many celebrities are gathering here. It feels like no one can stop this kind of momentum."

And yet, despite the odds (youth fashion is not a game for the faint of heart), 6%DOKIDOKI's influence only continued to expand. In 2009, they opened a pop-up shop in San Francisco and tours of Europe and North America followed. Sebastian became a spokesperson for Harajuku and Japanese street fashion, boldly proclaiming that "kawaii culture can save the world" at talk show events.

In 2011, Sebastian was the art director on Kyary Pamyu Pamyu's "PONPONPON" music video, a viral smash that helped to reenergize Harajuku yet again. Sebastian became in-demand as an art director on TV commercials and new projects like the fondly remembered Kawaii Monster Café. He had also embarked on a career as a visual artist, creating work outside of the 6%DOKIDOKI banner for gallery shows around the world.

The last time I saw Sebastian was in the fall of 2021, when I bumped into him in the streets of Shibuya. We recognized each other from afar even with our COVID-19 masks on. He told me that he had some big news: he was set to move to New York City. Still, 6%DOKIDOKI will remain open for the foreseeable future, as it has through earthquakes, pandemics, and fast fashion attacks.

Still, I wondered what Harajuku will be like without one of its biggest icons. Then I remembered something Sebastain Masuda once told me: "Harajuku style was created by the passion of a young generation of people who gathered here and made their own culture," he said. "It's more than just a look; it's a spirit. Maybe it would nice if that spirit left Japan and went on to inspire more people around the globe."

TUNES & VIBES

The unique sound of Japanese pop blends a wild cocktail of influences. The result? Masked wrestler rocker girl groups, space-age greasers, and holographic idols.

The Feminine

January 2006

Inside a dark club in Hatagaya, Tokyo, three young women are on stage, dressed in matching black and gold china doll dresses. There's a lead guitar and a bassist, and behind them is the drummer. They look a bit nervous, like cute little woodland creatures caught in the headlights. But that's understandable. Tonight is only the second time that their band, The Feminine, has ever played a show for a paying audience.

Suddenly, the guitarist, Reina, rips into her strings. Coarse, hot sounds come blasting out. The thudding caveman stomp of drummer Nao's beat backs her up. The music is primitive, borderline moronic. But there's no mistaking it. This is real rock and roll. Dig the lyrics:

"*My baby does the hanky panky...*"

The band breaks into a full-throated scream; the same howl that's been heard in a million frat houses and juke joints. Now it's official: The Feminine rock.

The garage rock scene is small in Japan, although it's had a shot in the arm from the internationally known band Guitar Wolf and the appearance of girl group The 5,6,7,8s in *Kill Bill Vol. 1*. But the

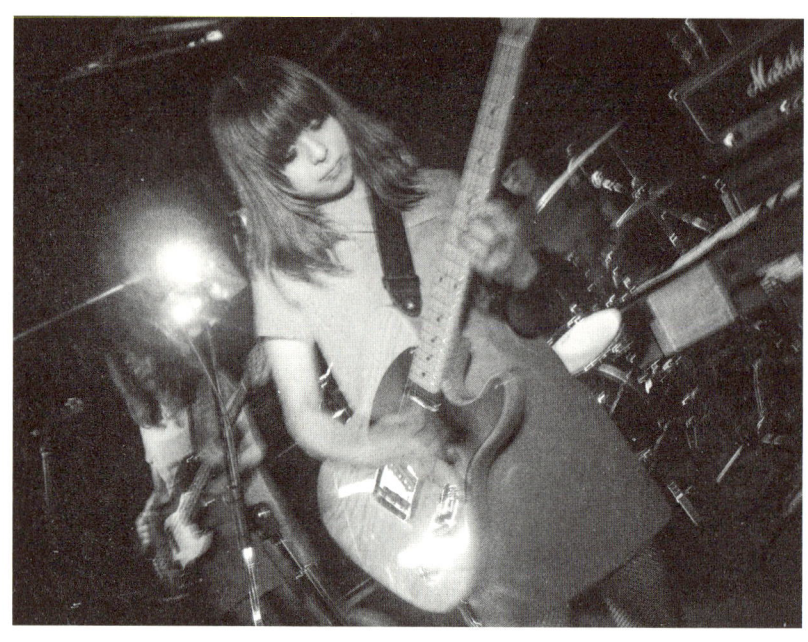

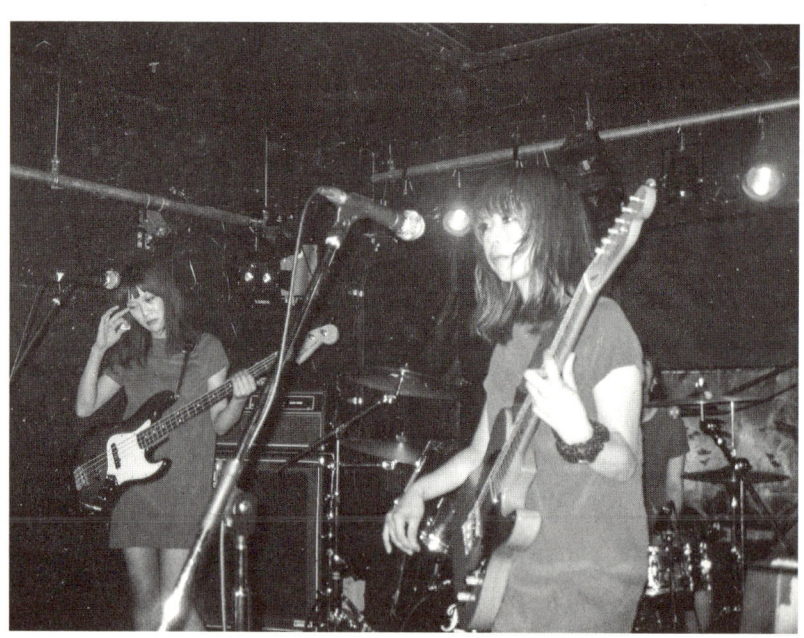

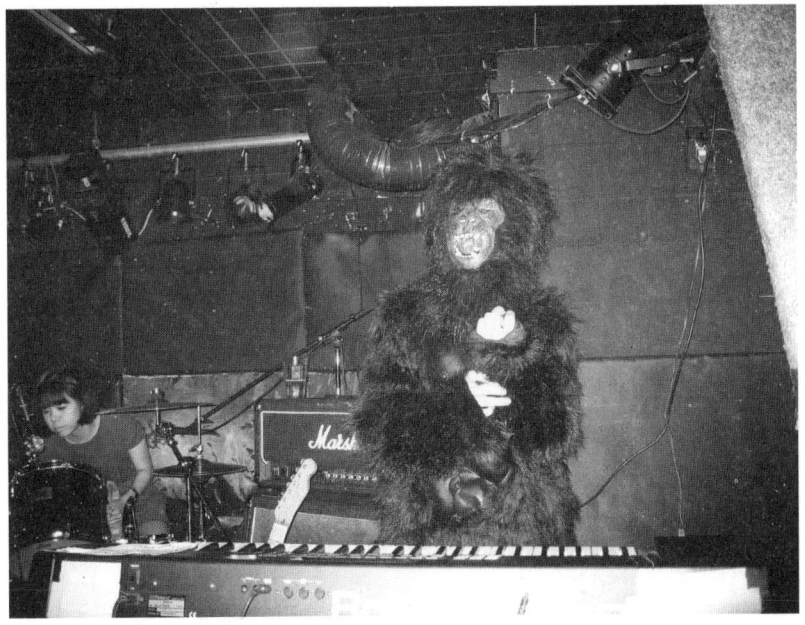

members of both those bands are in their 30s and even 40s: old enough to have been alive when rock dinosaurs ruled the earth.

The question that the existence of a band like The Feminine begs is this: what is it about old American music that appeals to young Japanese girls?

"I like this kind of music because it's simple and easy," says bassist Yoshimi, clad in after-concert vintage clothes that look like they were pilfered from Laverne and Shirley's wardrobe. Simplicity is a crucial factor for someone who has been playing her instrument for a total of three months. Her favorite band is The Sonics, a 1960s era R&B combo from the American Northwest. They're the kind of band known only to record collectors in their own home country. But that's how it works in Japan. If you want an alternative to karaoke-ready J-pop, you have to dig deep to find what you love.

Reina, coiffed with a Beatles haircut, is the best musician of the bunch. She's been playing guitar for five years now, long enough to be able to effortlessly toss out Chuck Berry riffs and honed her own sound. "I plug the guitar directly into the amp and turn the gain all the way up."

Yoshimi and Reina, both 21 years old, have been friends since junior high. Their lives were changed after they heard a CD by maximum Japanese rock and roll combo Thee Michelle Gun Elephant (sic) when they were teens at the local library. Soon, they found themselves taking the train from the suburbs to Tokyo's Nishi-Shinjuku, a prime destination for record collectors. Forming a band was the next logical step.

The Feminine have been around for all of three months, playing live about once a month, on average. Do they dream of someday becoming huge rock stars and playing arenas, even if that would mean giving up the garage rock sound?

"We like this kind of music because it's not A-class. It's B-class; a junk sound. We just want to keep playing live and having fun," explains Reina, who also has a message for America, the land where The Feminine get their inspiration.

"Let's twist the night away," she says.

"Thanks for the music," adds Yoshimi.

And then they're off to catch the last train home.

The Feminine were featured in Season Three of Johnathan Ross's feature documentary series Japanorama in 2007. They vanished soon afterward with only two official releases: a 45 rpm single and an appearance on a various artists garage rock compilation. I'd like to think Reina is still out there somewhere turning up that gain.

The Roots of J-Pop: Ten Bands to Explore

February 2008

Japanese popular music outside of Japan used to be a mysterious and obscure no-man's land accessible only to record collectors and people with enough money to blow on pricey imports. But now, thanks to YouTube, it's as easy as punching the following names into a search engine to get a sense of pop and rock's evolution in the Land of the Rising Sun. With such unlimited resources just a click away, I offer the following roll call of Japanese pop bands:

The Tigers

In the late 1960s, America had The Monkees and the UK had The Beatles. But over in Japan, the leading local merchants of teen freakbeat were The Tigers: five lads dedicated to making youth believe that all you needed to enter the pop sweepstakes were tight trousers and long hair. The music wasn't half bad either, and The Tigers ruled the charts with songs like "C-C-C," in which lead singer Kenji Sawada informed the listening public: "I'm so high." As if to prove

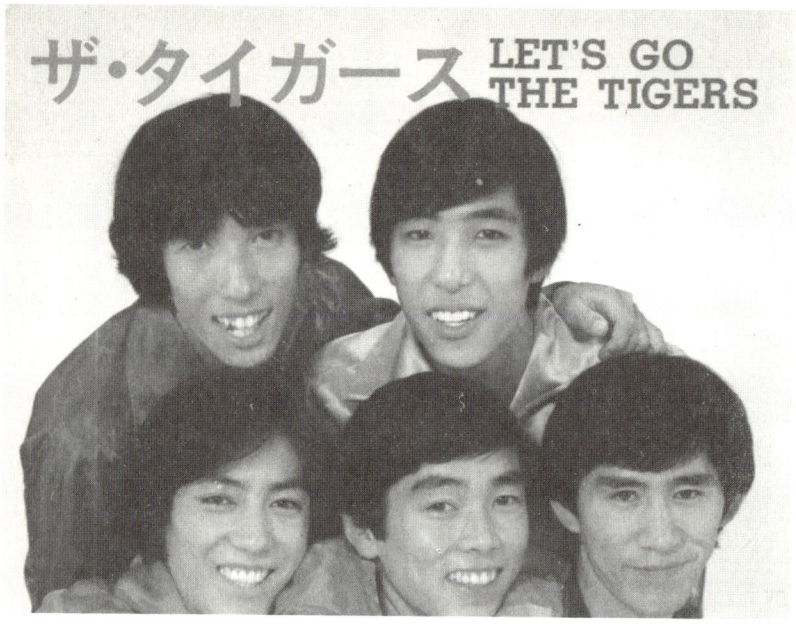

it, once The Tigers broke up in the 1970s, Sawada liberally applied eyeliner and lipstick, requested that everyone call him "Julie," and promptly sold more records than The Tigers ever did!

The Chanels

Direct from "the funky streets of Omori," The Chanels spent the 1980s imitating the sounds of American doo-wop and R&B. Unfortunately, they took the job a little too seriously: most of the band performed in offensive, minstrel-esque blackface. The Japanese public proved to be just as ignorant of racial sensitivity as The Chanels were, and their singles "Tonight" and "Hurricane" dominated the charts.

The band did get into hot water, but not because of their adopted skin color. One member was repeatedly arrested for voyeurism and others were caught with underaged groupies. But instead of changing their act, The Chanels merely changed their name to "Rats&Star"

and lived to croon another day. As recently as 2006, members could be seen on TV performing "Hurricane," still flaunting the ill-advised *Jazz Singer* look.

C-C-B

Ah, the 1980s ... peroxide hair, sweatbands, shoulder pads, and wheezing keyboards. Boy band C-C-B (full name deciphered as "Coconut Boys") was an undisputed master of all four. Ingratiatingly catchy hits like "Lucky Chance mo ichido" and "Naimononedarino I Want You" would win C-C-B little praise from music critics, but less demanding teenyboppers were knocked out. However, as their fan base began to grow up, C-C-B started to sound like the epitome of everything that was embarrassing about bubble economy era J-Pop. If you don't change with the times, what used to make you cool will suddenly make you lame. They managed to find some redemption, though, when their 1985 hit song "Romantic ga tomaranai" was prominently featured on the *Densha Otoko* TV drama.

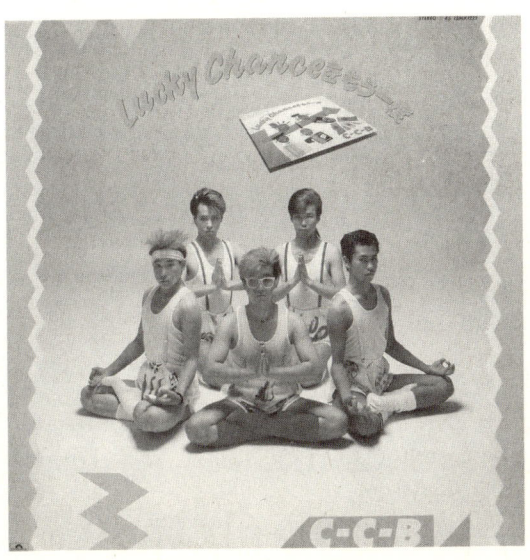

The Cools

Japanese pop acts had traditionally been as inoffensive as a basket of kittens until The Cools showed up in the mid-1970s. Roaring onstage in concert astride Harley Davidson motorcycles, this eight-member pack of Fonzie-esque greaseballs flaunted tough guy attitude and bad boy charm in spades. Studiously clad in leather and pomade, they belted out early R&R classics like "Long Tall Sally" and originals like "First Is Machine, and Second Is You" while girls in poodle skirts collapsed around their vintage Levi's jeans. Rebellious and mean-tempered, the band required no lessons in method acting when they appeared in the 1974 film *Violent Classroom*, sniffing paint thinner and reading porno mags in class. The title of their best-of record handily put their legacy in perspective for future generations: *Everything We Said Was Cool*.

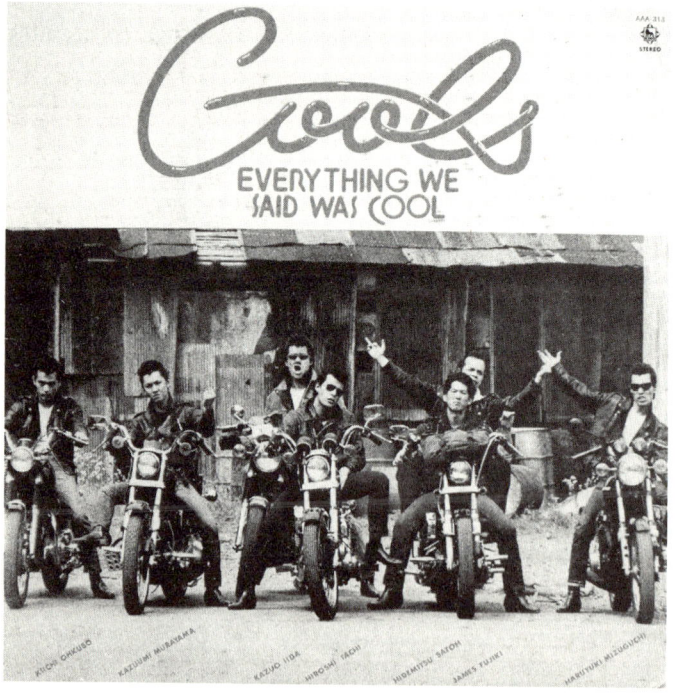

Hikaru Genji

It's hard to imagine a more potent symbol of Japan's remarkable ascension to economic power in the postwar era than this: seven half-naked boys singing and dancing around on roller skates. It almost didn't matter what their music sounded like; a shocked and awed public snapped up the late-1980s singles like "Stardust" and "Winning Run" anyway. Masterminded by pop Svengali Johnny Kitagawa, Hikaru Genji helped set the standard for the visually overwhelming concerts of successive "Johnny" monster acts like Tackey & Tsubasa and NEWS.

Godiego

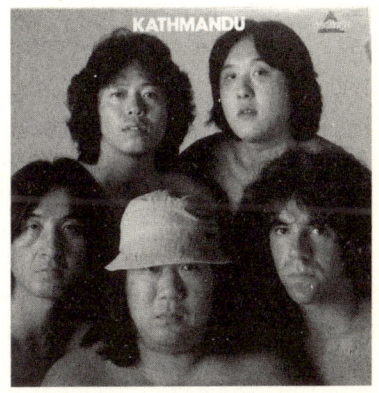

Problem: By the late 1970s, foreign rock music threatened to outsell domestic-produced Japanese pop. Solution: Godiego, a bilingual Japanese band that not only produced original songs in the exotic tongue known as "English," but who could count a genuine white boy among their number as well. The group wanted to be taken seriously as artists, but the biggest hits were mostly tie-ups with anime (such as their theme for the *Galaxy Express 999* movie) and kids' shows. Still, their song "Monkey Magic," written for the much-loved *Saiyuki* (known in the UK as *Monkey*) TV show, is ensured a place in history—if not for its synthesizer supernova opening, then most deservedly for lyrics like "What a cocky saucy monkey this one is."

Yokohama Ginbae

The Cools may have set the standard for bad motor scooter rock in the 1970s, but the following decade would require its own special breed of bike-riding grease monkeys. Yokohama Ginbae (full name: Crazy Riders Rolling Special Yokohama Ginbae) celebrated the lowbrow, speedtribe lifestyle of the "yankii"—trashy kids from the suburbs who zipped around on choppers at night making ungodly amounts of noise. With songs like "Tsuppari Rock and Roll" and "Yankii Mama," Yokohama Ginbae managed to make the sort of racket that could just barely be heard over their core audiences' "ah-oogah" horns. As such, they provided the soundtrack for uncountable acts of joyful juvenile delinquency.

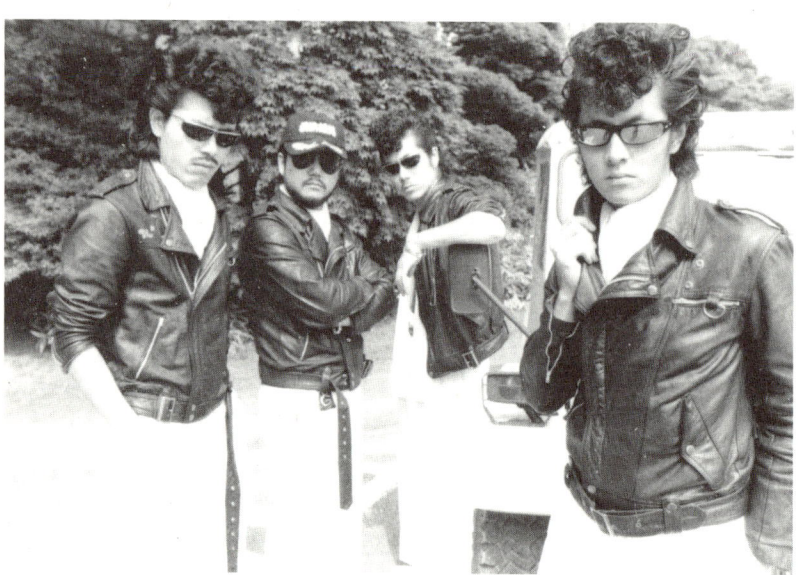

YMO

Three rich kids with keyboards managed to change the course of Japanese music forever. Since their 1980s salad days, the Yellow Magic Orchestra's pioneering techno sound profoundly influenced legions of knob twirlers. They were a national treasure of sorts, as early instrumental singles like "Rydeen" and "Technopolis" proved to be the equal of foreign masters of robot rock such as Kraftwerk. Even better, they were also the first (and last) Japanese band to ever hold court before a slightly baffled but ultimately appreciative audience on US TV's *Soul Train*.

Finger 5

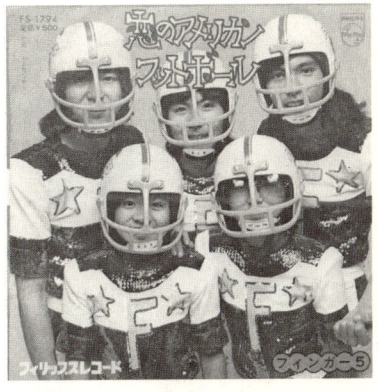

Okinawa's Finger 5 did everything in their pint-sized power to convince the record-buying public that any resemblance between themselves and the similarly named and sounding Jackson 5 was purely intentional. In hindsight, performing "ABC" live in concert wasn't such a good idea, especially since lead vocalist Akira (sporting hilariously oversized glasses) sounded more like South Park's Eric Cartman than Michael Jackson when straining for the high notes. Still, several of the Finger's original songs have become kitschy classics in their own right, including their stirring ode to telephone stalking "Koi no dial 6700."

The Checkers

Japan's answer to the New Kids on the Block, The Checkers made their media debut in 1983 in a storm of hair products and acid-washed jean jackets. There were seven members in all, although two were on the payroll to do nothing but dance on stage. Meanwhile, a team of hired songwriters provided the tunes. It would be easy to write off the band's material as textbook examples of disposable teen pop, but the songs, especially "Giza-giza Heart No Komoriuta" and "Namida no Request," remain inescapable in Japan to this day. Fans continue to clamor for a Checkers reunion, but such an event remains unlikely.

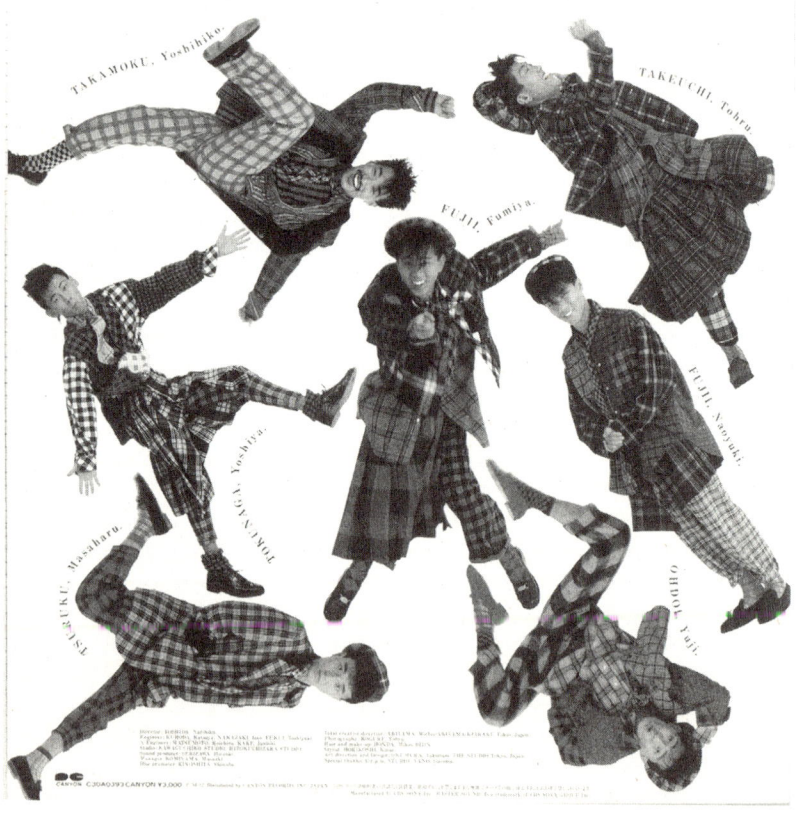

Shinjuku Freakbeat

March 2008

Shinjuku, Saturday night, and I'm making the long crawl from West exit through Kabuki-cho. You've gotta nudge through a wide trail of pleasure lovers and profit seekers on your way to NATURAL BORN ROCKERS night at the live house known as Shinjuku Red Cloth. A line of vintage scooters emerges from out of the velvety dark. Kids in skinny jeans and greasy hair stand around sucking on Marlboro Reds and guzzling Yebisu beer tall boys. This must be the place!

Inside, the Romanes—a three-piece female Ramones tribute band who mix up covers with familiar-sounding originals—are already on the stage doing their thing, slugging out 1-2-3-4 *dum dum rawk*. The look is vintage CBGB: leather jackets, stripey shirts, dirty sneakers. No one uses their real names, opting instead for monikers like "Johnny" (guitar), "Joey" (bass), and "C.C." (drums). The Romanes play in town a lot and recently had their first CD come out on the Deckrec label. But this is the first time I've seen them and I'm forced to pass a quick judgment. The act is a bit of a gimmick and just on the right side of amateurish. But the girls, probably in their early 20s, look like they are having a blast. Maybe it's a kind

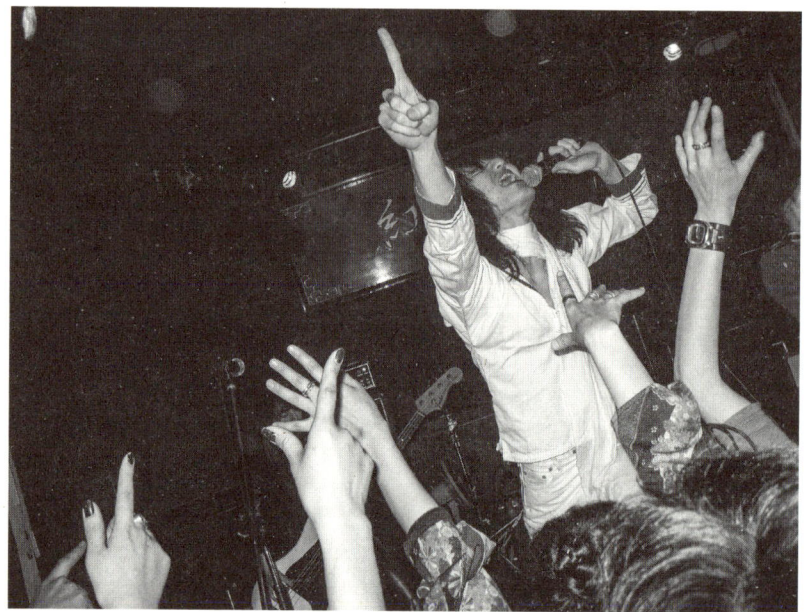

Above: Kegawa no Maries, 2008.

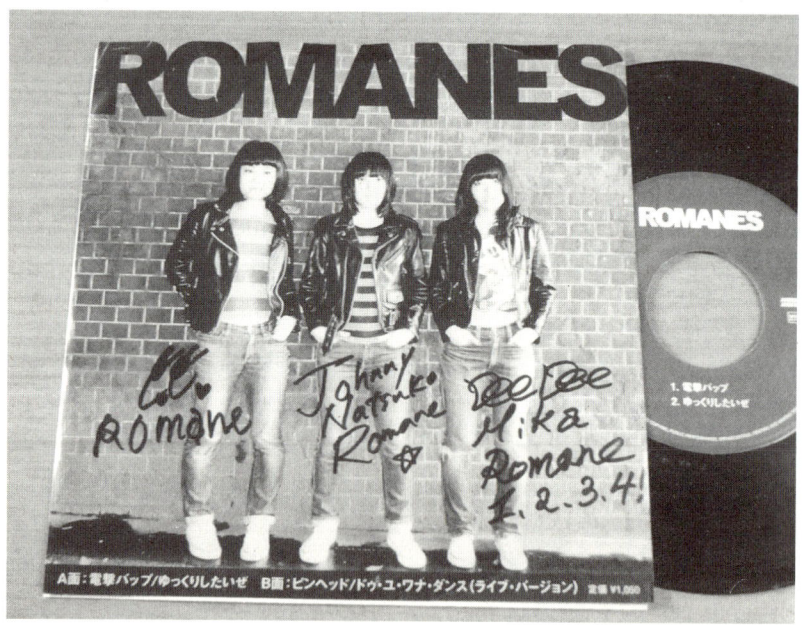

of gender-bending cosplay for people into old punk rock instead of anime. Still, there's a reason why the Romanes are on the bill as the opening act.

Old-time fixtures The Mighty Moguls are up next. They've ditched their usual caveman leopard skins for a Louisiana Hayride look tonight: overalls and string ties. The Moguls play wild and primitive frat rock (with just a touch of rockabilly) better than just about anyone and are blessed with one of the fiercest front women in the Tokyo garage scene: vocalist and bassist Miffy. She shrieks and wails her way through a set of greasy numbers that make the audience twist and shout, including a revelatory version of Disney's "Zip-a-Dee-Doo-Dah" (sounds weird, I know, but the strange power of Japanese rock and roll finds a way to make it work). Usually a three-piece, the band has a special guest tonight in the form of "Chucky" Nonaka, a long-lost member of the band who adds some crazy electric piano to the set. The crowd loses control and it's quickly becoming a big beery party in here—one that's about to go supernova.

The next band, Kegawa no Maries, stumbles on stage. The drummer, Fujio, is beefy, shirtless. He sports an inappropriate afro. Lead singer Ryohei looks like a shaggy-headed stork someone put makeup on and stuffed into a white sailor suit. Bassist Hiroko burns cool in a leather Emma Peel-meets-Planet X catsuit. Kegawa no Maries' music is more sleazy glam punk than studied retro rock, which is a very good thing. Their studio-bound 2006 debut CD was a bit disappointing, but the band is all aces live. In between thrilling Stooges-meets-Stones numbers like "Lovedogs" and "Velvet Gold May," Ryohei gobbles the mic and makes borderline incoherent (but oddly sincere) statements like "I love women! They don't care about politics or if something is cool or not! They just love cute things!" Their fans, mostly cute girls by no mean coincidence, eat it all up, while the boys can't take their eyes off that dreamy bassist. The group looks and sounds great. If it were 1973, they'd be selling out stadiums. Still, for those in need of authentic rock gods during these most desperate times, Kegawa no Maries might just have the goods.

But the real monster comes roaring out of the cage for the final act. Nylon is a four-piece all-girl band from Osaka wearing matching Reservoir Dogs suits and ties. There's no stage banter with this crew or even time to breathe in between bouts of their frantic, just-barely-melodic rock attack. All eyes focus on guitarist Shimano, a young lady seemingly possessed by the spirit of a young Pete Townsend. She doesn't play guitar so much as it plays her via windmills, duck walks, crowd surfing, and blank-eyed voodoo spazz-outs. The rest of the band struggles to keep up with her, and there's an element of "look at me too!" to the lead singer Meg's performance. But it's kind of hard to turn your attention away from the star attraction when Shimano leaps from the stage and onto the shoulders of a nearby spectator for a solo. Wait a second! That's no mere spectator. That's me!

Soon everyone spills out of Red Cloth sweaty and goggle-eyed, wanting more out of life. NATURAL BORN ROCKERS night did the trick. After a four-ring rock and roll circus, the remainder of this Shinjuku Saturday night seems positively tame by comparison.

Kegawa no Maries, the breakout band of this scene, signed to Columbia Records and did pretty well before splitting up in 2011. Nylon played their last gig in 2016. The Mighty Moguls are currently inactive but have played some reunion shows. There are still garage punk shows pretty much every week in Tokyo.

R.I.P. (Rest in Pixar) Perfume

June 2011

The girls of Perfume are graduating from the little leagues to be beamed into the very heart of the globalized entertainment industry. For, on this day most fair and foul, the Disney/Pixar film *Cars 2* opens in theaters across the world.

Perfume's 2007 hit "Polyrhythm" is featured on the *Cars 2* soundtrack, sandwiched in-between songs by their "new" contemporaries Robbie Williams and Weezer (remember them?).

Strange times. While holograms and virtual idols from Japan are stealing world headlines, last week's promotional splurge for *Cars 2* saw Perfume standing around in person at a Hollywood premiere for a CGI cartoon. One of them appears to have even made eye contact with an actual fan! A-chan, Nocchi & Kashiyuka sure have come a long way from their humble beginnings as starry-eyed dance students in Hiroshima. And while their techno sound—created by producer Yasutaka Nakata—isn't yet setting the world on fire, it is safe to say that their music (well, just this one song, unless Radio Disney deems otherwise) will soon be heard by a much wider audience, starting with little kids and their parents.

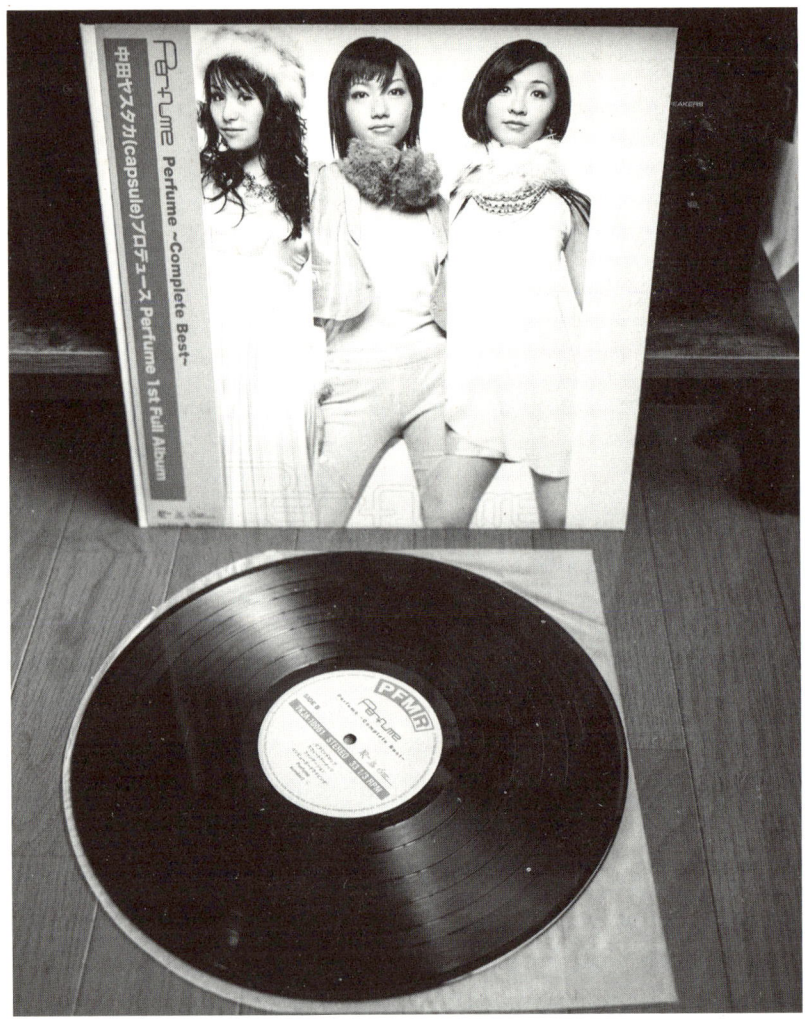

As an early fan of Perfume, and the type of guy who gets excited when Godzilla gets a star on the Hollywood Walk of Fame or when Tadanobu Asano wanders onscreen in *Thor*, I think I should be at least kind-of thrilled about this development. But my feelings are mixed at best.

Partially, this is because we are in the realm of a long and weird relationship between Japanese pop culture and the Disney Empire, which most recently has been playing out in their domestic handling of the Studio Ghibli films. And for readers who need reminding, Disney might have ripped off Japanese manga god Osamu Tezuka's *Kimba the White Lion* when they made *The Lion King*. More like *The Lying King*.

Much like Studio Ghibli, Pixar—also distributed by Disney—offers works that are high in production values and technical accomplishment; unlike Ghibli, they are also devoid of spontaneity or surprise, calculated down to the last pixel to affirm the most MOR of values. Formula seeks out other formulas to strengthen itself, so the already artistically tenuous electro-pop of Perfume has been cut and pasted into the mix.

Was "Turning Japanese" by The Vapors not available?

Japanese music magazine Oricon explains: "Director John Lasseter was searching for appropriate music to represent the Japanese party scene (in *Cars 2*) when Pixar staff members who were fans of Perfume recommended the group."

Why am I taking this so hard? I swear it's not merely a case of the fat hand of Hollywood taking a song I like and dropping it into a multiplex, thus endangering my emotional attachment to it by allowing total strangers in on the secret (see the entire Wes Anderson filmography). It's more that this crossover is happening at a moment when a once worthwhile musical act has become inessential.

I'll just come out and say it now: Perfume have arrived at the center of the world and all they have is a song that is four years old.

There's a good reason why "Polyrhythm" was cherry picked out of their discography. Their recent tracks don't stack up in terms of quality or novelty.

I first wrote about Perfume in 2007, when they hit it big. If you were in Japan in 2007, "Polyrhythm" was inescapable. It sounded like real music, unlike a lot of other Japanese pop girl groups, who sound like 48 hamsters all singing at once. Even W. David Marx, tireless critic of much of contemporary J-pop music, is willing to give the track a pass: "'Polyrhythm' instantly sounds like it was written in modern times by someone who likes modern music—not by some horrible committee of 50 year-old men who want to get the whole songwriting and production thing out of the way so they can get back to picking out the bikini styles that will force hapless nerds to each buy 500 copies of an upcoming single."

But now, Perfume has run its course. The band's sci-fi imagery (key tracks include "Monochrome Effect," "Liner Motor Girl," and "Computer City") and techno-pop style can be mimicked by any web-addicted *otaku* with his own "Vocaloid" singing synthesizer software, which simulates the human voice in an eerie, anime kind of way. These *otaku* fans can use Vocaloid to create their own virtual reality singers, and the results are increasingly outpacing the real thing. For example, the Vocaloid song "Just Be Friends" is clearly inspired by the Perfume sound but throws down the gauntlet with greater lyrical complexity and a very strong melody. Perfume's newer songs, by comparison, feel exhausted of ideas and composed of the same old knob-twirling tricks that producer Yasutaka Nakata presumably does in his sleep by now.

Perfume is destined to be as quaint to tomorrow's posthumans as 1970s soft rock feels to us today, and likely just as durable as a pop cultural landmark. The band and "Polyrhythm" will always sound like Japan circa 2007. This might be why Pixar was willing to export Perfume for *Cars 2*, way past the band's sell-by date. It's safe and tested and won't scare anyone off.

Without more songs to equal or surpass "Polyrhythm," Perfume now resembles Pixar's own would-be Hollywood blockbusters: every new release a carefully calculated tie-in, marketed months in advance for maximum exposure. Never mind the diminishing creative returns; gotta meet that quarterly report.

Ian Martin, who recently interviewed producer Nakata for the Japan Times, added some context: "With Perfume these days, I think Nakata's kind of working with his hands tied behind his back. He told me that since all the songs are pre-sold to advertising campaigns before he's even written them, he has to sort of work on them with that in mind."

In a shocking twist that no one saw coming (for once, I'm saying that with zero irony), *Cars 2* is now taking a beating from critics who were once convinced that the Pixar could do no wrong. *The Wall Street Journal* review lists off some familiar complaints that could just as well be applied to today's Perfume output: "a lack of variety, originality, subtlety, clarity and plain old charm."

That's all I have for now, but the song itself must have the final word:

とても大事なキミの想いは	Your very precious feelings
無駄にならない世界は廻る	Won't be wasted
ほんの少しの僕の気持ちも	The world rotates
巡り巡るよ	My little feelings
くり返す このポリリズム	Will circle again too

Despite my reservations about the waning quality of their music, Perfume has only continued to grow in global popularity. Now one of J-pop's big legacy acts, you can watch an original documentary about them on Disney +.

On "PONPONPON"

July 2011

The weekend finally started in earnest on Saturday night when Tokyo Fashion began spreading the word about the remarkable promo video for "PONPONPON."

"PONPONPON" is the first single by blogger, model, and all-around Harajuku Cinderella story Kyary Pamyu Pamyu. The song was produced by Yasutaka Nakata, mastermind of the groups Perfume and Capsule, for Warner Music Japan.

"PONPONPON" is exquisitely pitched right on the razor's edge between catchy and annoying, where real pop music resides. Half will love it, half will hate it. Either way, it sure makes an impression.

At the very least, the PON PON WAY WAY WAY PON PON WAY PON WAY PON PON chorus will probably take over your brain for a little while. So, mission accomplished.

If it were up to me, the song's music video would be recognized as a pop surrealist masterpiece on par with *Un Chien Andalou* or at least a gift shop calendar featuring Salvador Dali's paintings.

The visual landscape of the video—go watch it now—looks like one of those hallucinogenic everything-but-the-kitchen-sink photo

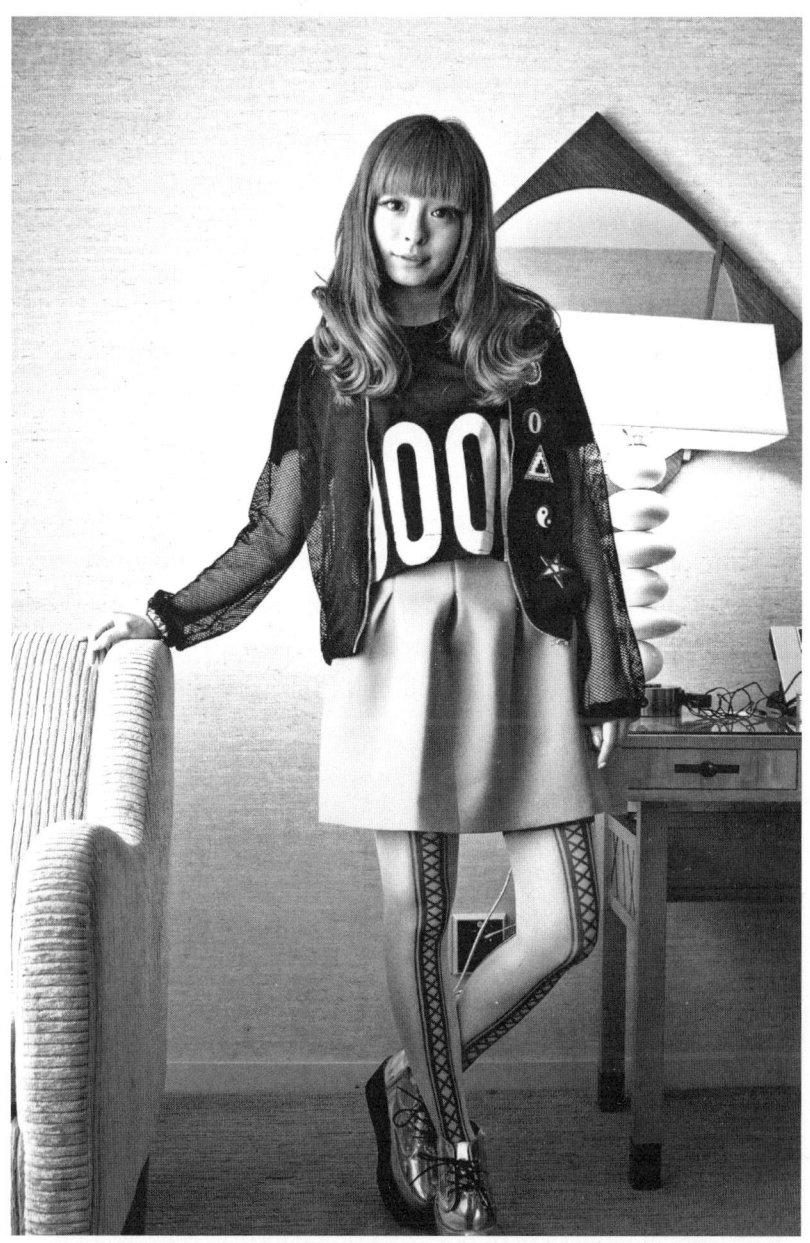

spreads in Japanese alternative fashion magazine *KERA*. The whole style is a balancing act between really *kawaii* or cute and really grotesque (a friend of mine describes it as "so *kawaii* it looks like a nightmare").

This absurd visual cocktail should come as no surprise when you consider the video's creative staff. Sebastian Masuda designed the set, after all; he has a background in avant-garde theater, which leads to a certain kind of aesthetic best typified by wild color, fancy goods, and accessory-littered rooms that form the backdrop for the strange and surreal lives of his female consumers. I recognize half the stuff in the video, including assorted toys and junk food wrappers, from the shelves of Sebastian's "sensational-lovey" Harajuku boutique 6%DOKIDOKI.

I always felt that Sebastian should create a mutant kid's show of some sort, maybe featuring 6%DOKIDOKI shopgirls Yuka and Vani carrying on the torch from Pee-Wee's Playhouse. While "PONPONPON" isn't quite a breakthrough on that level, I sincerely hope that it's a jumping off point for more adventures from all involved.

* * *

September 2021

It's been ten years since I wrote this little reaction to "PONPONPON"— after which it quickly went viral around the globe with zero marketing aside from a single upload to YouTube. It's not easy for Japanese pop music to get a big break overseas, and I shudder to think of all the time and money spent and lost trying to break other Japanese music acts abroad. But "PONPONPON" hit the right note at the right time: in the wake of this song came countless reaction videos, dance covers,

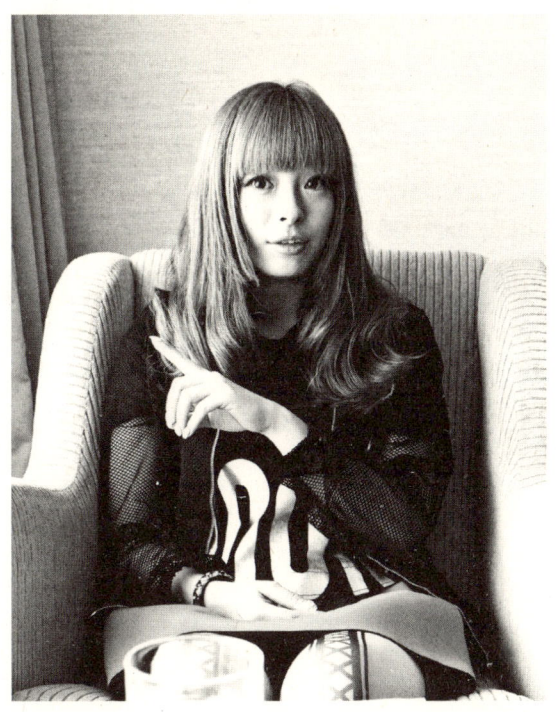

and makeup tutorials inspired by Kyary's unique look and crazy style. "Kids reacted," as they say. Over a decade later, "PONPONPON" has become part of internet history, joining the likes of "Chocolate Rain," the Harlem Shake, and Nyan Cat.

As of this writing, Kyary is nearly 30 years old. She still performs live and releases new music, but she is mostly a mainstream talent used to sell instant ramen, TV sets, and real estate in Japan.

Still, given the fact that people can't get enough of remakes and reboots these days, a trip back could always be in the cards. Before Kyary came along, only a handful of foreigners had ventured into the deep end where Japanese cuteness meets total lunacy. But now, we're all just a click on YouTube away from the epicenter. Stuff comes and goes, but "PONPONPON" will still be out there. Generations from now, still clapping along to some goofy beat.

Making a Virtual Idol: A Conversation with the Creators of Hatsune Miku

July 2011

Hatsune Miku is a virtual idol—an animated hologram—who sings using Vocaloid voice synthesizer software. On July 5th, three days after Hatsune Miku made her US concert debut at the 2011 MIKUNOPOLIS event in Los Angeles, her creators—Hiroyuki Itoh, the CEO of Crypton Future Media, and Wataru Sasaki, the developer of Character Vocal Series 01: Hatsune Miku program—passed through San Francisco. After I snuck into their hotel lobby, they graciously agreed to answer a few questions.

How do you think the MIKUNOPOLIS in LA concert went? Was it as you expected?

Wataru: I think it wasn't too "Americanized" or presented as American-style entertainment. It felt like a Japanese experience. It also wasn't too sophisticated, and that turned out to be a good thing. Simple is better.

Is Crypton looking to improve the hologram technology used in the concerts?
Hiroyuki: Our vision for these concerts is not "complete" yet. It doesn't exist in an idealized format yet. We're still evolving it. And we can't predict how the audience will react at each show. There is an experimental aspect to it, and the same goes for everything related to Miku.

Hiroyuki, you've said that "Understanding why Hatsune Miku is so popular with youth all over the world will also help us understand the future of the entertainment business." What do you think the future of the entertainment business looks like?
Hiroyuki: That's a tough question. We should ask, "What is the entertainment business?" Is it the business of entertainment? Maybe the future of the entertainment business is no longer business. For example, right now, a lot of people are enjoying YouTube. The content is made by users. The provider is not doing this as a business. The act of making content itself is already entertainment. It's just that there's not so much money involved. But the consumers respond to the creator by replying with comments and clicking "like" buttons. Eventually the creator or provider might get some kind of reputation or value and can finally end up making a business out of it.

By leaving comments and interacting, consumers aren't just consuming. They're now shaping the entertainment business. That means, to consume entertainment is now equal to creating entertainment. So, we need to redefine the meaning of what the entertainment business is. That is the future of the entertainment business. And Hatsune Miku is one of the experiments.

So the ability to create things for yourself will change what entertainment means.
Wataru: Right now, a lot of young people are consuming energy drinks and playing games on the internet. But who made the games

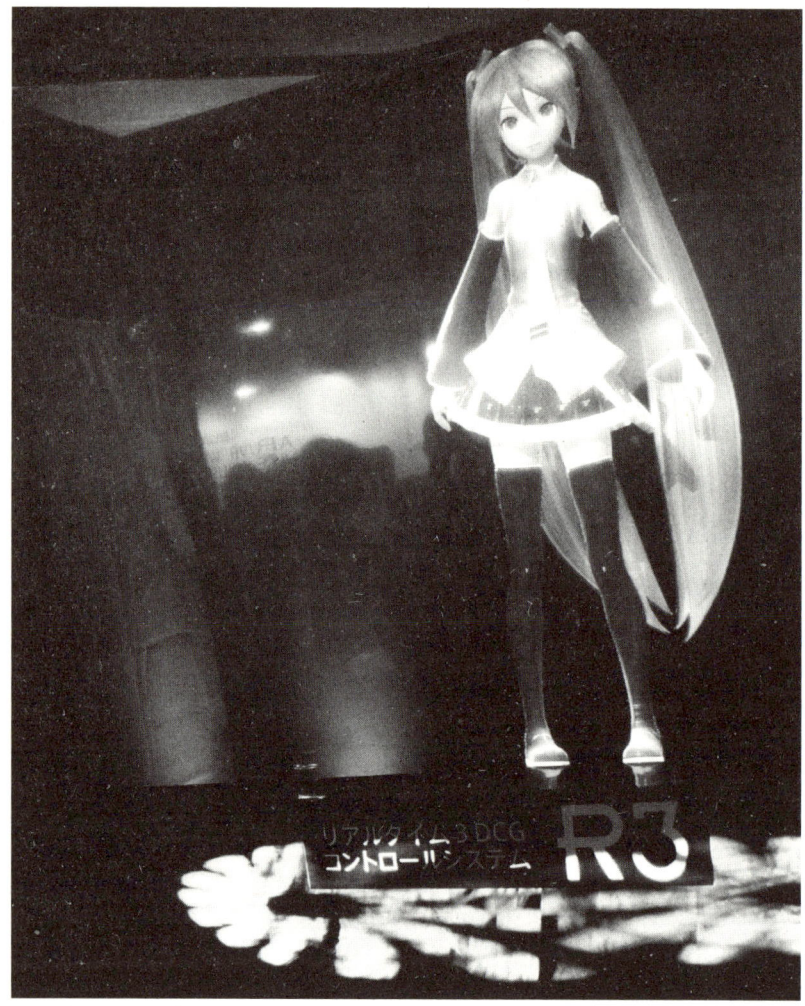

A holographic Hatsune Miku appears.

they play? The game producers. Who ends up making money? Maybe the owner of the game company. If you have a lot of kids enjoying a game, spending their money on it, you'll have even more old guys making money, even though they had nothing to do with creating that entertainment. I simply think that's not cool. People that you don't know, people that the game user has no relationship with . . . the more you spend your money, these strangers gain your money. That's a fact. This leads to a situation where it is harder and harder for creators to make a living.

So, to create a good situation for creators and producers means to offer strong entertainment that a lot of young people enjoy. That's why we want to redefine what "entertainment business" means. We want to change the way the world thinks about these things.

What has surprised you the most about the Hatsune Miku phenomenon?
Hiroyuki: It's only been about ten years since a lot of people started using the Internet. And I think we are still in the process of discovering what can be done with it. During the process of distributing the Internet to people, many things and industries will be replaced by newer forms. For example, music, e-commerce, or social networking sites like Facebook. Maybe an older institution like the telephone will shift into a totally new industry sometime soon.

I won't say that Hatsune Miku might destroy the music industry, but . . . I am looking forward to making some kind of impact. I feel like we are involved with something very new. I want Miku to be some kind of symbol or icon for change. I hope that Miku will be recognized for that, pointing us to a bright future.

Sounds like the discovery of the atom . . .
Hiroyuki: Yeah, that's right, just like the atom.

The tech behind Hatsune Miku helped open the door for a host of similar virtual music acts, including holographic resurrections for the likes of 2Pac and Freddie Mercury. The VTuber boom, where anyone can become a virtual character or just a fan of one is now underway as well.

Masked Marvels: The Strange World of Kamen Joshi

March 2016

How to explain Kamen Joshi ("Masked Girls"), Japan's latest experiment in mind-melting underground pop idol music acts? Perhaps it is best to let band member Nanaka Kawamura throw the first volley: "Kamen Joshi is a new type of idol that you have never seen before; we wear masks, do head-banging and dive into (the) audience. It is a very extreme and cool group."

You need a gimmick to stand out in Japan's crowded pop idol sweepstakes, and Kamen Joshi has too many to count: their world is a stage full of girls in slasher movie-style hockey masks, wearing eye-popping day-glo outfits, singing and dancing while swinging around weapons as though in a demented fighting video game.

"We also use toilet paper guns," says Nanaka Kawamura, who is wearing a schoolgirl uniform along with colossal Crocs-style sandals shaped like monster feet that squeak when she walks. "These guns can shoot a roll of toilet paper during our live performances."

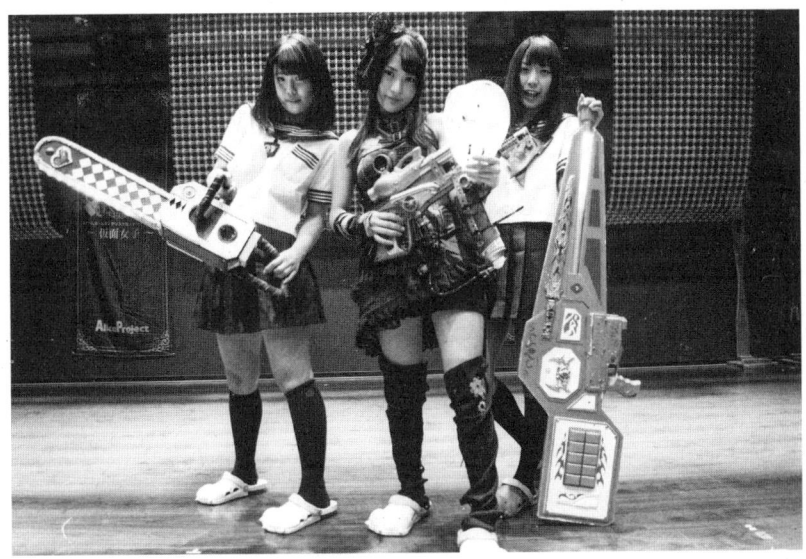

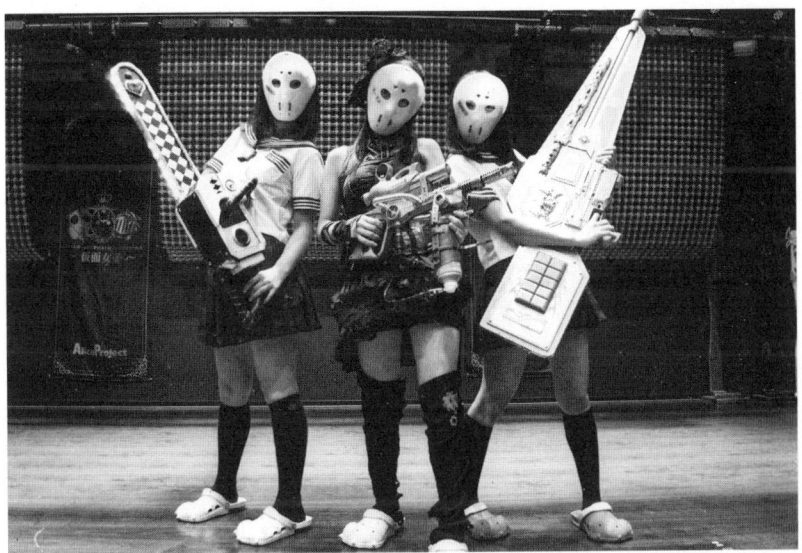

Originally formed in 2013, Kamen Joshi assaults the senses like a pop girl group seen through a postapocalyptic lens, shot out of a cannon through a Mad Max movie. They're here to challenge the

Tokyo Robot Restaurant for the title of greatest show on earth, and naturally, there is a growing cult of fans who adore them.

Kamen Joshi is actually made up of three subgroups: Alice Juban, Steam Girls, and Armor Girls, each of them performing in a slightly different style. Everyone syncs up at the official Alice Project Theater at the Pasela building in Akihabara: a multistory maze of karaoke rooms, colossal honey toast desserts, and bizarre-themed restaurants.

Here in the Alice Project Theater, at an ersatz tropical bar decorated with giant teddy bears, I have burning questions to ask about the function of leisure and entertainment in Japanese society. But right now, with three members from Kamen Joshi (Nanaka Kawamura, Moa Tsukino, and Erina Kamiya) seated directly across from me, I'm really just curious about the masks. Ladies, what is up with the masks?

Says Nanaka Kawamura: "Kamen Joshi is a group made up of people who failed the audition for other major idol agencies. Since we can't get by on our looks, we became a group, and wore masks. We also wear masks because we need to fight together as a mass of people, rather than as individuals."

Moa Tsukino explains, without a trace of irony, "We gave up on cuteness and instead we *rock hard*, using the power that comes from the bottom of our hearts to do our live performances."

Erina Kamiya, who is dressed in stunning head-to-toe Steampunk fashion (part of the look assigned to the Steam Girls subgroup) sums it all up thusly: "By doing this, we can make ourselves appealing in a different way than other idols."

So far, the appeal seems to growing. Kamen Joshi began marching out of the Akihabara underground and into the Japanese mainstream music charts in January 2015 when their single "Genkidane☆" hit the top of the weekly Oricon ranking (I'm trying to think of the last masked musical act that accomplished this feat and am coming up empty). And it's not just the usual idol otaku crowds supporting them, either.

Kamiya explains, "If you go to other artists' live performance, the audience is just watching the stage. But the good point of our live performance is that you can feel a sense of unity throughout the whole venue."

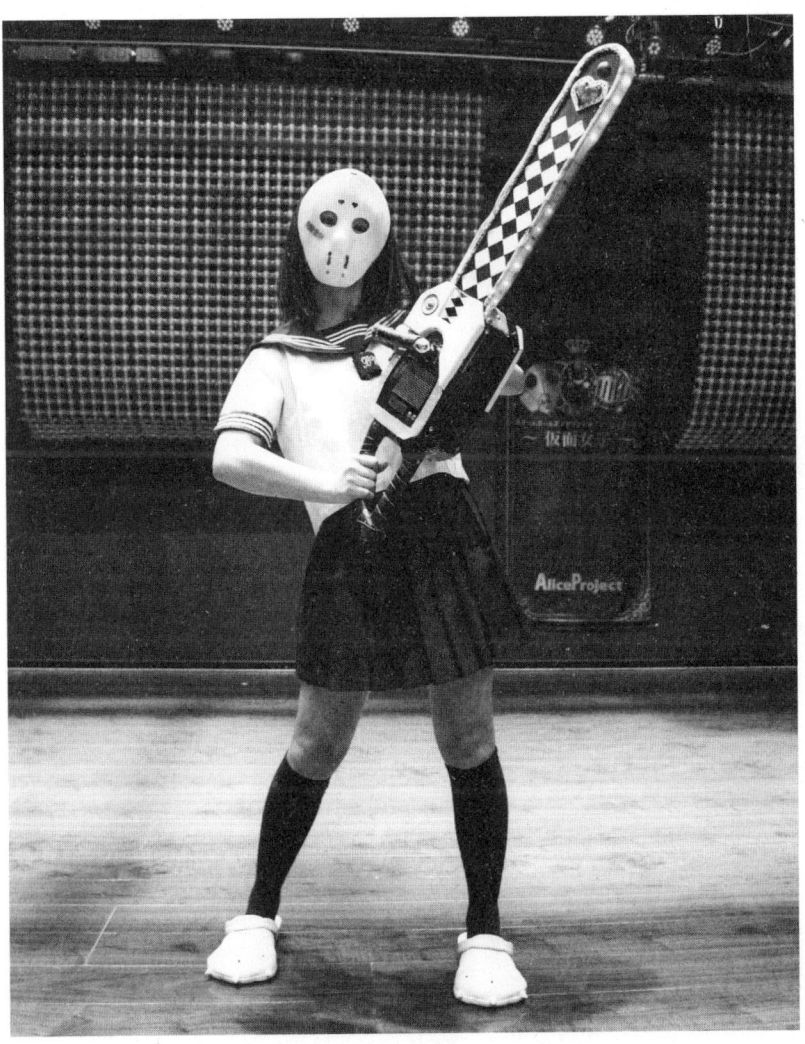

Kamen Joshi's penchant for "Boat Sailing" best demonstrates this very special relationship: during the frenzied peak of a particular song and dance routine, an inflatable raft is brought from backstage for one of the masked girls to climb in. A team of fans then hold the raft aloft and walk it around the venue while the singer continues warbling away inside. Pretty simple: No fans = no boat ride.

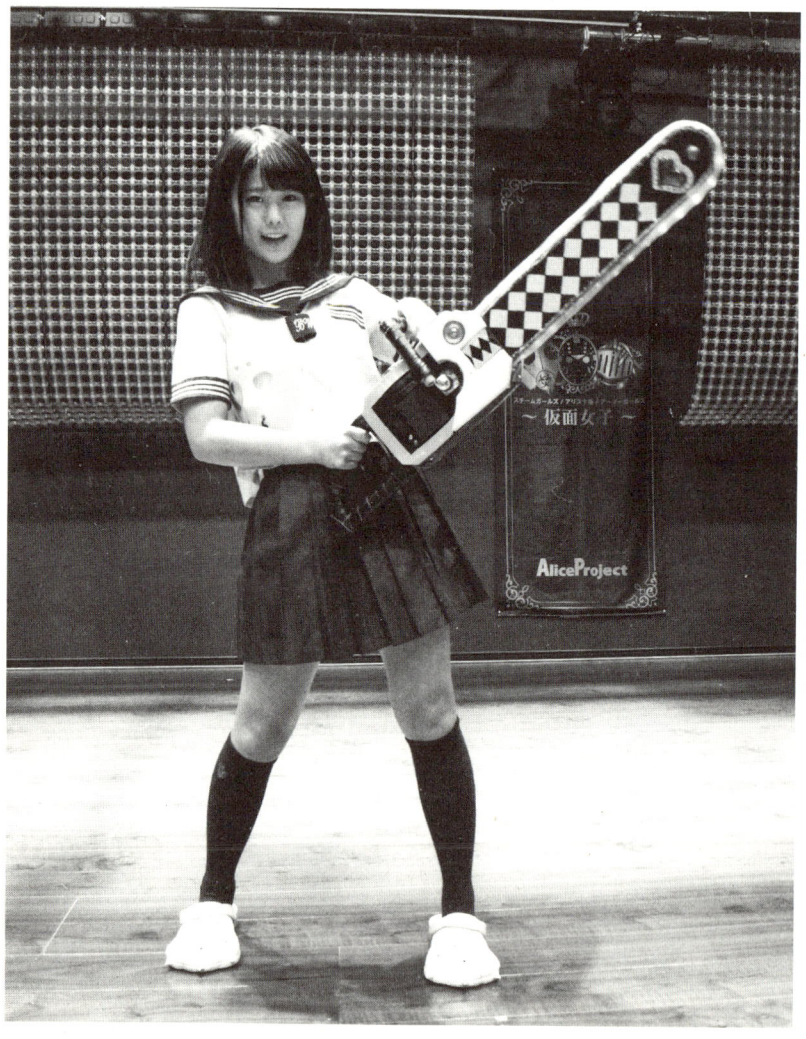

"You can find our fans easily when you are walking around Akihabara, because you hear the squeaky sound of their sandals," Nanaka Kawamura explains, referring to the trademark monster-mutant Croc slippers all three girls—and now their fans—love to wear. "Many shops in Akihabara carry them, so it's becoming a hit."

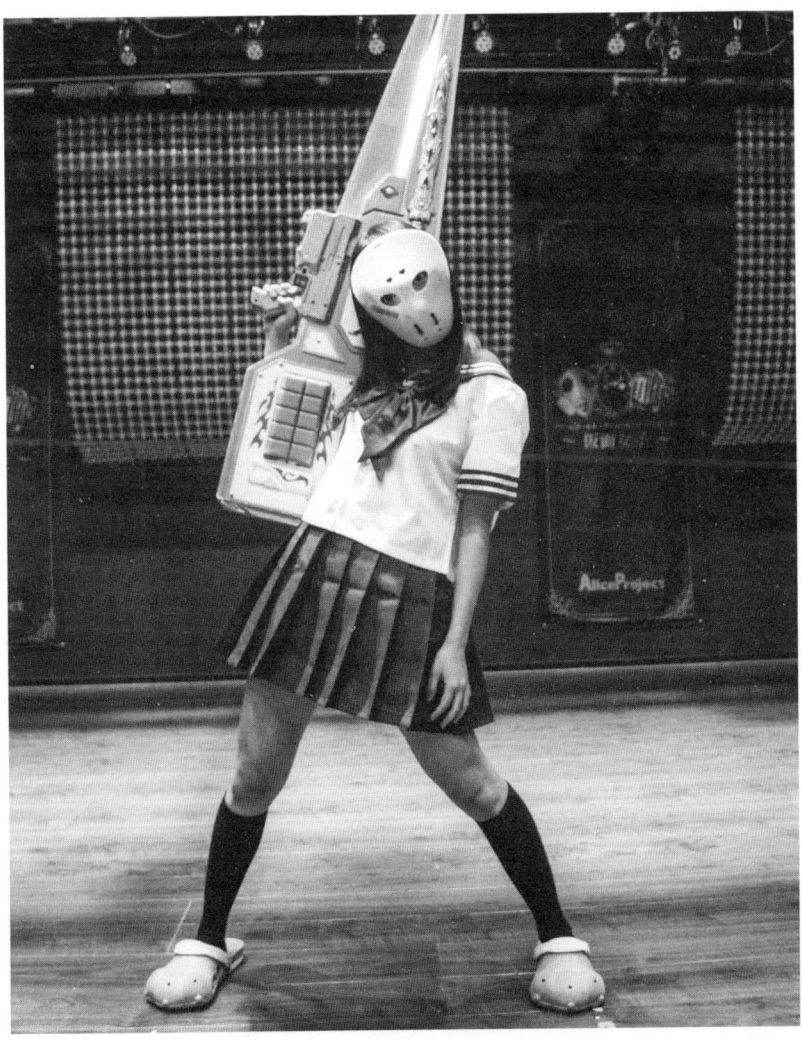

Before the girls run off to get ready for their next hard-hitting performance at the theater upstairs, they have a message for everyone reading this. Kawamura chirps, "I'd like you to come to this theater and enjoy our live performance. We actually see many overseas fans who are excited to tell us that they had fun!"

Moa Tsukino adds pragmatically, "We stream our videos on YouTube every day and our 'Junketsu' series has English subtitles. You can watch the segments featuring our live performance and our daily lives, so please search for them on YouTube."

Erina Kamiya knows there's a whole wide world out there, some of whom may be intrigued by the idea of gangs of wild masked idol girls, so she says: "Most of the people reading this must live outside Japan. So when you visit Japan, please come to Akihabara in Tokyo to see our live show. It's better and more exciting than watching our videos."

Kamen Joshi are still active and made world headlines for endorsing Donald Trump during his 2016 campaign on their YouTube channel. Erina Kamiya left the group to become a gravure idol in 2018 and received death threats from fans who didn't want her to quit.

Idolized

November 2019

Shibuya, Tokyo. A night on the town.

I am inside Club Asia, a medium-sized venue on rowdy Dogenzaka street, for the live debut of a new idol group called AiDOLOXXXY: a five-girl, all-singing, all-dancing sensation produced by the Japanese fashion brand galaxxxy.

Minutes before showtime, nervous event staff skitter across the stage, on the floor, behind the soundboard, and backstage, making sure everything is perfect. A pro camera crew takes their positions and adjusts their equipment to film this auspicious occasion for a music video.

Despite this being AiDOLOXXXY's first-ever live show, the house is full, with nearly 100 warm bodies waiting patiently to be entertained before the main stage. As with most idol shows, the audience is primarily male: guys in their late 20s to middle age. Some have just gotten off work and are still in the same suits they wear at their boring day jobs. Others are lost in the deep end. For these guys, idols are a lifestyle, not a hobby. They are part of the elite team of shock commandoes known as "Idol Otaku," decked out in concert T-shirts of their favorite groups (underground idol sensations such as You'll Melt More and BiS), backpacks festooned with logos and pin badges, and plenty of battery-operated glow sticks in their mitts.

The lights go down and AiDOLOXXXY debuts in a roaring blast of EDM beats, pop vocals, and highly choreographed dance steps.

The audience has probably seen better and probably seen worse. Either way, they begin to do what idol concert audiences do. They shout out loud call-and-response cheers of encouragement, frantically wave those glow sticks and eventually make conga lines and weave around the floor in train-like formations.

Even though no one has ever seen AiDOLOXXXY live before tonight, the idol fans know just what to do, like headbangers at a metal concert or salmon at a spawning. It is the ritual. It just always happens this way.

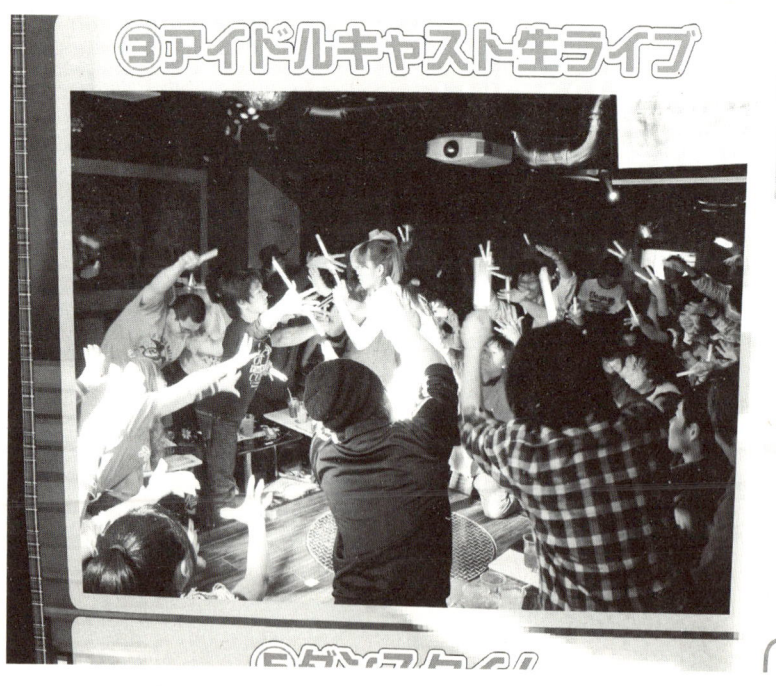

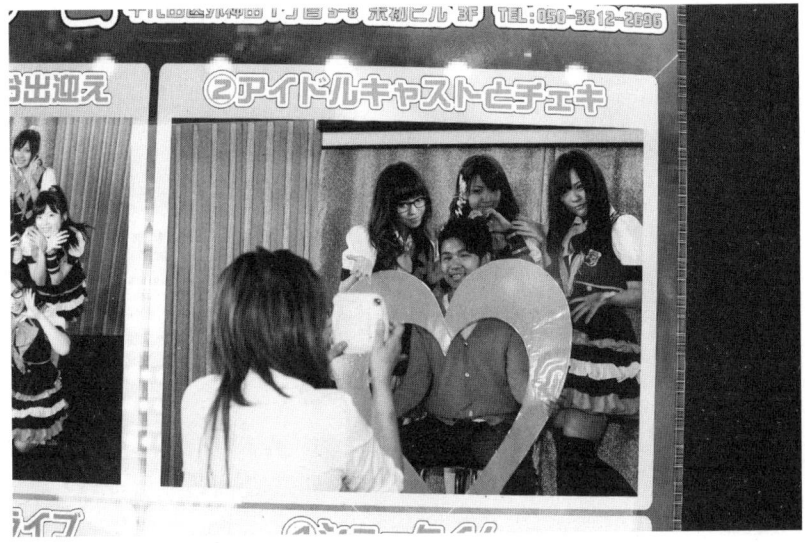

Photo op at an idol event.

It's funny.
It's awkward.
It's high energy.
It's an idol concert.

Japanese idol groups—so-called because their members are idealized and almost worshipped by adoring fans—began in the 1970s, when attractive young women dressed up in flashy outfits and grouped together to sing pop songs. Think the Spice Girls, but younger, cutesier, and with a very different audience (male, older).

Why and how do people become idols? For me, it is one of the great mysteries of Japanese pop culture. You ask the idols themselves about their motives and methods and you won't usually get much more than "I wanted to be an idol since I was a little girl." Male fans are even less self-reflective, giving cryptic statements such as "idols help cheer me up" without ever taking time to address the weirdness or compromising position of being a dude who's into teen (and sometimes preteen) musical acts.

The best I can figure is that idol groups and their fans are a dance between opposite forces: youth and age, male and female, spectator and spectacle.

I watch the concert leaned up against the wall, shifting my focus between the writhing crowd and the AiDOLOXXXY girls jumping around on stage, trying to take it all in. I'm half-laughing, half-shaking my head in disbelief. Hundreds of these kinds of events seem to happen every week across Japan.

After a few songs and some pre-rehearsed banter, AiDOLOXXXY say goodbye and exit stage right (being a new group, their repertoire is a bit limited at the moment). In time, COVID-19 will strike and idol concerts—and the proximity they allow between performers and fans—will become an endangered species. But for 15 minutes tonight, for an audience 100 strong, AiDOLOXXXY was the most important thing in the world.

ICONS

AKB48: Smells like Teen Spirit

When it comes to being in the right place at the right time, I've been lucky exactly twice.

I saw Nirvana live in concert in the summer of 1991, four months before they released their breakthrough album *Nevermind*. The crowd went wild. Kurt Cobain dove off the stage and landed on top of me, twice. I still have mild hearing damage from the show.

The other time was in 2006, when I got to see the first incarnation of the all-singing, all-dancing musical idol sensation known as AKB48 and lived to tell the tale.

It began simply enough. A TV producer at NHK had nabbed free tickets to an AKB48 concert and invited me along. We were not making a program about AKB48 or even working on a story about idols, but we *were* chasing a buzz.

The Akihabara neighborhood was in the media spotlight, thanks to the maid café boom and the popularity of *Densha Otoko* (Train Man), a multimedia franchise about the adventures of a lovelorn otaku guy who bravely helps out a young woman on a train. Everyone wanted to know what the wacky otaku would get up to next.

Producer Yasushi Akimoto—one of those show biz empresarios who periodically emerge from the shadows to rewrite the rules of the game—had the answer. He took over a floor of the Don Quijote chain discount store in Akihabara, already a hothouse of seriously bad taste, and converted it into a theater for his new idol group: AKB48. It was comprised of several rotating teams of young girls who performed in concert to small but adoring nightly crowds.

The group's tagline was "The idols you can meet" and the inevitably male audience was encouraged to stick around after the show and interact with the girls in the lobby, which was filled with consumables in the form of food and merch.

Breaking down the walls between idols (who previously maintained a distanced status at all costs) and their weirdo fans was then a novel idea. It would have major repercussions later on, when some fans got a little too close for comfort *and started attacking the girls with handsaws.* More about that later.

But for now, targeting otaku on their own turf was a marketing innovation that would be relentlessly imitated by later idol groups like Dempagumi.inc, Momoiro Clover Z, and Kamen Joshi. All of them used the hearts and minds of the countless lonely men in Akihabara as a launching pad.

Only seven people were said to attend AKB48's very first live performance. A few months later, the place was selling out every night.

When I got to the AKB48 theater that evening, I was struck by how small it was. It looked like the tiniest theater at a multiplex cinema. There were only a few rows of seats down in front, all of them claimed already, and the stage wrapped around them like a horseshoe.

I had to stand in the back to see the show, and I wasn't alone.

A group of young dudes stood shoulder-to-shoulder all around me, like soldiers in a private military company. They wore long coats

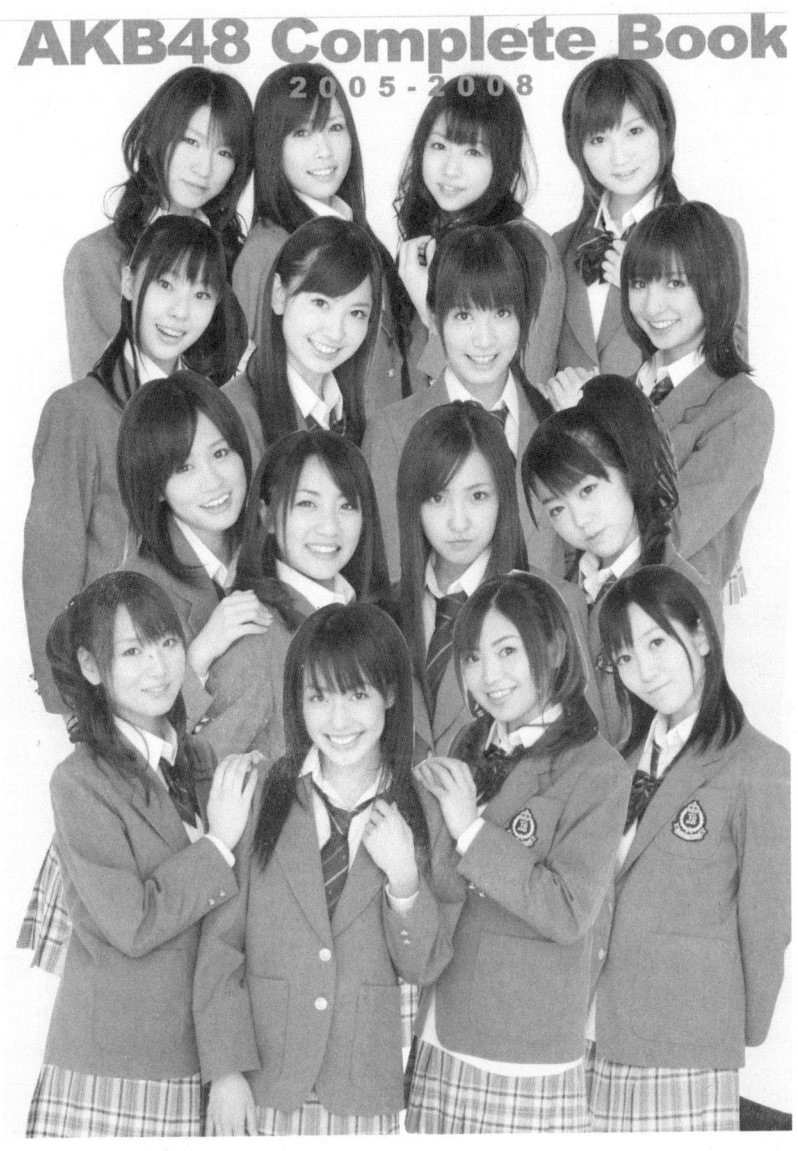

covered in pin badges bearing the faces of smiling girls: their favorite AKB48 members. This was their joint, they all appeared to know each other, and they didn't seem all that happy about having to share with me.

Looking at the folks in the reserved seating area, it became clear that this was likely some kind of special Press Night. Trendy media types of both sexes—adults, no less!—lounged in their chairs chatting, flippantly regarding the scene.

The dudes in the back looked me up and down. I imagined them thinking, "What are you doing here? What are any of you people doing here? This is our special place. Why is this happening?"

I probably would have felt the same way. These were the early adopters, the people who had made this phenomenon happen, and we were the mainstream, marching in to take over their subculture.

Then, 24 girls bum-rushed the stage all at once. The show began and it was impossible to think about anything else.

It's easy to scoff at idol groups when you see them shrunk down on a screen. *They can't sing! They can't dance! What's the big idea?* But in person and up close, watch out. The sheer amount of energy that an idol group generates can be overwhelming, even without AKB48's patented 48 members. Multiply that by the feedback

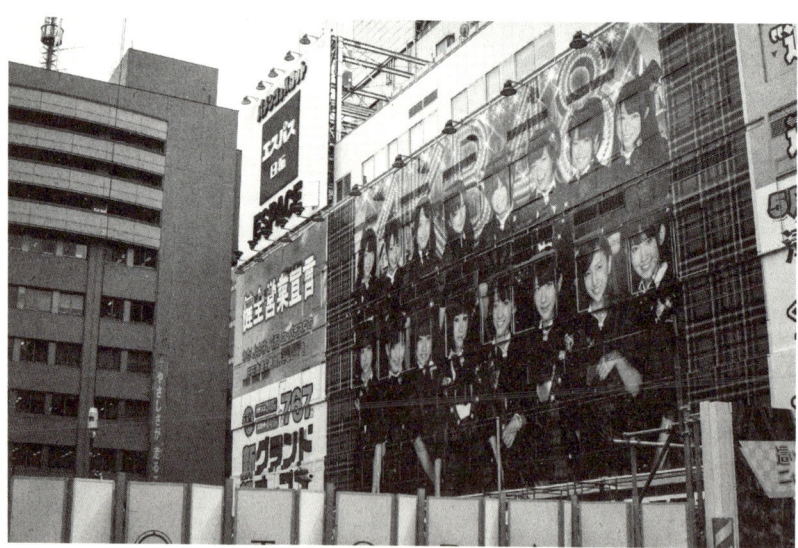

AKB48 building sized-ad in Akihabara, Tokyo.

generated by packs of adoring fans, and we're in the same ballpark as a peak grunge band in their prime . . . maybe even Nirvana.

After the show, the die-hard guys next to me gave me one final look over. I had made it through without incident. They allowed me to leave in peace. It was the end of an era for these hardcore dudes. They probably came back the next night, and the night after that, but AKB48's days as an underground phenomenon were numbered.

Scant months later, AKB48 blew up. They were suddenly Japan's number one idol sensation—the biggest thing since Morning Musume—dominating the music charts, karaoke rankings, and TV airwaves before multiplying into sister groups like SKE48 and NMB48. Fans now had literally hundreds of girls to try and keep track of.

In Japan, no one could escape them. But maybe the group members sometimes wanted to escape themselves.

In 2013, AKB48 starlet Minami Minegishi broke the band's strict "no dating" rule by spending a night with her boyfriend. As part of her punishment, she shaved her head and made a tearful apology on YouTube. It was not a good look. It looked like a hostage video.

In 2014, a 24-year-old man was arrested for attacking two members of AKB48 with a handsaw at a public "handshake event." One would think this would be a classic case of a crazed fan gone off the rails, but the perp turned out to be an unemployed man who was angry that idols were well paid (spoiler: they're usually not) while he wasn't making any money.

Crazy management. Crazy people. AKB48 only seemed to get international press for these extreme incidents, putting idols in the infamous category of Questionable Stuff from Japan; not as bad as tentacle porn, but not exactly Ghibli movie material either.

It didn't help that AKB48's music was not especially great, even though it still sold millions to captive fans who were expected to support their favorite girls by voting with their wallets. Not all idol music has to be unmemorable, as groups like Perfume can prove at their best, but AKB48 songs like "Flying Get" or "Heavy Rotation" all but define the middle of the road. Has the passing of time made their chipper girl-next-door style pop music any more appealing? I put on AKB48's *Greatest Hits* while writing this piece and didn't last long.

Yet, AKB48 themselves are still around, more or less. With old members constantly graduating and fresh new ones taking their place, the group has become something like those Japanese masked superhero TV shows, such as *Kamen Rider*, which have been on the air for decades: the names change and the details are different, but the rituals endure.

They may no longer occupy the center of the Japanese pop universe, but what they *do* still occupy is their exclusive temple for fan worship and musical excess. The AKB48 Theater in Akihabara remains open for business, high in the sky, on top of a chain discount store.

I'm hoping those old die-hard fans finally got their good seats back.

ICONS

Eiichi Ohtaki: The Wizard of City Pop

Diving into a swimming pool on a perfect summer day. A European boulevard preserved in time beneath a crystal blue sky. Lovers kissing in silhouette against a glittering Tokyo skyline.

These are the images that helped sell the sound of City Pop, a loosely connected genre of *smooth music* recorded in Japan during the late 20th century, a time and place of aspiration, prosperity, and *nouveau riche* consumption. These urbane and extremely chilled out visuals can also be found on the LP jackets of musician Eiichi Ohtaki, a City Pop pioneer who remains obscure in the West, even as the genre he helped to create has finally begun to receive global attention.

   The soft rock, jazz-infused sound of City Pop arose in Japan in the early 1970s, peaked in popularity during the bubble economy 1980s, and began to wind down once the bubble popped in the early 1990s. Since then, as J-Pop and J-Rock took over the charts, City Pop became a cult genre for record collectors. In the West, where Japanese music acts seldom get much attention, City Pop remained pretty much unknown.

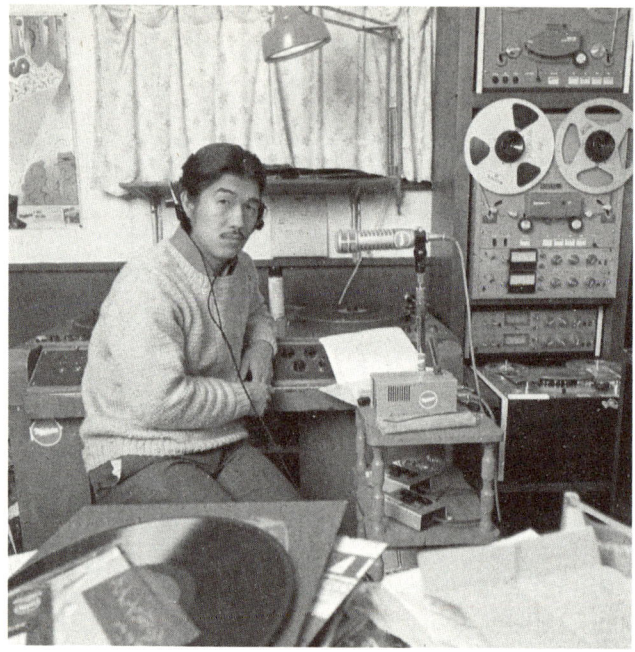

But in 2017, something strange happened. YouTube's almighty recommendation algorithm began heavily pushing Mariya Takeuchi's 1984 song "Plastic Love." Suddenly, as if obeying on cue, the Internet embraced City Pop. New City Pop fans started surfing YouTube and online auctions in search of more buried treasure. As "City Pop Night" DJ events began popping up in major cities from California to New York and City Pop tribute acts began covering old songs for clicks, I kept waiting for one name to get its due. Now, a few years into the global City Pop craze, I am still wondering: *where is the love for Eiichi Ohtaki?*

In the early 2000s, noting my love of old Japanese pop culture, several Japanese friends urged me to check out Eiichi Ohtaki's back catalog, starting with his bestselling 1981 LP *A LONG VACATION*. Hearing the very first track on the album "Kimi wa Tennen Shoku" was like hitting a widescreen wall of sound packed with huge melodies and head-spinning tempo changes. I immediately fell in love with Ohtaki's music and City Pop by proxy. The two were forever after linked in my mind.

Eiichi Ohtaki only released six solo albums during his lifetime, but as an all-round creator, he contained multitudes. Not only was he a singer-songwriter, but he was also a live performer, a producer, a record label owner, an engineer, and a radio host.

"The Japanese Phil Spector" is how friends initially sold him to me, mostly for the over the top, everything-but-the-kitchen-sink productions often featured on his records. But Ohtaki had none of the obsessive and dark energy of super producers like Spector or Joe Meek, both of whom he often paid tribute to in his music. Ohtaki's output was instead, as one of his song titles puts it, "FUN x4." His music was playful, but not insubstantial. As a kind of living encyclopedia of mid-20th-century popular music, Ohtaki used the sounds

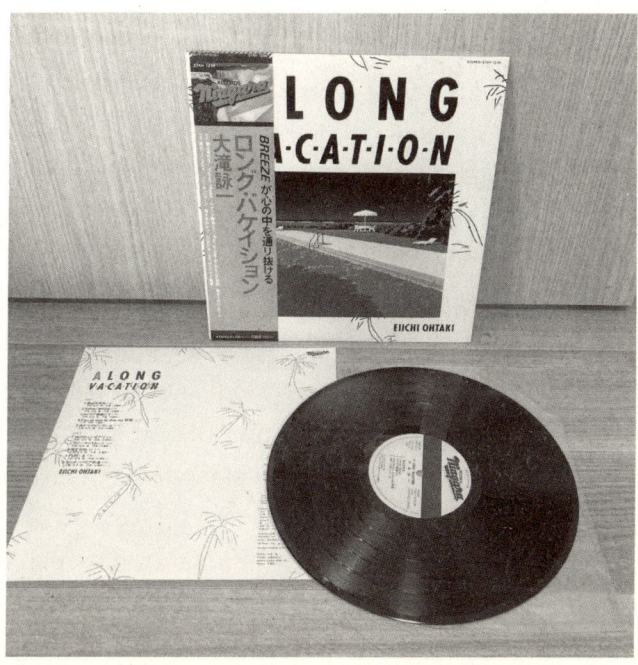

had loved since childhood to infuse City Pop with its sense of good times past and a longing to escape to faraway locations. This sense of nostalgia would quickly become hardwired into the DNA of City Pop music and style.

Eiichi Ohtaki was born in Iwate Prefecture in 1948. He became obsessed with music after hearing Connie Francis's "Lipstick on Your Collar" on the radio in 1959 on the Far East Network. Through this US military radio station, Ohtaki tuned into the new rock and pop music coming out of America, like Elvis Presley and Neil Sedaka. He also fell under the sway of native Japanese acts, like *kayokyoku* crooner Akira Kobayashi and the singing comedy group Crazy Cats. All these influences would help form the core of the later Ohtaki sound.

Ohtaki learned to play the drums, and while attending college in Tokyo, he met fellow musician and music fan Haruomi Hosono. Ohtaki was invited to join Hosono's new band, which he had formed with Takashi Matsumoto and Shigeru Suzuki. Originally called April Fool's Day, the band would change its name to Happy End and become folk rock superstars.

Happy End was a seminal Japanese band, but they only lasted three years before splitting up in 1972. Prefiguring the City Pop revival to come, Happy End finally got noticed in the West when their song "Kaze Wo Atsumete" wound up on the *Lost in Translation* film soundtrack in 2003.

After releasing his first post-Happy End LP in 1972, Ohtaki formed his own label, Niagara Records, in 1974 and began releasing more solo albums. He also coproduced and released the record "Songs" by the band Sugar Babe (sometimes called "the first City Pop record" by people prone to make such statements). Ohtaki's early solo LPs, like *Niagara Moon* (1975) and *Go! Go! Niagara* (1976), are almost too eclectic to qualify as City Pop. From his small recording studio in Fussa (home to a major US Air Force Base), Ohtaki mashed up doo-wop, mambo, exotica, piano boogie, surf music, and

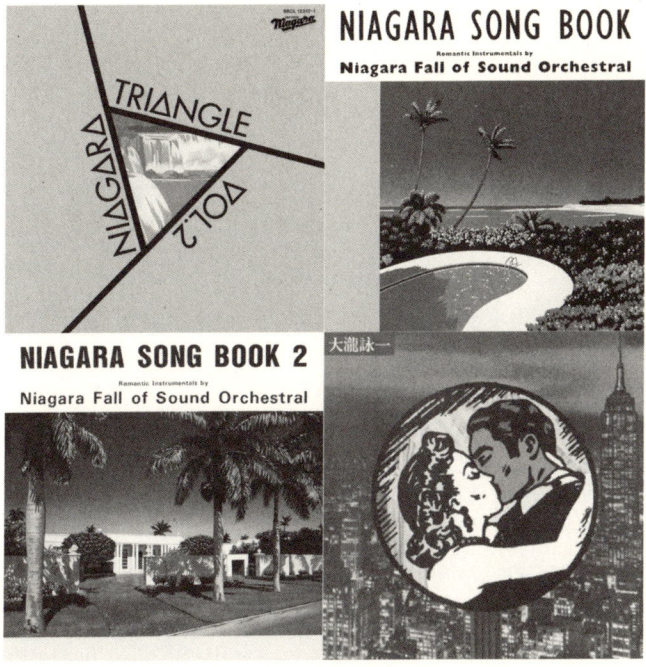

traditional Japanese *ondo*. It was genius pop in a way that prefigured the sample-heavy Shibuya-kei sound of Pizzicato Five and Cornelius in the 1990s. But while they were musically dazzling, Ohtaki's initial solo works didn't sell well. His biggest successes of the 1970s came from the songs he wrote and produced for pop singers like Hiromi Ota and radio-friendly jingles for products like fizzy, refreshing Mitsuya Cider . . . literal pop music for soda commercials!

Ohtaki's breakthrough came in the summer of 1981 when his fifth LP, *A LONG VACATION*, was released. Working from rejected jingle demos, Ohatki finally delivered his proper City Pop masterpiece. Recorded at CBS Studios in Tokyo's Roppongi district (a prime Bubble Economy location) with live instruments, synths, and an entire string section, *A LONG VACATION* preserved the playful mix of styles from his earlier LPs, but now presented everything on a much bigger, more polished stage.

Ohtaki's singing voice had become expressive and confident during his solo years and is almost unrecognizable compared to the ragged folk rock he made with Happy End. The iconic, much-imitated LP cover art of *A LONG VACATION*—a painting by Hiroshi Nagai that depicts a luxurious beachside resort—screams Bubble era relaxation and leisure, yet the mood of the album's music is melancholic. The lyrics, by former Happy End member Takashi Matsumoto, are loaded with heartbreak, rainy Wednesdays, lonely nights, and memories of old flames fading away. It is the Japanese soundtrack of the 1980s par excellence.

A LONG VACATION peaked on the Japanese charts at number two, but became a long seller on vinyl, cassette, and CD. Like all great music, *A LONG VACATION* is both of its time and timeless. Many of its songs became standards, covered by other singers to this day, or endlessly repurposed for TV themes and ad campaigns.

Ohtaki released just one more solo LP (1985's *Each Time*) before leaving recording behind in order to produce other artists, repackage his back catalog, curate oldies compilations, and guest on talk radio. Ohtaki had spent decades working on a general theory of pop music when he unexpectedly died of an aneurysm at the age of 65 in 2013.

Modern City Pop fans, instigated by YouTube, seem to prefer the funkier, rhythm-forward side of the genre as typified by Takeuchi's "Plastic Love" (66 million views and counting, as of this writing). Female vocalists like Takeo Ohnuki and Junko Yagami tend to top lists of "Best City Pop Records ... Ever!" made by Westerners, leaving out guys like Ohtaki, Haruomi Hosono, Chu Kosaka, and even groups like Sugar Babe. With so much old-time rock'n'roll in its foundations, a lot of Ohtaki Eiichi music probably sounds prehistoric to someone expecting something "totally awesome!" in the "I love the 1980s!" sense.

In some ways, an imagined City Pop "aesthetic" has overshadowed the reality of the music. Fans lock onto the visuals found on LP jackets—the beach resorts, the bayside skylines—and merge them with other bits of Bubble Economy ephemera that can be easily converted by Vaporwave DJs: 16-bit SEGA videogames, Sony Walkman commercials, convertible cars. Anyone can make City Pop nowadays. Take a photo of the sky. Add pink and purple filters. Tag it. Post it. Like and subscribe.

Nostalgia is key to unlocking both sides of City Pop: the reality and the fantasy. Ohtaki Eiichi recreated the music he loved as a kid and spread it across Japan during a mythic moment in time. Now, this past calls out to new generations searching for a timeless sound.

Ohtaki Eiichi's *A LONG VACATION* is out there. Go and take it.

MONSTERS OF THE SCREEN

Giant beasts rampaging through Tokyo, hotheaded gangsters, deadly delinquent girls, and the men and women who bring them to life.

Directing with Napalm: The Ryuhei Kitamura Interview

January 2008

Born in Osaka in 1969, Ryuhei Kitamura, a self-described "movie otaku," left high school at the age of 17 to follow his *Mad Max*-inspired dreams of becoming a director by studying at the School of Visual Arts in Australia. After returning to Japan, where he established the independent production studio Napalm Films, Kitamura hit a home run with his independently produced *Versus* (2000), a stunning mix of zombie horror, gunplay, comedy, and kung fu that won instant acclaim around the world. Now a hot property, Kitamura was tapped to helm the manga-inspired, big-budget action films *Azumi* and *Sky High*. Both released in 2003; the former was one of the highest grossing movies of the year in Japan.

    Kitamura had his pick of options and began eyeing projects in Hollywood. Meanwhile, Toho Studios sized up Kitamura to helm *Godzilla: Final Wars*, their 50th anniversary celebration of the Godzilla series and so-called "final" film of the franchise. But the experience of making the 2004 epic, which has both fans and detractors, soured Kitamura on the Japanese studio system. After delivering one more independent production—the wild action-comedy *LOVEDEATH* (2006)—Kitamura finally made the move to Hollywood. His first film made in America was a Clive Barker adaptation called *The Midnight Meat Train* (2008).

The Midnight Meat Train is your US debut as a filmmaker. Were there any new challenges you had to face on the set?
It wasn't that difficult for me. I was expecting a bigger difference between making movies in Japan and in Hollywood. But I was always kind of an outsider in Japan too. It was always hard to make movies there. But here, I felt really happy going into preproduction surrounded by all these experts and a clever and talented crew. The hard times mostly came when we were developing the script.

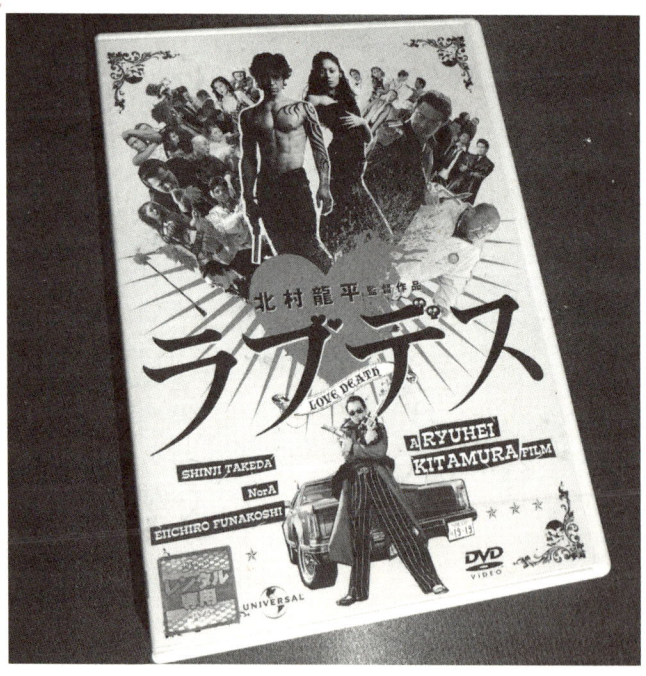

DVD for Ryuhei Kitamura's 2006 film LOVEDEATH.

Somehow Clive Barker read one of my in-progress drafts and he got pissed. There was all this stuff missing from it and he didn't know that I was going to put new stuff in it. Once I explained what I was going to do, we were okay and we got along great. But that was really scary (laughs), making Clive Barker angry!

However, it's not a big budget film so we only have a very limited amount of money and time. One of the producers even told me, "Hey, I'm sorry, but this is kind of impossible with the money and time we got. There's too much stuff in this script." Now this is a very experienced producer and even he was asking, "How are we going to do this?"

I've read interviews with other Japanese filmmakers who go to Hollywood and it seems like they immediately have problems dealing with the system.
Well, if you don't speak English and if you've never lived abroad, it's going to be much harder. I don't believe in making movies with a translator. But it's more about personality. I've always had problems with the Japanese staff anyway . . . not the crew, but mainly producers. They don't want to do anything challenging, they're afraid, and they don't take responsibility.

What do you think are the problems with the Japanese film industry?
The problem is a lack of good producers and directors. That's it. I like Japanese movies from the 1960s to the early 1980s, but I'm not a fan of Japanese movies at all now. TV has more power these days than the film industry in Japan. Whatever you make needs to be based on a TV show, or at least on a book or comic. When I originally tried to make *Versus*, which was an original idea, nobody wanted to get involved. I went to see everyone in the Japanese film industry and nobody gave me a chance. Even after *Versus* finally got

made and become a hit, everything I've made since then, like *Azumi* and *Godzilla: Final Wars*, was based on a comic or an established series. Japanese producers are really afraid of doing something original. The same thing has happened in Hollywood. There's very little chance for an independent filmmaker in that environment.

Does the same thing apply to actors?
In Japan, talent management companies make their actors and actresses work like horses. They do commercials and TV series every day and they sleep about two hours a night. That's how they make money. It's completely different from the system in the United States. When I made *Azumi*, I wanted to make a great, great samurai action movie, so, of course, I wanted Aya Ueto, who played the heroine, to get trained with swords and martial arts. I knew asking for six months was unrealistic, but I actually only needed her to receive about three months of training to really make it work.

I've never revealed this before, but in the end, they only gave me three fucking days. It wasn't the actress's fault; it was all the dirty liars around her. During preproduction, I got her alone and told her, "If a shitty movie comes out, everyone blames the director and the lead. That's it. Nobody else. You and me have to stay together. They only gave you three days for training, so take your wooden sword with you everywhere you go and practice whenever you can. And after shooting, I have to train you. It's going to be a hard schedule." We woke up at 4 in the morning and shot until 6 pm, went back to the hotel at 7, took a shower, ate something, and after 8 pm, me and my action director trained her. The shoot lasted for three months, so when you watch the film, you'll see she's much better at doing action scenes at the end than at the beginning. I'm really proud of that movie, but that was a really weird way to make something.

MONSTERS OF THE SCREEN

How about the difference between audiences in the United States versus Japan? I've heard that in the US, viewers were standing up and cheering during the monster battles in *Godzilla: Final Wars*, but the Japanese reaction was colder.

I don't know if it's because of the education system, but we Japanese are raised so that if everybody is looking to the right, you have to look right too. If nine people agree on something, you have to agree too. Here, in the US, you have to have your own opinion, but in Japan, it's better not to have one. If you open your mouth and say what you really think, people will think you are troublesome. That's what everyone says about me. You go to Japan and ask all those executives at the studios and 80% will say, "Kitamura is a scary guy. He's going to punch and kick you." And I've never even met 99% of them. The other 20% love me and that's the way it goes. That's

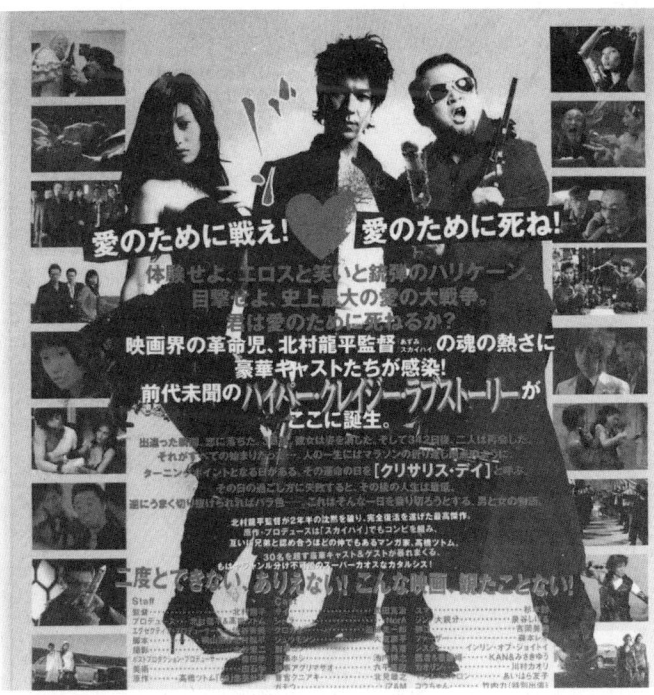

because I always open my mouth and say, "What's wrong with you guys?"

I get a lot of support from overseas movie fans. They are the guys who love my movies and give me energy. But if Japanese movie executives aren't willing to go out on their own and do something original, Japanese audiences will stay stuck with the same old stuff, and they won't know any better. That's why so many live-action Japanese movies don't travel outside of Japan. When overseas audience think of Japanese pop culture, they think about music, video games, anime. But our movies just aren't up to snuff. It makes me angry and I feel like I have to do something about it.

You haven't given up on Japan?
I still know lots of great people there like comic artists and designers. But there are no producers or companies that can introduce them in a strong way to a worldwide audience. Maybe only Taka Ichise (producer of *The Ring* and *Ju-on*), but he's part of the Japanese horror movies trend that has become cliche. Doing the same thing over and over is going to kill us. I'm producing this samurai-zombie movie that we are going to start shooting in a few months. I wrote the script and the director is my right-hand guy (Ichiro Kiriyama). He wrote *Azumi* and *Final Wars*. I'm doing it because it's not just another Japanese ghost story; its more direct and it's bloody. No mysterious phone call, no computer. Everyone is going to get their head chopped off!

You started out as a movie otaku who managed to make it to the director's chair. What advice do you have for young filmmakers who would like to follow in your footsteps?
Every time I go to conventions, I get a lot of DVDs from these guys who want to be the next Tarantino or the next me. And I watch them, because I'll feel bad if I don't, and unfortunately, I've never

met someone who is good, whether in Japan, the US, or wherever. If they are good, then I'm going to call them and give them a chance. That's what I've done my whole life. I'll try to make it happen somehow. But there's a huge difference between being an otaku and being able to please otaku. Just because you've watched thousands of action movies doesn't mean you can make a great action movie, right? That's tough. And a lot of what I get are bad rip-offs of *Versus*, which isn't what people should be doing. I never want to compare myself to someone else. I always try to fight the enemy within. I'm always telling myself, "No, it's not good enough, you have to try harder, more, more, more."

I'm in the middle of preproduction right now and I'm also writing four scripts and reading three books and reading four scripts at the same time. I feel like I'm going insane. I'm also working on six other projects with different producers. Each time I meet with them, I have to be prepared, otherwise I don't get the job. If Clive Barker thinks I'm a dickhead, it doesn't matter if I'm a fan or not. If I get respect from Clive Barker, it's not because he's a nice person. He sees how hard I've been trying with my career and on this movie. There's no real advice I can give except: try hard. Do 100% more than your best. I never say negative things to young filmmakers who ask me for advice, but it is extremely hard. But don't listen to people who tell you never. I've been through armies of people who tell me, "No, you can never be a director." Since I was 17, thousands of people told me, "You never can become a filmmaker." Then after I became a director, thousands of people told me, "You're never going to make it to Hollywood." But I made it because I tried my best.

Ryuhei Kitamura has continued to make feature films in both the US and Japan, including a live-action Lupin III movie in 2014.

WE WILL BE RAMBO

May 2008

On May 24, *Rambo*, the greatest American movie in recent memory, will finally explode across Japan like a carefully placed Claymore mine. The extensive PR and tie-up campaigns have begun in earnest, and the only way to keep up with the dizzying number of promotions, poster designs, celebrity endorsements, and food tie-ins is to follow the official Japanese blog for the movie: WE WILL BE RAMBO. It seems that all of Japan is literally starving for action and only a Guy Named Sly can satisfy their hunger pangs via such delicacies as:

The Rambo Hot Dog, deployed on camouflage cardboard for "sneaky snacking." More deadly than a .50 caliber machine gun at close range. Free limited edition button with purchase.

The Rambo Set, now available at Janqoo restaurants: a giant fucking beer and your choice of sizzling "horumon" offal or Genghis Khan-style lamb. Free bandanna and stickers for the first 100 customers or until someone dies of food poisoning.

Not to be outdone, Sly's Planet Hollywood Tokyo (wow, it really is the 1980s all over again) is offering their own Rambo Last Battlefield

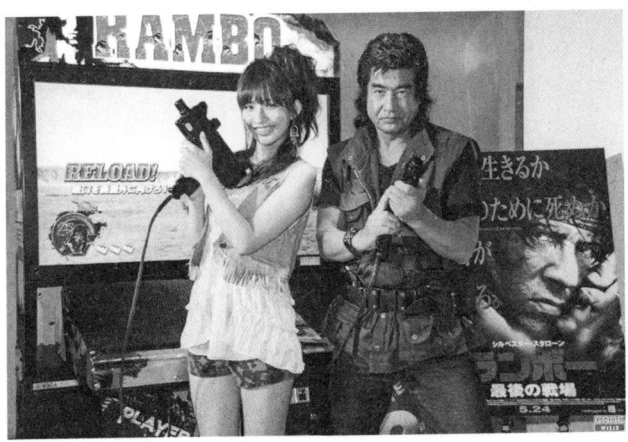

Action star Hiroshi Fujioka and friend celebrate the launch of the Rambo *video game in Japan, 2008.*

Original Menu . . . an incredible CROCODILE BURGER served on an eco-friendly palm leaf! Advertised rightfully as "a violent challenge to food and beverage."

Then there are *Umaibo* snacks for the kiddies, with the tagline "rise to the battlefield with an exciting flavor . . . HOT!" It can probably cauterize an open wound better than gunpowder, in line with what happens in *Rambo III*.

Rambo has also teamed up with delicious Kyokyo Daha carbonated coffee-based energy drinks for "a tie-up promotion of hard blow destruction," more or less guaranteed to keep you from "breaking down on the battlefield." No word on how it will help you deal with impotence, a divorce from Brigitte Nielsen, or a really bad hangover. Look for these awe-inspiring ads on over 2,000 taxi cabs in Tokyo and Osaka and on the Marunouchi line subway.

Always remember, WE WILL BE RAMBO!

Planet Hollywood Tokyo closed in 2009, but Stallone keeps making Rambo movies.

We Are the Japanese Fantasy Film Society: Kaiju 'Zines circa 1980

December 2010

I'm sitting next to a stack of newsletters for something called the "Japanese Fantasy Film Society" dating from 1980. They consist of four pages of Xeroxed, high-contrast, black and white images and text. Although they were produced mere decades ago, they look and feel ancient: the nerdy equivalent of the Dead Sea Scrolls.

First of all: nope, I was not a member of the "Japanese Fantasy Film Society." I didn't even know such a thing ever existed until I procured these newsletters a few years back from . . . I can't remember where. eBay? A convention? Did they just spontaneously materialize out of time and space onto my desk?

Welcome to the Japanese Fantasy Film Society!   with a number of impressive orchestrations. The

MONSTERS OF THE SCREEN

While the origin of these papers remains mysterious, the cover of the first issue of the Japanese Fantasy Film Society tells you pretty much what you need to know about the people who made this and where their heads were: a drawing of Japan is front and center. Around it drifts a veritable bestiary of everything great about it: Godzilla, Mazinger Z, Gamera, Space Battleship Yamato, *yokai* monsters, Astro Boy, King Ghidorah, and many others.

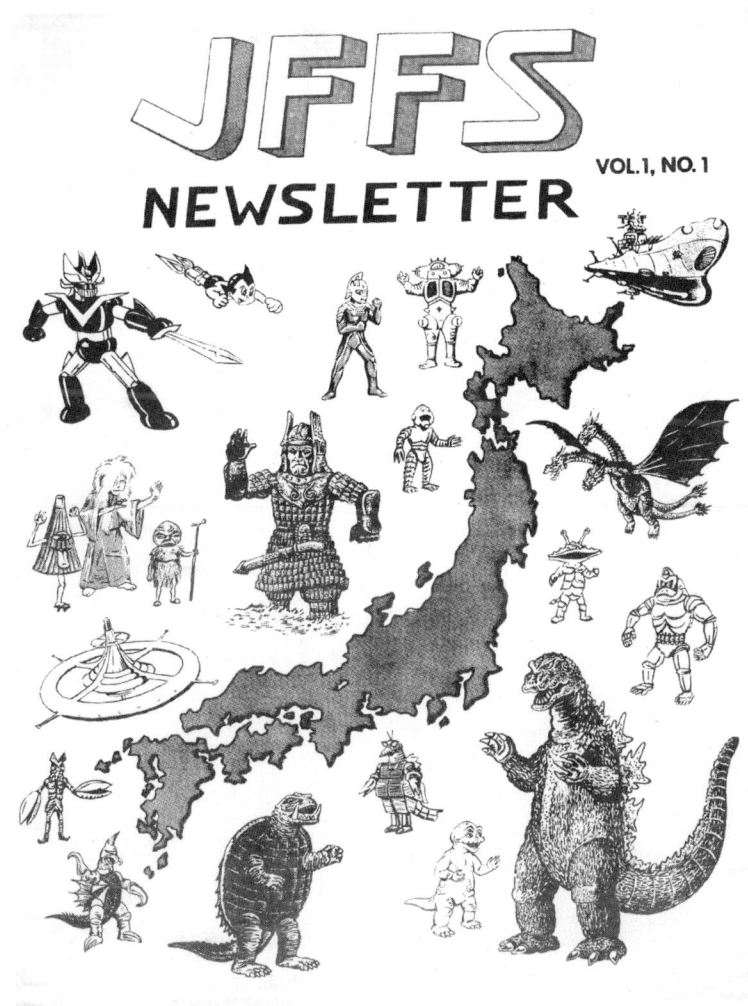

A quick flip of the page and the reader must navigate a tiny typewriter-created font: the punk rock look of classic homemade 'zines, way before desktop publishing and personal computers made this sort of thing a snap. What burning and obsessive passions the founders of the Japanese Fantasy Film Society must have had! All I

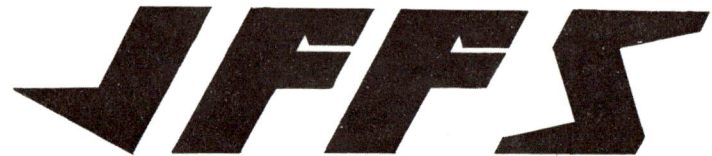

JAPANESE FANTASY FILM SOCIETY NEWSLETTER

November-December-January 1982   Vol. 3, No. 3

GODZILLA, CHINESE STYLE? As was first reported in Vol. 2, No. 4 of the JFFS Newsletter in 1980, a Chinese Kung-fu film distributor had taken out ads in the film trade papers to announce a film titled STAR GODZILLA. At the right is a copy of that advertisment, depicting Godzilla (styled after SON OF GODZILLA), Angilas (barely discernable at Godzilla's feet), and a Di Laurentis style Kong. As far as can be determined, this film has never been made--if it was, it was without the knowledge and approval of Toho Studios. In light of the way in which Japan's other popular series monster, Gammera, made his return to the screen in recent times (see article within), perhaps it is for the best that Godzilla remains in retirement.

REIJI MATSUMOTO's latest tv series, QUEEN OF A THOUSAND YEARS, is going down in the ratings game with a big splat. This 'unprecedented space fantasy', as the publicity materials refer to it, concerns the exploits of another Maeter/Yuki look-alike as she travels about time and space. This show exhibits many similarities to GALAXY EXPRESS 999 in both characters and content, but seemingly lacks theappeal and drama of its predecessor. On the other hand, Matsumoto's SARABA GALAXY EXPRESS 999 feature film of the summer of 1981 did quite well. The film featured some striking animation, providing a fitting finish to the space fantasy series. Leaving Tatsuro behind, Maeter boards the Galaxy Express, never to see her little companion again.

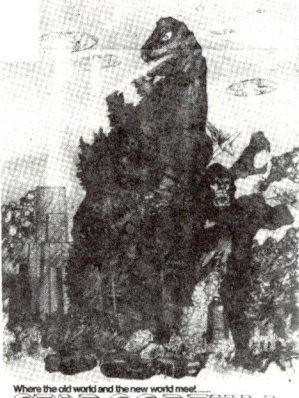

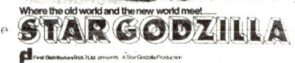

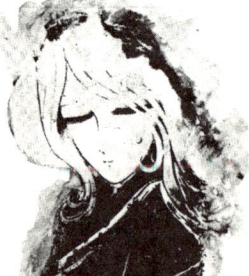

Queen of a Thousand Years

know about them is that they were based in the Chicago area. The regular issues don't have any editorial credits. It really IS like these things popped out of nowhere!

The first issue has four names scribbled in by hand (note to future self: always include your printed name in addition to your signature). One of them is Alex Wald, who is still active as an amazing illustrator of sci-fi/monster/rock and roll-themed art. The other—I think—is Ed Godziszewski, a name familiar to monster movie fans who published the seminal (and miraculously still active) kaiju 'zine *Japanese Giants*.

I get why people want to watch Japanese fantasy films, but it takes a whole different level of crazy to grind out and mail a newsletter over the course of several years (the last issue in my stash is marked Winter 1983–Summer 1984).

What made them do it?

According to the introductory essay in the first issue, "For one reason or another, a widespread, unified fandom has not surfaced to encompass all areas of Japanese fantasy fandoms . . . It is our desire that, circumstances willing, the JFFS will be able to achieve the goal of a unified following for the Japanese fantasy film product." And in a pre-desktop publishing, pre-Internet world, this could only be achieved one hand-typed word at a time.

Back in 1980, there were US-produced 'zines and newsletters for anime and for live-action special effects films of the Godzilla ilk, but no one was really embracing both fronts at the same time. By contrast, the JFFS liked to swing both ways, and the December 1980 January 1981 issue of the newsletter proves it. The first item concerns rumors of a new Godzilla film in development at Toho Studios—it helps to remember that back then, a new Big G film hadn't been produced since 1975 and Godzilla fans were on the verge of death-by-starvation as the new decade began. Up next was info about the then-new color Astro Boy TV series and the feature

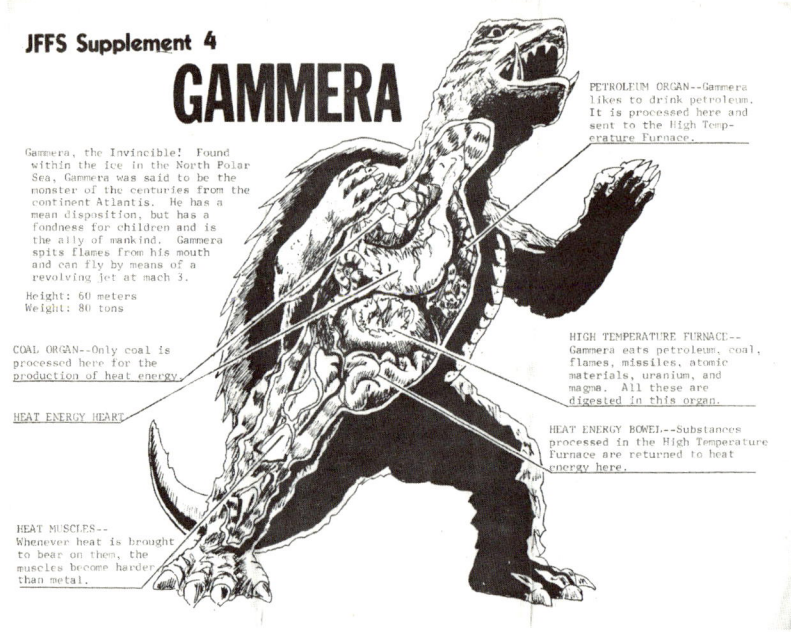

anime film *Cyborg 009: Legend of the Super Galaxy*; then there's some info about the live-action-by-way-of-puppets *X-Bomber* TV show, which points out that the show had just been picked up by the BBC to air in the UK under the name *Star Fleet*. How did the JFFS even learn about this stuff in the days before the Internet?

Looking back at these dusty newsletters of yore, I have to ask myself: do I really miss this achingly analog era of fandom?

Obviously, it's nice that modern folks get the latest news about anime and special effects movies at the speed of light through the Internet, insta-translated at the press of a button. JFFS members must have experienced an agonizing wait between issues in the snail mail environment of the early 1980s.

But modern fans sure seem to take a lot of shortcuts now, whether that means reducing their critical thinking skills to sharing lazy memes or conversing in contrarian "hot takes" with zero nuance.

What's ultimately gone is the grind: the day-to-day struggle to make an actual physical artifact crafted out of pure obsession and then drop it into the ocean like a message in a bottle, in the hopes that someone will find it and understand what the hell you're talking about.

I don't want to romanticize the Dark Ages too much . . . but what the hell. I'm going to romanticize it a lot. Try and stop me. I'm out in the back building a time machine. Set the dial for 1980. The Japanese Fantasy Film Society and its mission to unify anime and live-action fandom under a groove has only just begun to fight.

Outlaw Obituary: On Bunta Sugawara, 1933–2014

December 2014

Bunta Sugawara's death marks the end of the modern yakuza movie, the last shot of the machine gun dragons, and the final police sweep of the Showa era.

I first discovered Bunta when I saw the 1972 yakuza flick *Street Mobster*. It wasn't subtitled, but you didn't really need to understand the language: Bunta's **hellfire persona** was more than enough to go on. There was the **face**, twisting and contorting with overclocked emotion. Then there was the **voice**, which could go

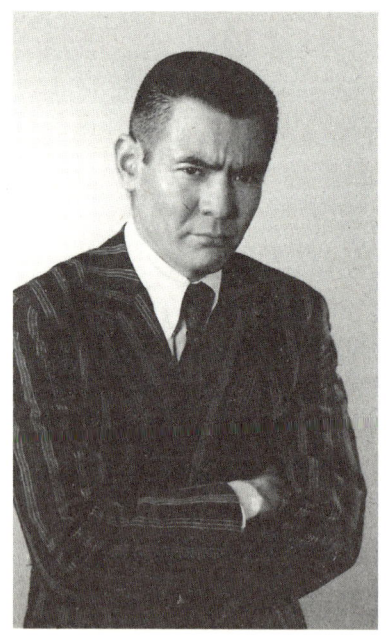

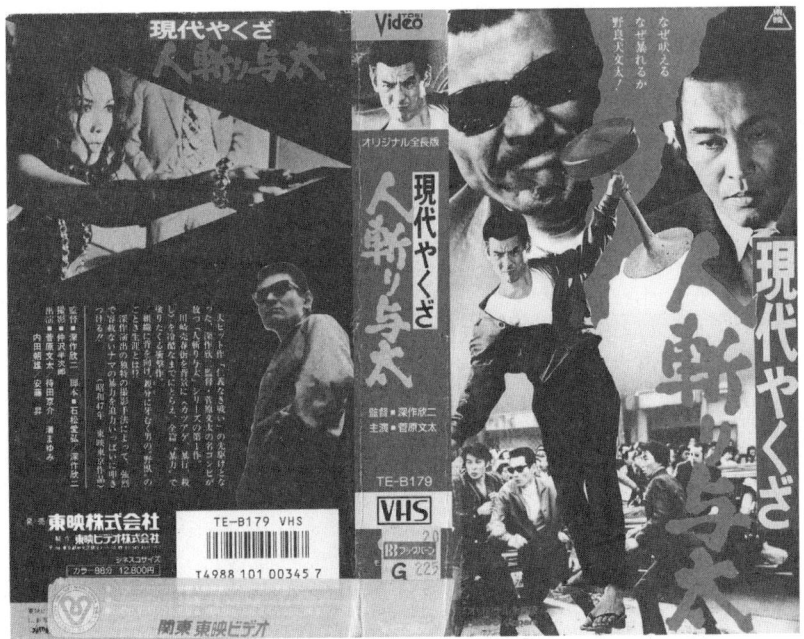

from a deep menacing rumble to something like the sound of an entire room filled with beer bottles breaking and ramen bowls shattering (usually over someone's head) all at the same time.

I had to see more. I raided the shelves of movie joints throughout San Francisco's Japan Town, hunting down un-subtitled VHS tapes. Bunta starred in dozens of yakuza and cop flicks with wild titles like *Bloodstained Clan Honor, Outlaw Killers: Three Mad Dog Brothers,* and *Battles Without Honor and Humanity.* Many of these films were directed by cult filmmaker Kinji Fukasaku, who would later receive international attention and Quentin Tarantino's seal of approval by directing the bloody headtrip *Battle Royale* at the age of 69.

Why was I so drawn to Bunta's movies? Looking back, I think I saw something of my own father when Bunta and all of those yakuza movie tough guys were mixing it up. My dad wasn't an abusive person, but he could project explosive rage mixed with remote coolness

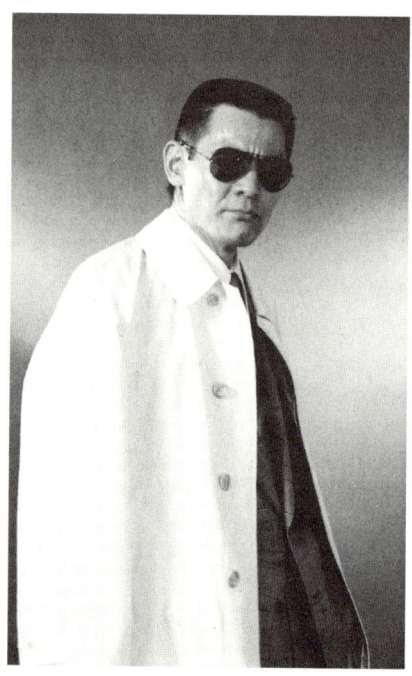

in the same way that Bunta radiated a sense of boiling, detached energy. I experienced my father's personality up close on several occasions, and it left a big effect on me. Bunta's persona helped me to understand the terms and conditions of violent masculinity so that I could make sense of it and figure out where it came from.

It might seem counterintuitive for an American kid from San Francisco to look for answers to his personal identity in movies about postwar Japan's criminal underground, but I think this speaks to how thoroughly and deeply guys like Bunta and directors like Kinji Fukasaku were trying to work out their own past traumas in these films. To hear Bunta's characters tell it, postwar Japan was a lawless hellhole where there was easy money and dead bodies on every street corner. It was a time when being a man meant a constant fight for survival and life was an endless battle for respect as well as basic necessities.

MONSTERS OF THE SCREEN

Bunta's death comes mere weeks after the loss of fellow icon Takakura Ken. Together, they were the alpha and omega, the *ninkyo* and the *jitsuroku*, of Japan's movie tough guys. Ken was stoic, suffering, and deeply connected to the crisis of modernization as Japan progressed through the twentieth century. He was a brooding, thoughtful outlaw. Bunta, however, was more primal: a libidinal Frankenstein monster hatched from Japan's anxieties that couldn't be tamed with law and order. Even when Bunta's characters were part of a gang, they were always outsiders.

Bunta and Ken are gone, so we're on our own now: death claims victory in yet another cynical freeze-frame ending. But, at least, we'll forever have these role models, real and imaginary, for how to fight battles without honor and humanity.

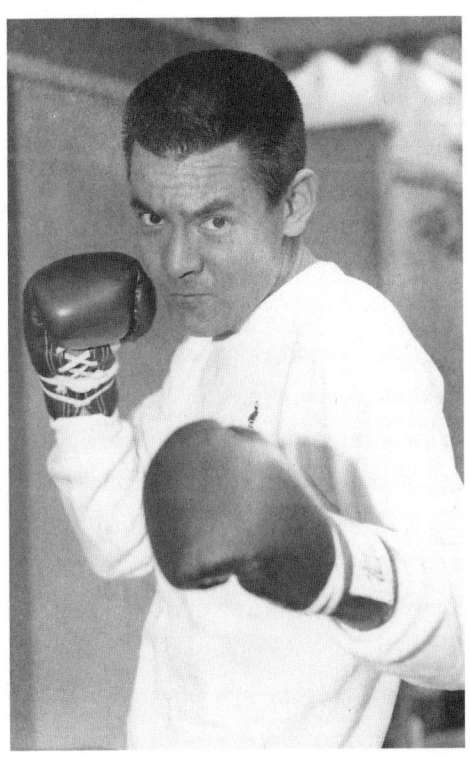

The Harajuku Line: Forgotten Fashion Monsters of Japanese V-Cinema

November 2019

Twenty years ago, Japan was overflowing with movies: some good, some bad, many now totally forgotten. It was an era in which the direct to video market, known domestically in Japan as "V-Cinema," supplied entertainment in the form of grungy cassette tapes to countless rental shops and consumer VCRs.

Many of these direct to video productions were made outside of the traditional distribution channels of movie theaters and television; in order to be profitable, they moved fast to capitalize on new trends and often targeted niche audiences. In addition to established Japanese genres such as yakuza movies, J-horror, and samurai films, there were also original V-Cinema titles made especially for pachinko players, mahjong players, golfers, and host and hostess club workers. Even long-distance truck drivers got their own original films to enjoy!

The good news is that there are *entire genres* of V-Cinema ripe for rediscovery. Chief among them is a handful of films known as

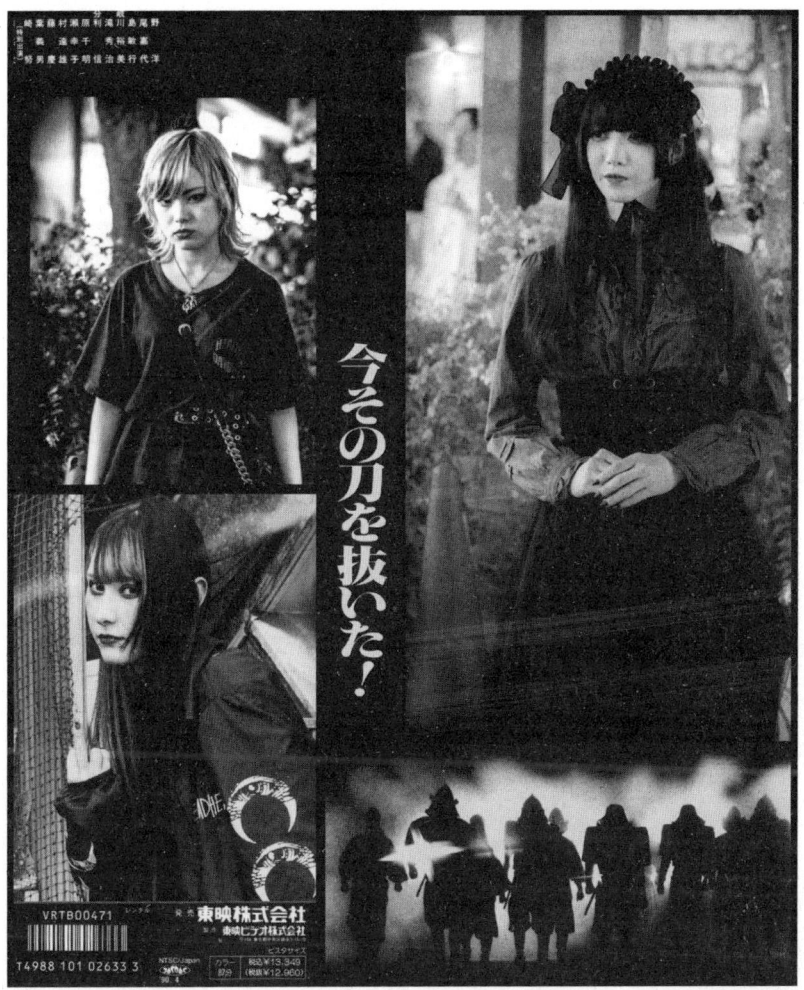

the "Harajuku Line." These were a series of films set in and around Tokyo's famed fashion district in the late 1980s to mid-1990s, just as new strands of Japanese youth culture were beginning to emerge from the underground. In addition to preserving a time and place before the area was taken over by international fast fashion brands and real estate development, the Harajuku Line titles were unique in how they freely combined multiple film genres, class and generational conflicts, street fashion, and strong female perspectives.

One of the best of these films was *Takeshita Street Proxy War*, the first of the Harajuku Line productions. It kicked off the genre with an original twist on the yakuza thriller movie formula. A big year was 1989 that marked both the dawn of the V-Cinema era *and* the

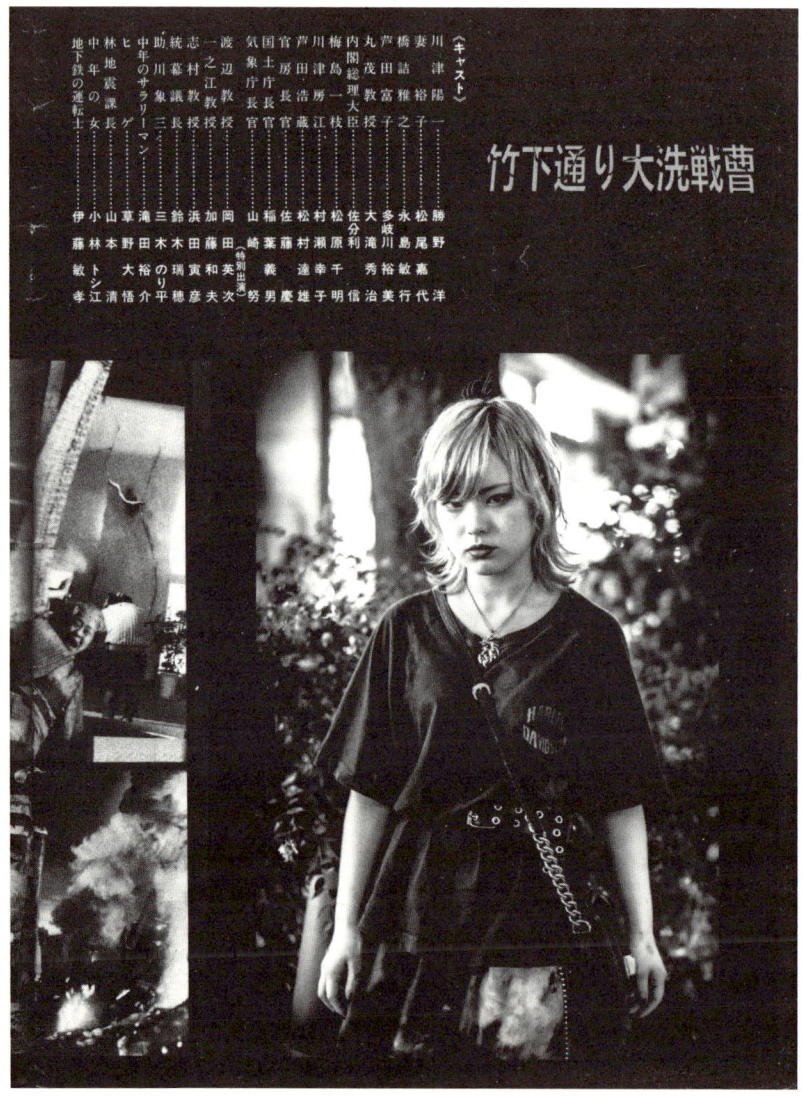

Video store flier for Takeshita Street Proxy War.

opening of "Pedestrian Heaven"—when bands and dancers would gather in the car-free streets surrounding Harajuku station.

Takeshita Street Proxy War features Mai (played by *Popteen* magazine cover girl Hiroko Harada), a young fashion designer who makes the mistake of borrowing money from a loan company to achieve her dream of opening a boutique on Harajuku's famed Takeshita Street. Unfortunately for her, Mai soon discovers that the seemingly legit loan company is actually a front company for the local yakuza. While preparing her shop for the big opening, Mai finds herself under constant harassment from goons sent by boss Takekuma (played by V-Cinema regular Hitoshi Okura). His plan is to make sure that Mai defaults on her loan and goes into debt: if she can't open her store, she must pay back double what she's borrowed. Overwhelmed, Mai goes to the local police, who are useless and refuse to help (this will come as no surprise to anyone who has seen a few yakuza films).

Very bad things begin to happen in quick succession: the thugs smash up the store and later try to set it on fire. Mai's best friend and business partner can't handle the stress and abandons her. Finally, her salaryman father ends up in hospital with critical injuries after a brutal beating.

In a wordless sequence, Mai decides enough is enough and buys a large kitchen cutting knife at a household supply shop. This leads to a bloody showdown with boss Takekuma and his henchmen, filmed guerilla-style, without permission or legal permits, in the center of Takeshita Street.

The film, directed without fuss by Toei Studios veteran Kojiro Abe and written by J-pop lyricist Miyuki Toki, concludes with a chilling epilogue set months later. Mai has opened her store and is doing brisk business, but we can tell something about her is a bit off. Seconds after cheerily saying goodbye to a customer, the film ends on a sudden freeze-frame as Mai looks directly into the camera and at us with a cold hard stare. Our heroine has fought back against her tormentors and has won her independence, but at a terrible price: her humanity.

* * *

Although fashion was not a driving feature of the next film, *After School, I Fight the Devil* (1990) was filmed on location in the Harajuku and Yoyogi neighborhoods and was funded by the La Mer department store, where many international and Japanese indie brands can be found to this day. La Mer's deep commitment to the arts, seen in the complex's museum space that puts on massive exhibits from the likes of outsider artists like Paul Laffoley and Henry Darger, briefly crossed over into an anti-establishment mode, resulting in a film that explores the psychological and sociological tensions of the area.

Yuri (played with sullen intensity by half-Japanese actress Julia Omori) is a high school student on the edge, about to drop out of the fictional Jingumae High School. She's a juvenile delinquent and apparently an ex-gang member who now prefers to drink and smoke on her own instead of going to class. Yuri lives with her single mom in a tiny residence on Cat Street, a relic of when the area was a haven for foreign diplomats and servicemen (Yuri's dad was an American GI who abandoned the family soon after she was born). Yuri's mom can't stand her daughter's bad attitude and downward trajectory and wants her to either get a job or move out. When those demands fail to make an impact, Mom calls on one of her old acquaintances, Murota, who is now a local government official, and begs him to intervene. Soon, Murota begins randomly appearing at Yuri's home "to check in on her." When they are alone, he becomes verbally and physically abusive, flipping back to being genial and polite as soon as her mother is around.

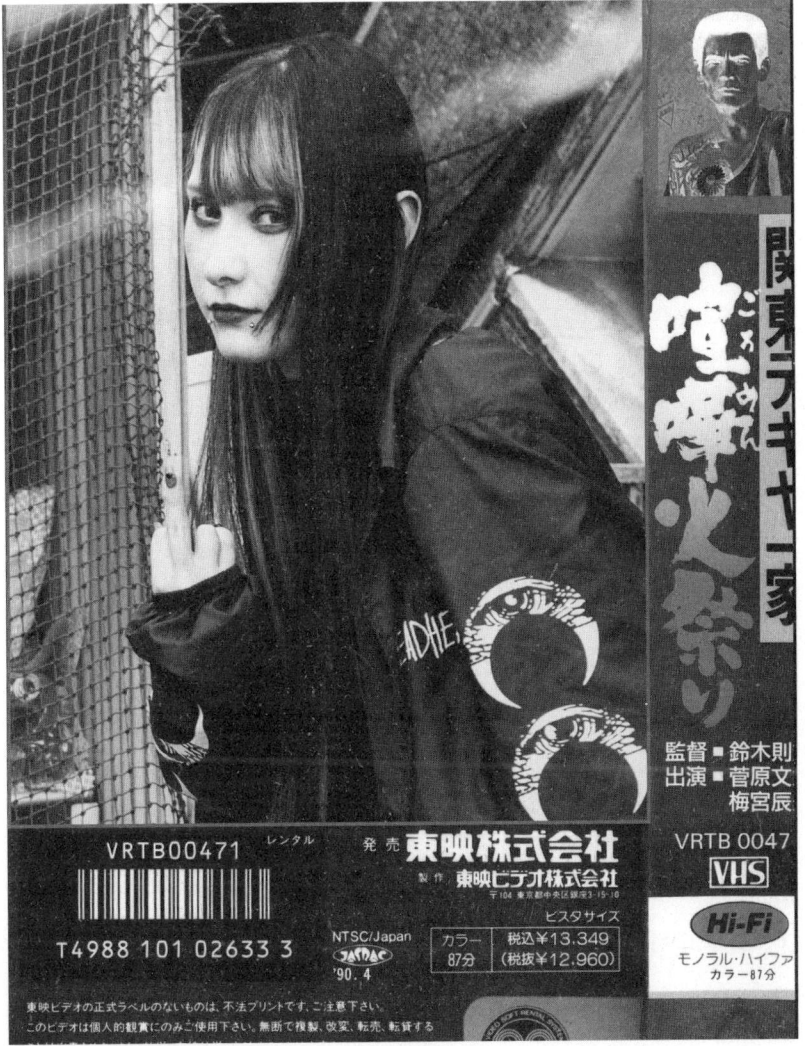

VHS box for After School, I Fight the Devil.

Yuri, of course, does not take shit from anyone, and so begins an epic battle of wits between a teenage girl and a corrupt politician. Yuri quickly discovers that Murota has managed to turn the entire community against her, but since she's already such an outsider already, trying to ostracize her further doesn't achieve anything.

Meanwhile, Yuri trails Murota, wielding not a deadly weapon but an instant camera. She winds up capturing a typical day in his life: exchanging money with underworld figures, taking methamphetamines, and capping off the night with a visit to a high-end brothel. On election day, Murota announces his win at a public ceremony (held at Yuri's high school no less). Yuri shows up and hands over the packet of photos she took of Murota to the media, but not before naming his misdeeds to the entire community through a megaphone.

Chaos ensues. Murota snaps and begins choking Yuri in front of a live TV crew that is broadcasting nationwide. Yuri is hauled away by the cops for disturbing the peace. Murota himself is now ostracized by his voters and party members, and as we see him get smaller and smaller in the rearview window of the police car, we sense it's only a matter of time until he will himself is behind bars.

While driving away, one of the cops asks Yuri why she did it: throwing away her life like that. She replies triumphantly, "The only reason a warrior is alive is to fight, and the only reason a warrior fights is to win"—a famous quote from Musashi Miyamoto's "Book of Five Rings."

With that, director and screenwriter Masa Katsuki connects to the masterless samurai of old. Actress Julia Omori, who retired from show biz after this one film, plays a character who is part of a long tradition of anti-heroes that cannot conform to the strict rules of Japanese society . . . and the audience cannot help but root for her as a result.

Former TV comedian Ken Takahata gives something of a dual performance as Murota, showing off an amiable nature as a well-liked man about town, but also a terrifying figure who pathologically cannot stand anyone who refuses to submit to his authority.

* * *

MONSTERS OF THE SCREEN

Floating in the Dark Mirror (1996) is something of a Harajuku film noir, full of mysteries both onscreen and off. Shot on Super 16mm at a time when most productions had moved to video to save costs, there are no credits for the main cast aside from the name "Saito."

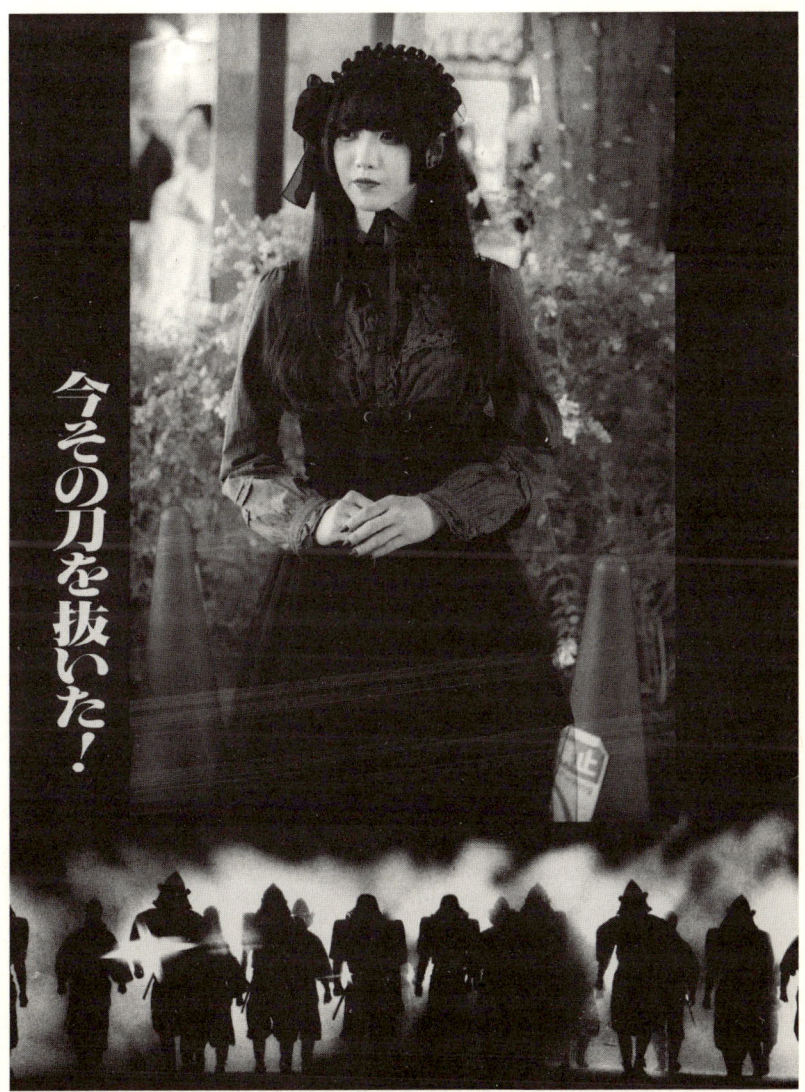

Film poster for Floating in the Dark Mirror.

Casting real kids instead of professional actors, this indie film explores how personal identity is constructed through fashion and how Harajuku operates as a place where people can reinvent themselves, or disappear, completely.

Yuka is an ordinary girl from a small town in Niigata who wakes up to find that her more stylish and outgoing twin sister Mariko has vanished from their home without a trace. Yuka hires the town's low-rent private detective to do some sleuthing, and he explains that the missing girl's trail leads to the backstreets of Harajuku. Something of an introvert (and a bit of a Plain Jane), Yuka takes her first big trip outside of her comfort zone and makes for Tokyo. Once there, she is immediately mistaken for her identical twin sister by punks and goths hanging out on Harajuku's famed Jingu Bashi bridge. Yuka soon realizes that the fastest way to get information about what happened to Mariko is to try and impersonate her sister. Over a three-day weekend, Yuka does some shopping on Takeshita Street and transforms into the spitting image of her missing sibling: a Gothic Lolita.

But pretending to be someone else only leads Yuka further down the rabbit hole and into smoky and crowded Visual Kei concerts, meet-up photo events, and awkward encounters with the opposite sex.

Eventually, all clues point to Shibuya, specifically the nightclubs of the Dogenzaka district. Located only a short walk from Harajuku, it is seemingly a world apart and a place where the Harajuku kids fear to tread. After all, this is the stomping grounds of hip-hop "Teamers," hard partying rich kids, druggies, and even more dubious characters. In this film, the goths can only handle decadence when it is served up via props at a photoshoot and subculture magazines, but Shibuya is shown as a stronghold of genuine darkness that Yuka has no choice but to infiltrate in order to complete her quest.

Once again, she goes shopping to disguise herself in her sister's last-known style choice and emerges from the Shibuya 109 department store clad head to toe in gyaru fashion. The final act takes place over the course of one rainy night as Yuka goes from club to club, only to discover that the detective she originally hired has trailed her to Tokyo and that the true fate of her missing sister is far stranger than she could have imagined. The story concludes with Yuka essentially trapped in her sister's identity: the charade of being someone else must now be forever maintained or else she will suffer severe consequences. It's a dark ending, but it helps to remember that Yuka/Mariko need only play dress-up again for another chance to escape. Not all fates are certain. Especially when you can buy a new one off the rack in Harajuku.

* * *

Alright, I've got to be honest: the Harajuku Line studio and *Takeshita Street Proxy War* don't exist. They are just products of my imagination, conjured after too many hours spent watching real V-Cinema junk like *Bodyguard Kiba: Apocalypse of Carnage*. What I tried to capture here is the *vibe* of what V-Cinema movies were about at their platonic ideal: the dirty, subversive surprises that lurked in the stained video tape shells sold in Japan's back alleys.

My Top Five Godzilla Movies

January 2020

As far back as I can remember, there have always been Godzilla movies to keep me company. Maybe I had to turn the UHF dial on the TV, or line up for a movie ticket, or flip over a Laser Disc, but He was always there. Hang out with me too long and Godzilla flicks are going to be on heavy rotation. But after nearly 60 years, there's a lot of celluloid wreckage to sift through, and not all Godzilla movies are created equal. Here is my personal list of the really super ones:

1. Godzilla, King of the Monsters (1956)

It's a monster on the loose movie . . . it's a somber warning for the atomic age . . . it's a moody postwar noir steeped in real-life tragedy. It's the first Godzilla film I ever saw (at the age of five) and it happened to be the first one ever made.

Much as I love *Gojira*, the original and uncut Japanese version, the American edit is carved into my brain: I recorded the movie's audio off the family TV set and then played the cassette over and

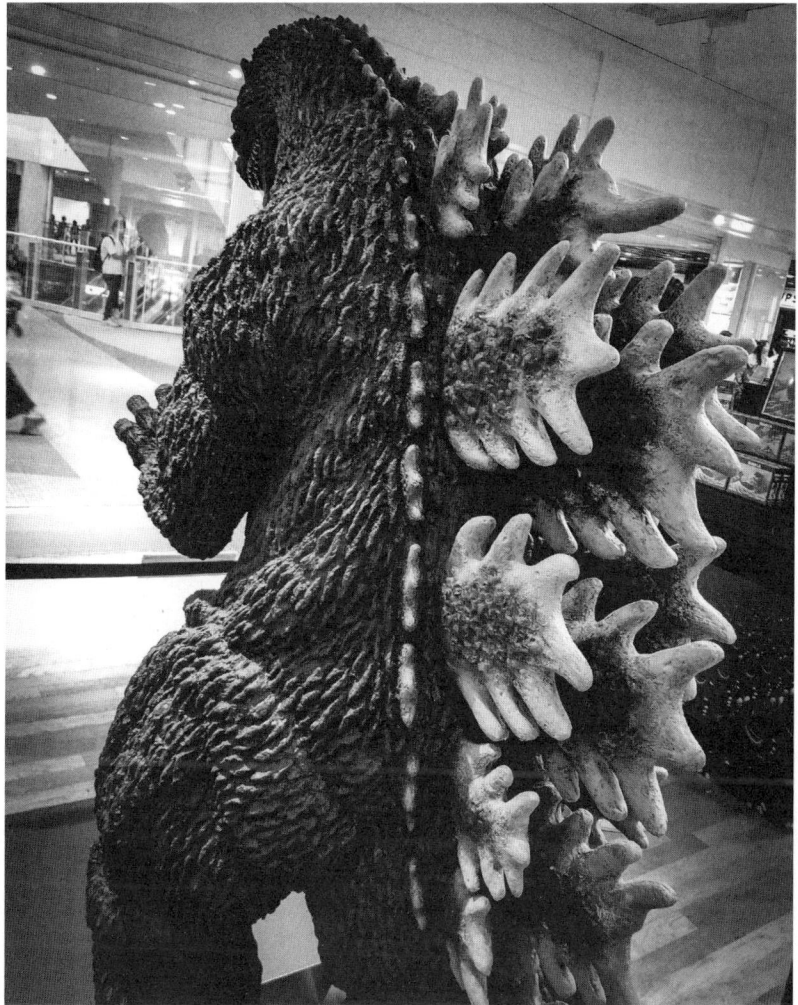

Godzilla statue at a Japanese shopping mall.

over again. Even with English dubbing and missing scenes, the thick atmosphere, dense sound mix, and Akira Ifukube's monumental score still seep through.

Toho Studios could have easily made this a mindless creature feature, but instead, director Ishiro Honda approached the material like a documentarian. The resulting film has an immediacy and emotional range that you don't find in many other monster movies before or since.

Meanwhile, Godzilla looks like he's smiling through it all with a big toothy grin. It's the face of a little kid causing trouble and having fun. I know it well.

2. Invasion of Astro Monster (1965)

Should we trust a bunch of weird aliens from Planet X who just want to borrow our world's monsters and take them off our hands for a bit? Sure; what could go wrong?

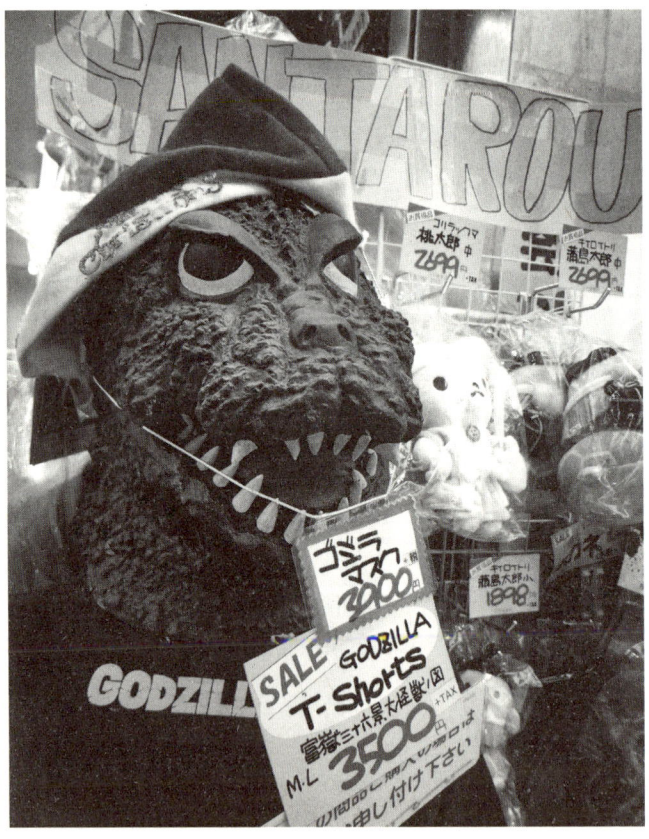

Mashing up elements from earlier alien invasion epics like *The Mysterians* and marrying them to the monster movie genre was a slam-dunk move that only Toho Studios could have pulled off. As if Godzilla, Rodan, and Ghidorah, the Three-Headed Monster, on the bill was not enough entertainment on its own, interplanetary sci-fi action and cool mid-1960s style make *Invasion of Astro Monster* (aka *Monster Zero*) a movie that's a lot of fun even when the Big G isn't on screen.

Then there's the emotional core of the film: a love story of epic proportions between American astronaut Nick Adams and doomed space lady Kumi Mizuno that threatened to leap off the screen and into real life.

Adams slays every time he opens his mouth, giving us line delivery that's something like Ed Wood by way of the Bronx: brash, full tilt, making a bigger cinematic impact than even Godzilla himself.

3. Terror of Mechagodzilla (1975)

More aliens, more Mechagodzilla, more problems.

Director Ishiro Honda came back to the monster movie scene after a long absence and injected the pessimism of his first Godzilla film into a franchise that had, at this point, basically degraded into kiddie fodder (I like *Godzilla vs Megalon* just fine, but wouldn't want to live there).

The 1970s downbeat bummer atmosphere comes in the form of a mad scientist who is haunted by his past, a cyborg girl struggling with the last embers of her humanity, and the general feeling that things will not end well, despite the King of the Monsters fighting on our side.

The secret sauce holding everything together is Akira Ifukube's musical score, which is heavy and lumbering in the best way possible: like an orchestra doing *Vol. 4* era Black Sabbath.

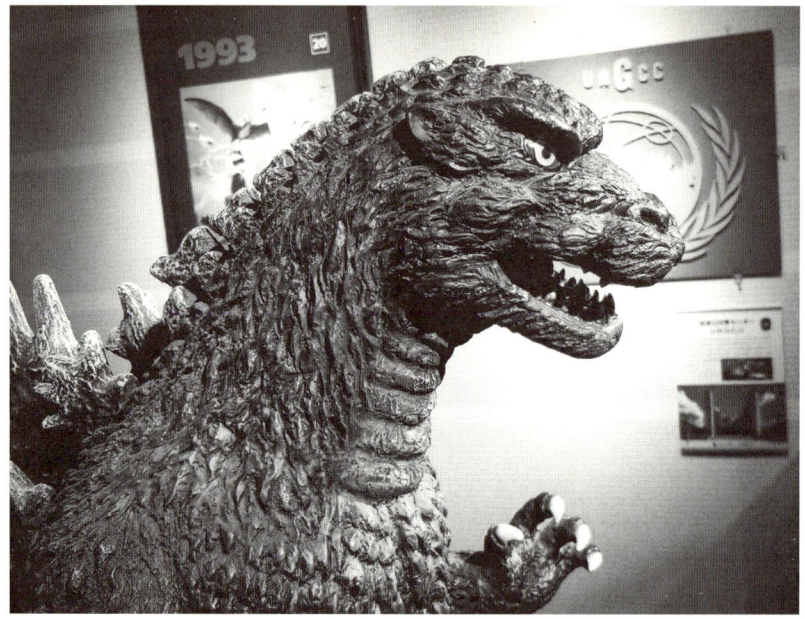

Not a hit when it originally came out, but it still packs a feel-bad wallop today, despite the goofy monster fights. I went to a screening of this movie in Tokyo and all the adult Godzilla freaks came out on the other side totally drained.

4. Godzilla vs Biollante (1989)

With many of the franchise's original filmmakers out of the picture (except for producer Tomoyuki Tanaka), it took Godzilla some time to find a new direction in breezy bubble era Japan.

Under the supervision of writer-director Kazuki Omori, *Godzilla vs Biollante* lets loose at the restless pace of a Hollywood blockbuster, but with really good practical miniature and monster effects.

The tone, pitched at general audiences, might annoy some Godzilla purists, but this movie still routinely tops fan polls in Japan when ranking the best of the series. There are more mad scientists,

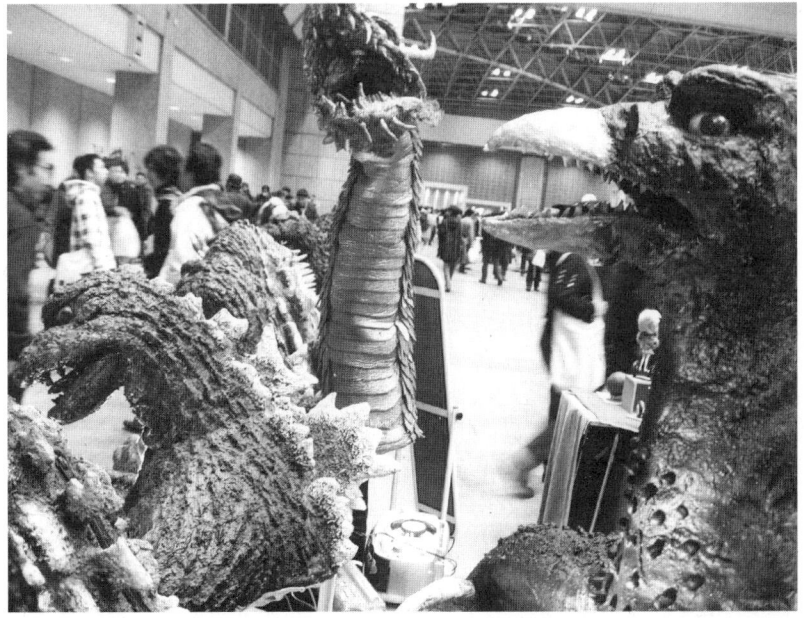

Godzilla puppets for sale at a Tokyo hobby show.

super weaponry like the Super-X2 flying tank, and Godzilla almost gets his head crunched like a Blow Pop by a massive plant monster that looks like something out of a John Carpenter flick.

The creative team and filmmaking style behind this entry would quickly flame out with increasingly messy productions, but this feels organic and fun, with a genuine sense of wonder. If only all the American Godzilla movies could try and hit this mark.

5. Shin Godzilla (2016)

It took the trauma of the 3/11 earthquake and tsunami to give Godzilla his first (and to date only) great movie of the 21st century.

Written and directed by Hideaki Anno of *Neon Genesis Evangelion* fame (also a lifelong monster movie fan), the first half of the film is a bitter black comedy on par with *Dr. Strangelove*, as bureaucrats choke on the rules and regulations while a monster mutates and eventually irradiates Tokyo. The second, less pointed half, where Japan strikes back, had some viewers moaning about "nationalism"—but hey, shouldn't the army *try and stop* Godzilla? It won the Japanese Academy Award for Best Picture either way.

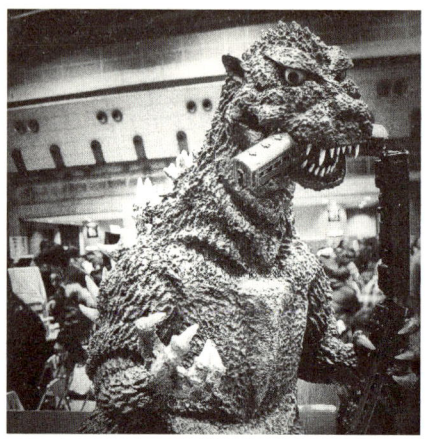

Living in Japan during the pandemic and experiencing the country's less-than-warp-speed vaccine rollout has been like watching *Shin Godzilla* every day in slow motion: bureaucrats stifled by what to do next as a monster grows and rampages outside.

Shuji Terayama's Notes from Underground

February 2020

There is a seemingly ordinary patch of urban street about a five-minute walk from Shibuya Station in Tokyo. You wouldn't know it from the way it looks now, but a genius of the Japanese Avant-Garde once operated a theater on this spot, in a building that looked like a cross between a circus and a surrealist art sculpture. Now, decades after the demolition of the original building, the location has transformed into a family restaurant from the "Johnathan's" chain of franchises.

Do any of the staff or patrons inside know that this is the place where Shuji Terayama's famed theater Tenjo Saijiki once stood, setting the film world on fire from 1969 to 1976?

Would they care? *Should they care?*

Despite being one of the leading figures of the Japanese Avant-Garde, Shuji Terayama's short films and features have never had a commercial release in the West, outside of screenings at museums and film festivals. Terayama, who is celebrated and studied by academics, remains largely known only to cult movie fans. This is too bad, because Terayama made mind-bending movies with surrealist

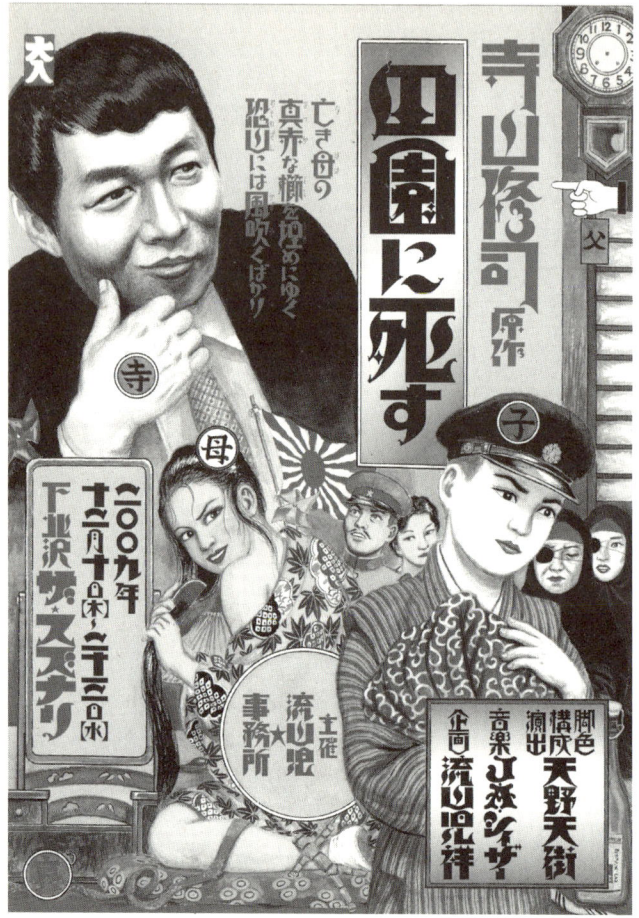

abandon that should put him in the same renowned company as Luis Buñuel, Federico Fellini, and Alejandro Jodorowsky.

I would rank two of Terayama's films, *Throw Away Your Books, Rally in the Streets* (1971) and *Pastoral: To Die in the Country* (1974), among the greatest movies ever made, full of ruminations on time, memory, and rousing calls for rebellion. They offer viewers a chance to take a time machine back to a wild era in the Japanese underground art scene when subculture was in full flower . . . before the dark times . . . before the free refills at the family restaurant.

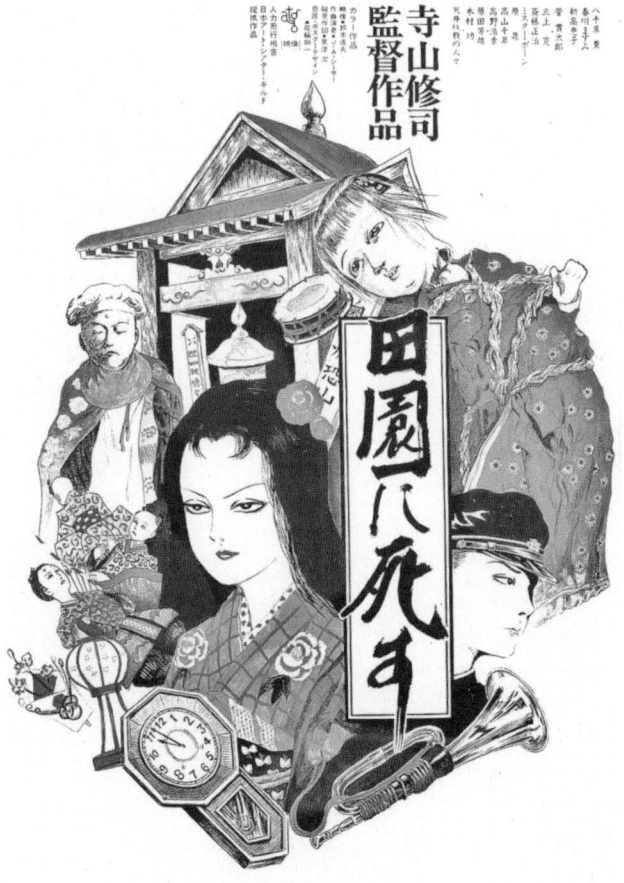

Movie poster for Pastoral: To Die in the Country, *1974.*

Shuji Terayama was born in 1935 and raised in the northern countryside of Aomori Prefecture. He attracted notice as a poet while still in high school and attended Waseda University in Tokyo, where he composed verse in the traditional style of Japanese poetry known as *tanka*. Soon, Terayama became a hugely prolific writer, not only of poems, but also novels, essays, magazine columns, and plays. Terayama plugged into the new youth culture percolating in Tokyo during the late 1960s and early 1970s; his speciality was the

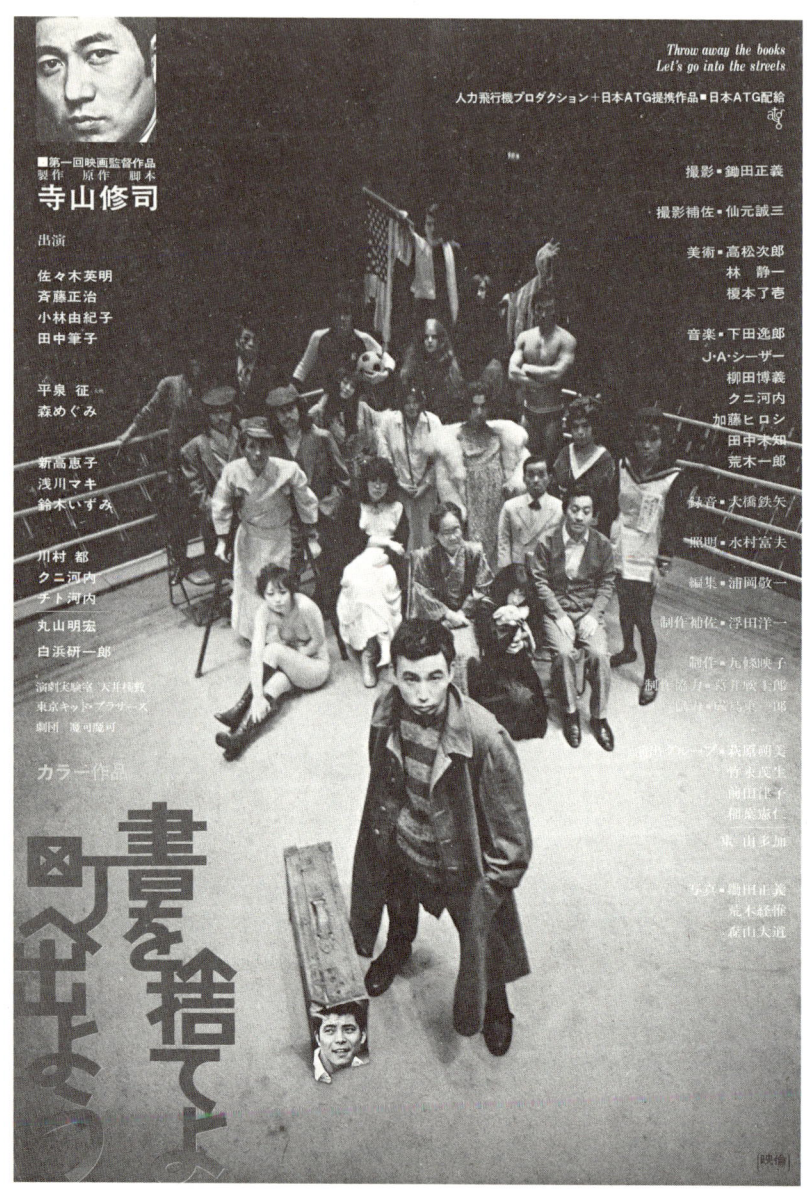

Movie poster for Throw Away Your Books, Rally in the Streets, *1971.*

marginal realm of radical student protesters, runaway kids who hung out in the Shinjuku area known as *futen*, plus sexual outlaws, glue sniffers, and just plain freaks.

Some of these folks joined Terayama's theatrical troupe—the Tenjo Saijiki—and starred in a series of plays and experimental films that Terayama wrote and directed.

His film *Throw Away Your Books, Rally in the Streets* was originally a book of essays and then a play, before it became the basis for Terayama's first feature film in 1971. The contents differ from version to version, but the theme of "youth in revolt" and the title remains the same across all media.

"What are you doing there? Hanging around a movie theater isn't going to make anything happen. The screen's completely blank . . ." That's the main character, Eimei, talking to us as the film begins.

Eimei, a young dude in the slums of Shinjuku, lives with his lowlife family, including his grandmother (a pickpocket), father (a former war criminal), and his sister (who prefers playing with her pet rabbit to men). Eimei wants to fly away from the dirty boulevard and imagines himself fleeing the scene on a human-powered airplane. But mostly, he just bums around the city, running aimlessly on train tracks or hanging out in a state of semi-disgust with his sports jock friend and his soccer team.

There's not much of a story or narrative drive to *Throw Away Your Books*. Instead, the film digresses into free associations, in the style of sketch comedy, through a series of surreal vignettes. An American flag is burned, drag icon Akihio Miwa shows up in a bathtub, Eimei loses his virginity, and something really bad happens to his sister's rabbit. The propulsive rock music of J.A. Seazer, a key Terayama collaborator in the theater and on screen, helps connect the many disparate parts. The result is a work of "angry young man" cinema that foreshadows *Quadrophenia* (1979) and Mike Leigh's *Naked* (1993) and that still cuts deep.

Terayama shows us the state of disaffected youth after the failure of the revolutionary dream of the 1960s. Belief in the family and social institutions have all been torn down ... now what? The city became an open book and Terayama wants people to scribble their names and stories in the margins, but a kind of inertia in the day-to-day grind has taken over. Eimei is stuck in the slums and can't get his airplane off the ground.

Like American yuppies, some kids from this era would join the establishment and enjoy the fruits of Japan's bubble economy. Others would try to keep the underground dream alive, preserving it just beneath the surface of mass culture (J.A. Seazer and several other Terayama alumni would later come up for air and work on the popular *Revolutionary Girl Utena* anime series). *Throw Away Your Books, Rally in the Streets* remains a wakeup call to anyone wasting their life in a movie theater. *Do something. Do anything. Fast.* The lights are changing.

Sadly, just over a decade later in 1983, Shuji Terayama died of kidney disease at the age of 47. New productions of his plays and reprintings of his books have continued ever since in Japan. Still, I can't get over the fact that his old theater is now a family restaurant. There's a bright side to this story: you don't have to dig in the dirt to find the Japanese underground anymore. Even if there isn't any Criterion Collection or Arrow Video DVD boxset of Shuji Terayama's best films, as of this writing, both *Throw Away Your Books* and *Pastoral: To Die in the Country* are on YouTube with English subtitles.

Watch them, rally in the streets, and freak out.

Kaiju Rhapsody

November 2020

It's 1978.

It's Saturday afternoon, I'm five years old, and I'm stuck in the house.

It feels like there is nothing to do.

My dad tells me there's a movie on TV called *Godzilla: King of the Monsters* that I (a dinosaur-obsessed kid who made it all the way through 1933's *King Kong*) just might get a kick out of.

The movie is in black and white and a bit on the slow and talky side, but something about it clicks deep inside me.

I spend the next week at school drawing pictures with green, black, and red crayons: Godzilla is destroying Tokyo and all the planes and tanks in the world can't stop him.

* * *

It's 1982.

I hate school. I don't like sports.

I scour the TV Guide every week for Japanese monster movies or TV shows to watch.

I run home from class to see *Ultraman* in the afternoons. I stay up late at night for a chance to get a glimpse of Godzilla or Gamera. To pass the time, I watch whatever is on the all-night movie main attraction. *Midnight Cowboy* and *La Dolce Vita* play alongside *Destroy All Monsters* and *Gorath*.

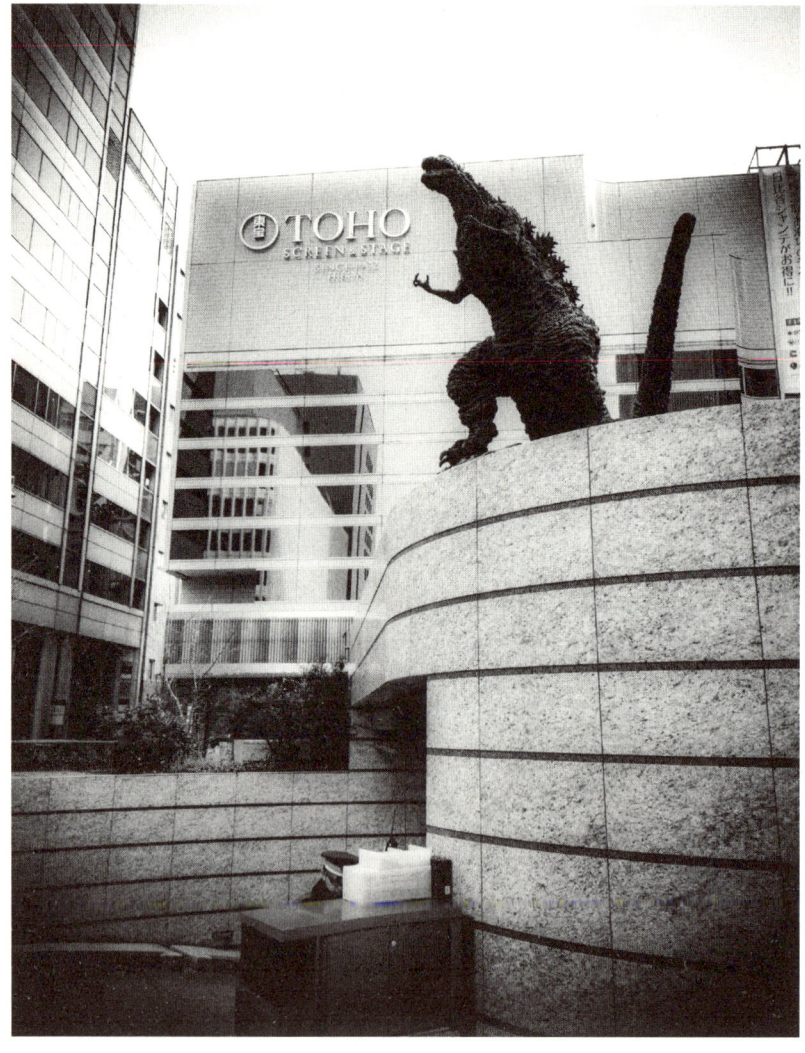

Godzilla statue in Hibiya, Tokyo.

MONSTERS OF THE SCREEN

Maybe one or two times a year, my family goes to San Francisco, and we stop at Japan Town. I buy a small-but-fat dictionary at a Japanese bookstore. It is a "monster dictionary," several hundred pages long, containing countless pictures of rubber creatures and their vital stats: height, weight, incredible powers.

I learn to read my first Japanese words: ゴジラ and 怪獣.

"Gojira" (Godzilla) and "Kaiju" (Giant Monster).

* * *

It's 2004 and I am in Japan.

I find myself at the offices of Toho Studios, home of the Godzilla movies. I am here to interview actress Kumi Mizuno, the luminous star of so many kaiju films, for a Japanese movie magazine.

In the bathroom, I stop and wonder: Is this really happening?

I gather up my courage and enter the room, and the lady from the Godzilla films is inside. I feel like something impossible has happened. I must have walked through the movie screen.

* * *

It's 2020, toward the end of a very tough year.

I live in Tokyo now. The landscape around me is the same one I saw destroyed by so many *kaiju* in the movies: Tokyo Tower, the Diet Building, the Ginza district. This city has survived many real disasters as well, like typhoons and earthquakes . . . but the subtle disasters, the ones that seem to happen in slow motion, do the most damage. As if the pandemic wasn't enough, political chaos in the US and my dad passing away at the age of 82 all happen within the span of a few perilous months.

I haven't been out much since February or so. I'm stuck in the house. It feels like there is nothing to do.

I turn on the TV. Every Godzilla movie ever made is now available to stream at the press of a button. So are lesser flicks featuring Gappa, Gamera, The X from Outer Space, pretty much everything.

Would the five-year-old-me be surprised at how things turned out, or was this the plan all along?

I guess I'll probably never know. Maybe I don't want to know.

What kind of a person lets his life be decided by Godzilla movies anyways?

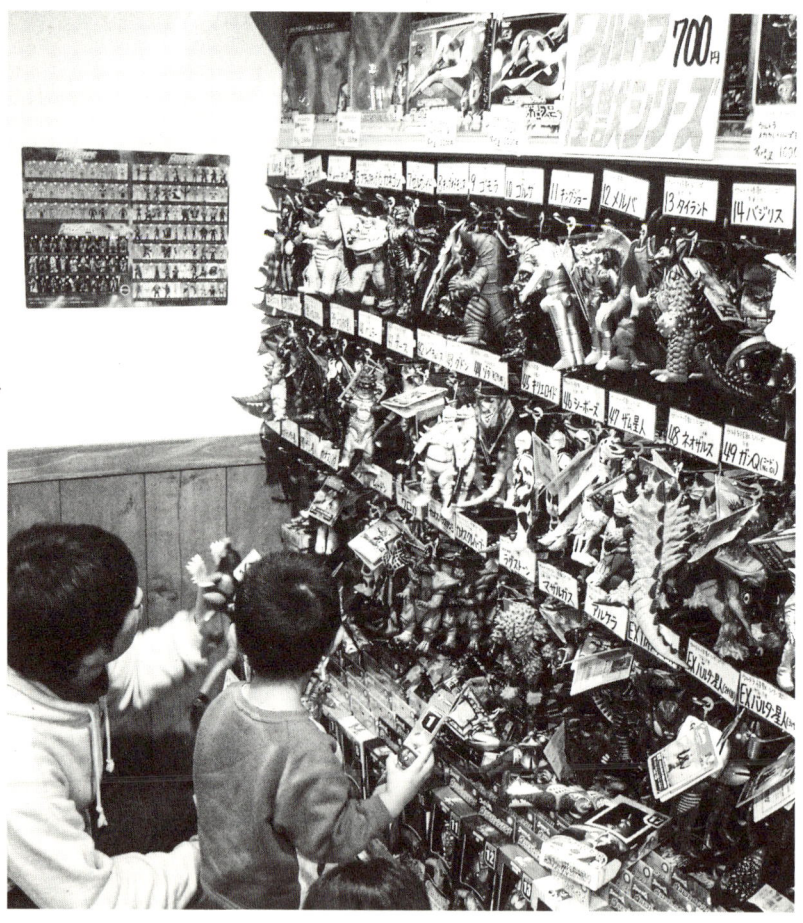

Kids buying kaiju figures at a Tokyo department store.

ICONS

Tetsuro Tamba: The Prince of the East

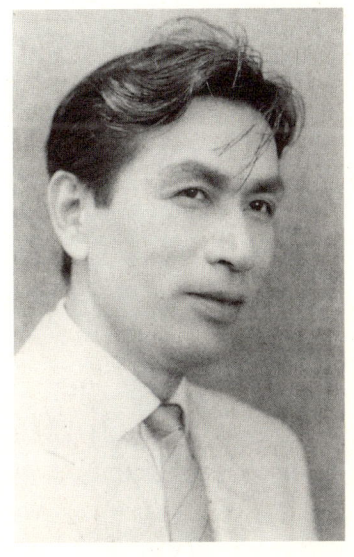

It's early evening somewhere out west on the Chuo line in Tokyo. I am walking through a supermarket with Takashi Miike. The prolific director of wild cult classic movies like *Dead or Alive* and *Audition* is wearing sunglasses at night and making a path through old women puttering about with bags of produce. We are on a mission to visit an iconic movie star—Tetsuro Tamba, The Prince of the East—at his home nearby. Miike knows the way and says that the best shortcut is through these aisles of spritely seniors.

Tamba was one of Japan's most legendary and notorious actors, having appeared in anywhere from 200 to 350 films (no one can seem to remember). He is best known in the West for essaying the role of Tiger Tanaka in the James Bond-in-Japan classic *You Only Live Twice* (1967), which was one of ten "foreign" films he starred in. Tamba often played authority figures: G-Men, scientists, professors, cops, army officers. But as someone who didn't seem to ever turn down a role, he would just as easily pop up in sexploitation and karate films as much as prestige pictures like *Harakiri* (1962) and *Kwaidan* (1965). If you've watched enough Japanese films—good, bad, and ugly—you've most definitely glimpsed Tetsuro Tamba and heard his deep baritone voice.

Tamba was a rich kid from a prestigious family, a troublemaker who stumbled into acting in the early 1950s. Five decades later, Tamba was still working and had recently appeared in several of

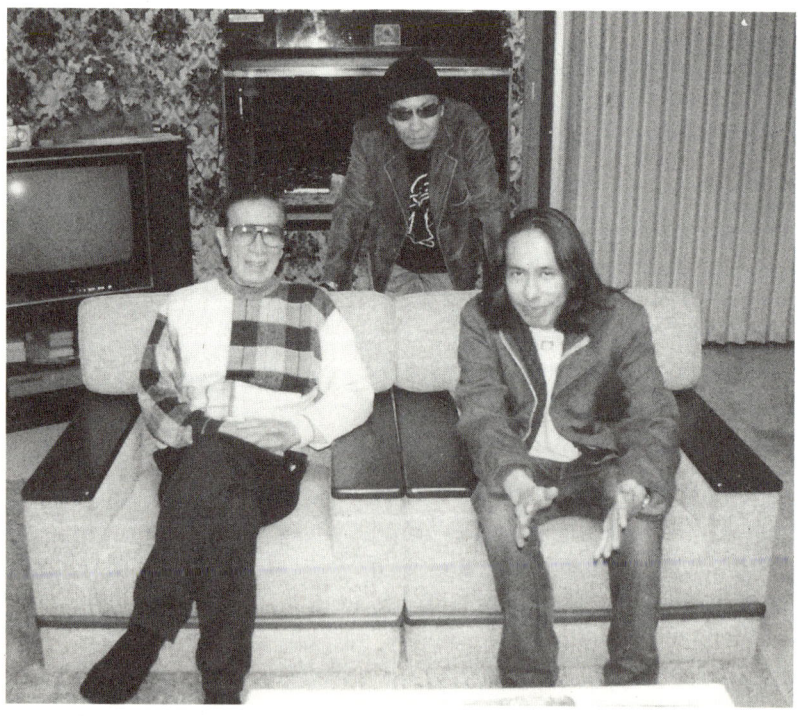

From left: Tetsuro Tamba, Takashi Miike, Patrick Macias.

Takashi Miike's movies, including *The Happiness of the Katakuris* (2001) and *Deadly Outlaw: Rekka* (2002).

Tamba spent so much time on screen that it was hard to believe he was a real person. His off-screen life was just as strange and mythic. In the 1980s, Tamba fronted a quasi-religion called *Daireikai* (Great Spirit World) which sought—through a series of bestselling books and bizarre films—to prove the existence of life after death.

Miike and I wander through an upscale neighborhood in search of Tamba's house. We're accompanied by the writer/editor Tomo Machiyama; Tomo's sister actually worked with Tamba on a short-lived TV talk show called *Tamba Club*, where the master of chaos himself held court in a room full of bikini girls. Apparently, he would sometimes wander around the set asking women: "I'm sorry but... did I fuck you before?" We could only imagine what he would say to us.

We finally find ourselves in front of a big white mansion surrounded by a fence. We are greeted by a sign that reads "Afterlife Research Laboratory." Miike assures us that this is it.

Inside, the entranceway is dominated by a life-size picture of Tamba in his prime: a black and white photo from an old *ninkyo yakuza* movie, where Tamba was clad in a *yukata* robe, clutching a deadly *dosu* knife, presumably about to kill someone.

"HELLO!" a booming voice shouts at me in English. Tamba springs into the doorway, nearly knocking us over like bowling pins. Given his age (80 at the time), I was expecting a tired old man energy, but Tamba is real GENKI!—still the same wild playboy that he always was!

The house is huge and we sit in Tamba's living room, which is done up in the "frozen in the 1980s" Western style that you'd expect of a Japanese movie star.

The day before this meeting, I made a strangely synchronistic find: I unearthed an old publicity photo of Tamba for sale in the Jimbocho district, an area of Tokyo where the streets are literally filled with movie memorabilia. It was a portrait of a stern-looking Tamba in an Imperial Navy uniform from one of the many war pictures he had appeared in. I ask him if he remembered the movie that it was from.

"I don't remember . . . I don't watch any of the films I appear in," Tamba says proudly. "I don't even read the scripts!"

During the getting-to-know-you phase, I tell Tamba that he starred in my favorite Japanese movie: Kinji Fukasaku's sci-fi epic *Message from Space* (1978), in which he played the President of the Earth Federation (pretty much the President of Space). But, despite sharing screen time with the late, great Vic Morrow, Tamba doesn't remember much about that movie either.

Time to pick a bigger target. I ask him what it was like when he first met Sean Connery, 007 himself, when *You Only Live Twice* was filming in Japan.

Now this is something Tamba remembers quite clearly: "I was in my hotel room having sex at the time." Miike, Tomo, and I audibly gasp. "There was a knock on the door. I went to answer it and Sean Connery was there. He had locked himself out of his room and wanted to use the phone to call the front desk, so I let him in."

During the swinging 1960s, Tamba travelled to Europe for business and pleasure. He tells us, "I learned English and French in bed. In England, I was sleeping with a maid. In France, I was sleeping with an actress named Capucine."

Tomo was the founding editor of Movie Treasures magazine and the name Capucine set off alarm bells for him. Capucine had starred in *The Pink Panther* (1963) and *What's New Pussycat* (1965), had dated actor William Holden, and was once rumored to be transgender. Had Tamba heard that before?

"I . . . didn't know that," Tamba intones somberly. "I'm hungry!" he shouts, quickly changing the subject. "Let's get something to eat!"

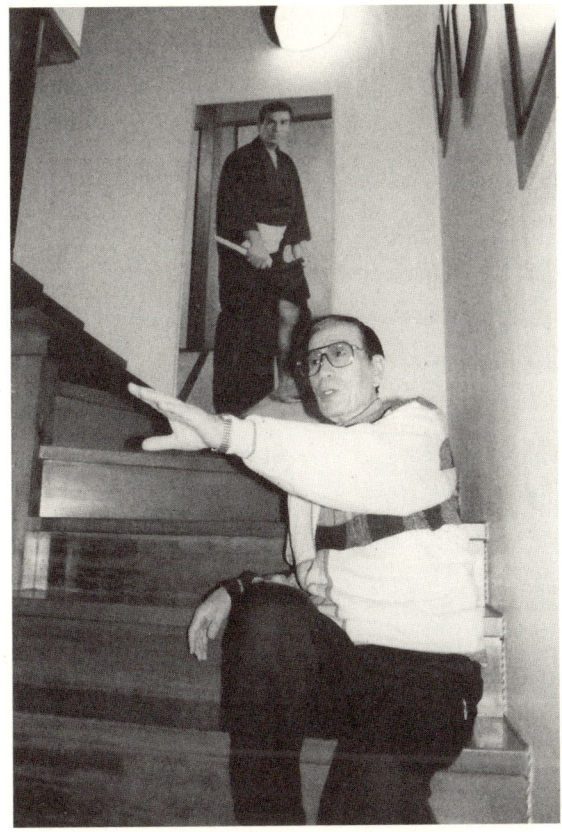

Tetsuro Tamba at home.

Tamba leads us to a *yakiniku* barbeque restaurant nearby. People on the street stop in their tracks and practically bow when they see the legend in their midst pass by.

Inside, the restaurant staff help Tamba put on his bib—traditional accoutrement for cooking and eating *yakiniku*—and Tamba jokingly makes a loud wailing sound, crying like a baby.

Miike stares and looks genuinely spooked. It must take a lot to freak out a guy who has directed some of the most extreme movies ever made. Miike's movies are about people getting cut to pieces and worse. Maybe an old man crying like an infant was just a bridge too far.

After dinner, I ask Tamba if he has a message for his fans around the world (I know I will write about this evening someday and that I'll need an ending). Tamba wastes no time in rising to the occasion. "I was known as the Prince of the East! I've been with many different kinds of woman . . . English, French, Spanish girls. And every day, around 6pm, I would have a massage."

I meant *message*, Tamba-sensei, not *massage*! Though if Tamba had starred in a movie called *Massage from Space* it would not have surprised me—he was that kind of guy.

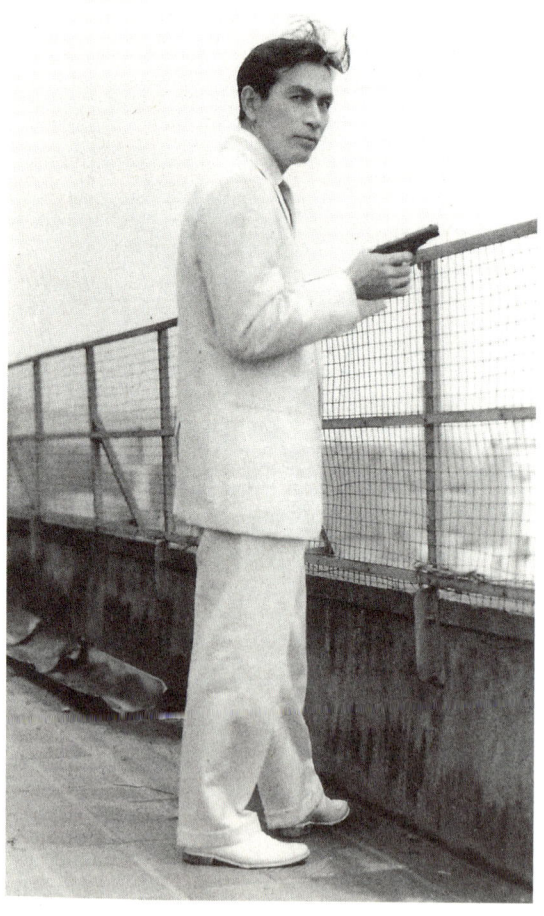

After our goodbyes, Tomo, Miike, and I walk away stunned, totally dumbfounded. Being in the presence of Tetsuro Tamba was even wilder than watching one of his movies.

Four years later, in 2006, Tetsuro Tamba passed away the age of 84. According to the rumors, a beautiful girl was trimming his locks at a hair salon when he departed once and for all for the Great Spirit World.

At his funeral, opera singer and spiritualist Hiroyuki Ehara claimed he saw Tamba's spirit sitting on his casket, looking at the hundreds of gathered attendees with a smile.

I want to believe.

ICONS

Sonny Chiba: The Last Action Hero

Shinichi "Sonny" Chiba died during the summer of bummers that was July 2021 in Japan.

People around the world mourned the loss of a man who seemed less like a human being and more like the titles of the movies he starred in: *The Street Fighter*, *The Killing Machine*, *The Karate Bearfighter*, *The Bodyguard*, *The Executioner*, and *The Champion of Death*.

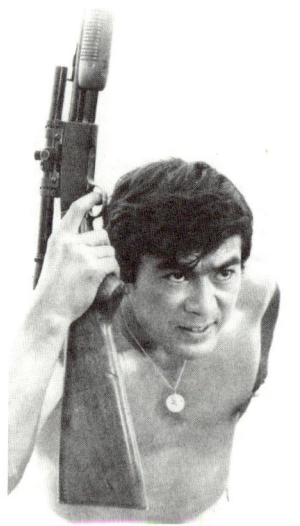

Sonny's death at the age of 82 was especially messed up. He died of pneumonia associated with COVID-19 at a time when most senior citizens in Japan had full access to vaccines. According to his talent agency, at the time of his death, Sonny had chosen to be unvaccinated.

There was minor scandal in Japan as tabloids reported Chiba as saying, "I'm healthy, I don't need to take the vaccine," only to then succumb to the disease himself. It's sad to think that the great Sonny Chiba would suffer a karmic twist of fate more suitable to a conversative radio host than the rough and tumble star of *The Street Fighter's Last Revenge*.

But Chiba was always something of a "think different" kind of guy. Born Sadaho Maeda in 1939, Shinichi "Sonny" Chiba had an epic life journey. After a back injury kept him out of the Olympics, he worked his way up the ladder of stardom in Japan during the 1960s, appearing in superhero productions (*Invasion of the Neptune Men*, 1961), action dramas (*Drifting Detective*, 1961), and lots of gangster films before finding his groove on action TV shows like *Key Hunter* (1968–1973) and early karate movies such as *Bodyguard Kiba* (1973).

Soon enough, Chiba would become a global movie star—even if only at the grindhouse. The martial arts boom of the early 1970s was in full swing, reaching its height with the 1973 *Enter the Dragon* starring Bruce Lee. Chiba decided to make a movie that was even crazier, grungier, and more violent than *Enter the Dragon*: a karate exploitation spectacular called *The Street Fighter*. It was a massive success, and it was soon clear that the biggest Asian action stars on the planet, able to sell tickets based on their names alone, were Bruce Lee and Sonny Chiba . . . and then suddenly Bruce was dead.

Bruce Lee was an impossible act to follow. He combined a charismatic screen persona and raw athleticism with philosophy and an almost scientific approach to ass kicking self-improvement.

By contrast, Sonny Chiba was something different. He was a wild card.

First of all, you had the crazy scowls that he would make in every scene. He was constantly chewing the scenery with mad snarls and primal grunts, squeezing out every bit of gnarled emotion from his

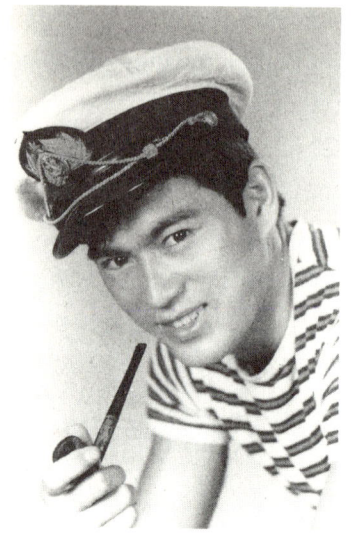
furrowed brows, whether he was thrashing his way through a room full of goons or hanging from a helicopter rope ladder.

Second, he was not a martial artist in the purest sense. He really did train in Kyokushin Karate under the legendary Mas Oyama and practiced judo as well as several other kinds of martial arts, but what he presented on screen was anything but authentic. Instead, his movies were awash in fake stage blood, jump cuts, cheesy rear projection, and unconvincing stunt dummies thrown from great heights.

There wasn't a ridiculous storyline or splatter gag that he thought was beneath him, and his golden years (which I would mark from the 1974's *The Street Fighter* to the 1977's *Doberman Cop*) produced some of Japan's wildest, most unforgettable movies.

No, Sonny wasn't a real martial artist. He was an *action movie star*.

Sonny owned and operated a stunt training school that he fittingly called "The Japan Action Club." The organization's goal was to create world-class action movie stars and stuntmen. It created a launching pad for the likes of Etsuko Shihomi (aka Sister Steetfighter) and Hiroyuki Sanada (*Roaring Fire, Avengers: Endgame*). But trouble came in 1990 when Sonny wanted to celebrate the Japan Action Club's 20th anniversary with a big budget movie about a killer bear called *Yellow Fang*. The self-financed film (which Sonny directed but didn't star in) was a flop at the Japanese box office, and Chiba was forced to sell off his assets, including the Japan Action Club, to cover costs.

MONSTERS OF THE SCREEN

The 1990s were lean years for many Japanese stars who had peaked in decades past, and Chiba's own career was at an all-time low. He renamed himself J.J. Sonny Chiba, with the new initials standing for "Justice Japan." Chiba spent a lot of time in Los Angeles looking for work, only to wind up in B and Z grade movies like *Aces: Iron Eagle III* (1992) and *Immortal Combat* (1994); in the latter flick, he played second banana to former pro wrestler "Rowdy" Roddy Piper.

Things started picking up toward the end of the millennium: producers realized that Chiba still had the charisma and nostalgic value to bring in audiences, and he appeared in high-profile Hong Kong movies like *The Storm Riders* (1998) and *The Legend of the Flying Swordsman* (2000) as well as straight-to-video productions back in Japan. Slowly but surely, Chiba was going back up the mountain, until he finally reached the top once again with his memorable appearance as Hattori Hanzo in *Kill Bill Vol. 1* (2003).

But even when Chiba was back on top, he never stopped the hustle. Fresh from his success in *Kill Bill*, he continued to shill for all

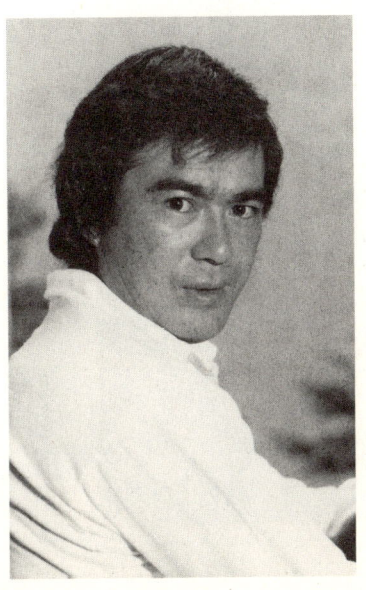

manner of dubious health and diet products in Japan. And just before coming down with COVID-19, he was slated to appear in a new zombie movie called *Outbreak Z* starring Wesley Snipes and Jessie Ventura (if that kind of company doesn't set off alarm bells, nothing will).

Along the way, I somehow managed to meet him briefly. It was at the US premiere of *Battle Royale* at the American Cinematheque in LA. I had just interviewed the film's director, Kinji Fukasaku, and was already in the auditorium. My friend Marc Walkow nudged me and pointed to a seat in the back: "Hey, is that Sonny Chiba?" We dared each other to get closer and take a look. Sure enough, it was the old Street Fighter himself. He was there to support Fukasaku, with whom he'd often collaborated, going all the way back to their very first films in the early 1960s.

Sonny Chiba stood up and greeted us like old friends. I hadn't been expecting to meet the Killing Machine that day. All I could do was yell out my favorite titles from the old films he'd starred in: "*Message From Space! G.I. Samurai! Okinawa Yakuza War!*" As Sonny heard each title, he yelled back "YEAH! YEAH!" as if to confirm it was really him.

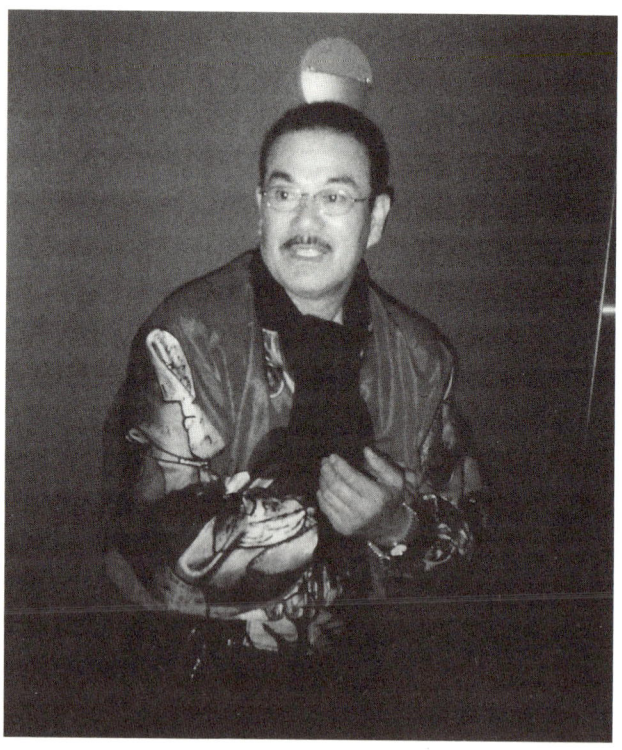

Sonny Chiba at the US premiere of Battle Royale, *2001.*

When Sonny died, my social media timelines filled up with pictures from people who had also gotten their own private Sonny Chiba experience. Chiba had spent his final years as a frequent guest at American movie and comic books conventions and posed with what must have been thousands of fans.

I want this to be a celebration of a life well lived, filled with ups and downs, and a sort of happy ending. I guess Sonny wasn't the type to live responsibly or to do what he was supposed to do. He was an icon of a time that no longer exists, when Japan was the second biggest economy in the world and made wild, outrageous movies that were perfectly suited to larger-than-life men like Chiba. His death really does spell the end of an era for Japanese cinema. It's tough to be the top action star in a country that no longer makes action films.

I suspect that, like Bruce Lee, Chiba's legend will only grow with time. But the next generation needs to be told: yes, there really was a Street Fighter, a Killing Machine, a Karate Bearfighter, a Champion of Death.

Viva Chiba!

ICONS

Kumi Mizuno: The Bride of Godzilla

Kumi Mizuno (born in Niigata, Japan, in 1937) was the belle of the Toho Studios' famed special effects movie series, appearing in *Gorath* (1962), *Matango* (1963), and *Godzilla Vs. the Sea Monster* (1966), among other titles. Mizuno is probably best known for her 1965–1966 "gaijin trilogy" (*Frankenstein Conquers the World*, *Godzilla Vs Monster Zero*, and *War of the Gargantuas*), in which the studio paired her with foreign devils Nick Adams and Russ Tamblyn. Her definitive appearance is in *Godzilla Vs Monster Zero*, where she plays "Miss Namikawa": a sexy alien spy from Planet X who winds up falling in love with a hot-blooded astronaut from Earth (played by me ... no, wait ... Nick Adams).

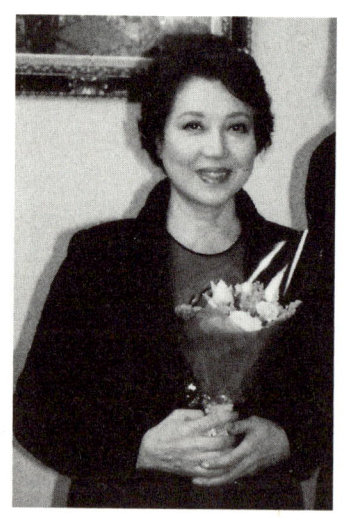

Kumi Mizuno, 2002.

This interview (which ran in the Janurary 2003 issue of *Eiga Hiho* magazine) was conducted at the Toho offices in Hibiya, Tokyo. It was done to mark the release of a new version *Godzilla Vs Mechagodzilla*, in which Mizuno plays the Prime Minister of Japan. The film marked her return to the *tokusatsu* (special effects) film genre after a long absence.

Present at Toho that day were hopeless Kumi Mizuno fanboys and interviewers Tamao Urayama, Tomohiro Machiyama, and yours truly (who presented Kumi with a bouquet of flowers, only to be told, "That's very American of you." Did Nick Adams get the same treatment?). Her son, Junichi Mizuno (who appeared on the *Kamen Rider Ryuki* TV show) was also in attendance.

What made you return to Godzilla movies after all this time?
Kumi Mizuno: They called me up and made the offer. It's been 36 years since I last appeared in a *tokusatsu* film and I said OK. It feels like the first time I've played a human being in one. I've played mainly non-human roles in the past.

You've played aliens, scientists, and animal-hybrid people before . . .
I even played a mushroom in *Matango*! But this feels like the first time I'm playing a normal person. But she's also exceptional. She's a female Prime Minister and someone who has gone through a lot of struggles in her life.

Do you approach acting any differently when you perform in a Godzilla film?
No, my motivation is always the same. Even if I face a human being or Godzilla, it's the same thing. If I open my heart up, then the other person will open theirs.

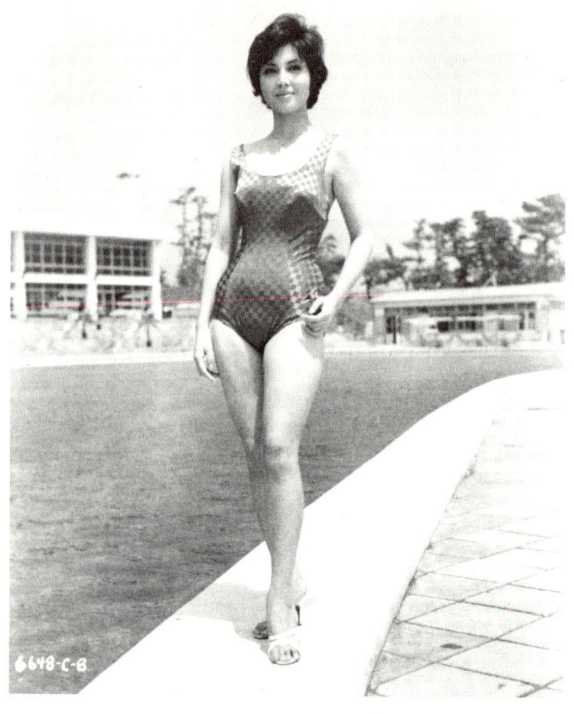

In *Godzilla Vs. the Sea Monster*, you were kind of a monster translator.
I remember I had the line, "Poor Godzilla." I had a lot of compassion for him.

Ok, I have a lot of questions about (former costar) Nick Adams.
Nick was known in America and I was known in Japan, so they put us together. We had a translator working on the set so we could communicate.

Was it difficult working like that?
No. Even though we didn't speak the same language, the basic emotions were the same. As long as I was paying attention to Nick's expression, I could understand what he was saying.

What kind of guy was he?
He was gentle, especially compared to (*War of the Garganutas* costar) Russ Tamblyn, who was cold. But maybe that was because Russ came to Japan with his wife and he couldn't get too involved with the staff and cast.

But Nick was very warm. I even invited him over to my house after the shoot. His gentleness somehow turned into a marriage proposal. He even told me, "I will divorce my wife to be with you!"

And then?
I turned him down.

There is a rumor in America that he went crazy after being turned down by you...[1]
No, no. I don't think so. When I turned him down, I knew that he had already proposed to *another* actress at Toho. Maybe he misunderstood me when I invited him over.

What else did he do to try and win you over?
While he was staying in Japan, he called me every night on the phone. Since I didn't speak English, I had to keep checking a dictionary to understand him.

What sort of things did he say?
(In English): "Kumi, I love you! I love you!"

Your son Junichi is also in the new *Godzilla Vs Mechagodzilla* movie.
Junichi: Yes, I play a pilot.

---

1 *Adams died of an apparent drug overdose in 1968.*

What was it like growing up as Kumi Mizuno's son?
When I was in kindergarten, I didn't really know what my mom did for a living.

You didn't know there were many crazy monster movie nerds who loved your mom? She is kind of an icon!
No, but recently, I noticed there are a lot of fans of her X-alien character. I've even seen action figures for sale.

Kumi, your special effects films are shown on television all the time in America and have been for decades. They are also beginning to come out on DVD.
Kumi: I didn't know that. I actually receive many fan letters from the US.

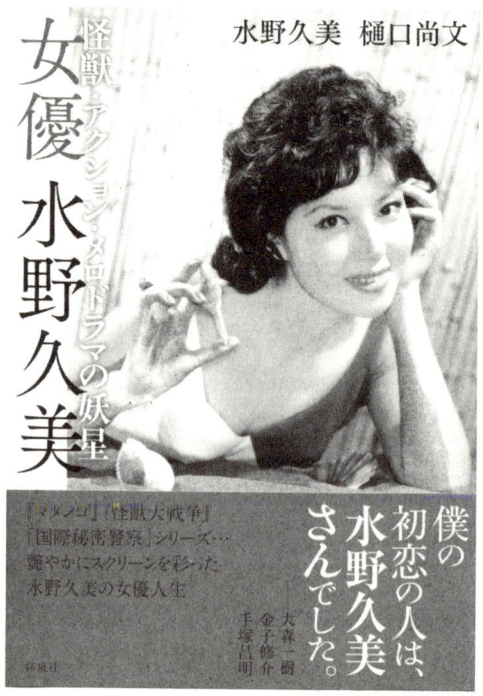

Just like fans in Japan fell in love with foreign actresses, fans outside of Japan feel the same way about you.
That's a pleasure to hear.

So, how does it feel to be appearing in a new Godzilla film after all this time?
I feel like I'm coming back home, and I feel very nostalgic.

Would you like to continue appearing in more Godzilla films?
Yes, because it's fun!

And she did just that. Kumi Mizuno appeared in 2004's totally amazing Godzilla: Final Wars.

Epilogue

It is winter 2023...

The book is almost done. Just a few more things to do and that's a wrap for Mondo Tokyo.

My old text and old photos have been rearranged across these pages, forming a map of another world that is fading away while a new one starts to take shape.

A lot of things have changed along the way...

On the day as I sit down to write this chapter, the news breaks that manga creator Leiji Matsumoto has died. Thirteen years ago, as detailed in this book, I sat next to him, watching in awe as he drew a picture of a character from his series *Galaxy Express 999*, a space-age fairy tale about how eternal life isn't all that's it's cracked up to be. Things are meant to be finite, people, places, and the points in between.

There's a line from the *999* series that says, "The time you spend must never betray your dreams, also your dreams must never betray your time."

Some of Japan's dreams and schemes haven't worked out so well recently...

The government-sponsored Cool Japan program, which kicked off in 2005, looks like it will be finally scrapped after squandering

EPILOGUE

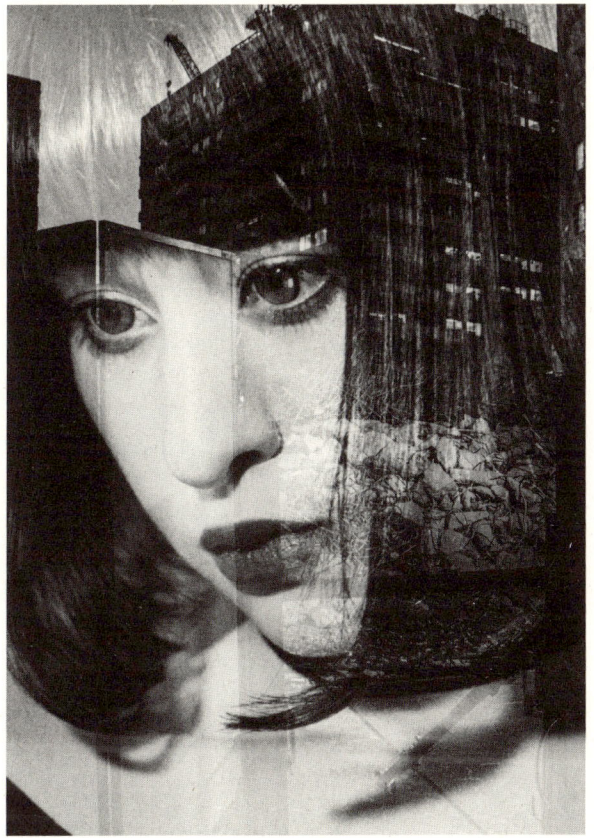

USD 789 million in public money into promoting things like anime, fashion, tourism, and food with little to no gain.

The long-awaited 2020 Tokyo Olympics turned into a series of arrests and scandals as various officials were caught taking bribes in exchange for lucrative deals.

Former Prime Minister Shinzo Abe, who once wowed folks with his Super Mario cosplay, was assassinated by a man with a homemade firearm. The fallout from the case drew attention to links between Abe and the Unification Church. Afterwards, it was determined that many other politicians besides had similar ties to the religious organization.

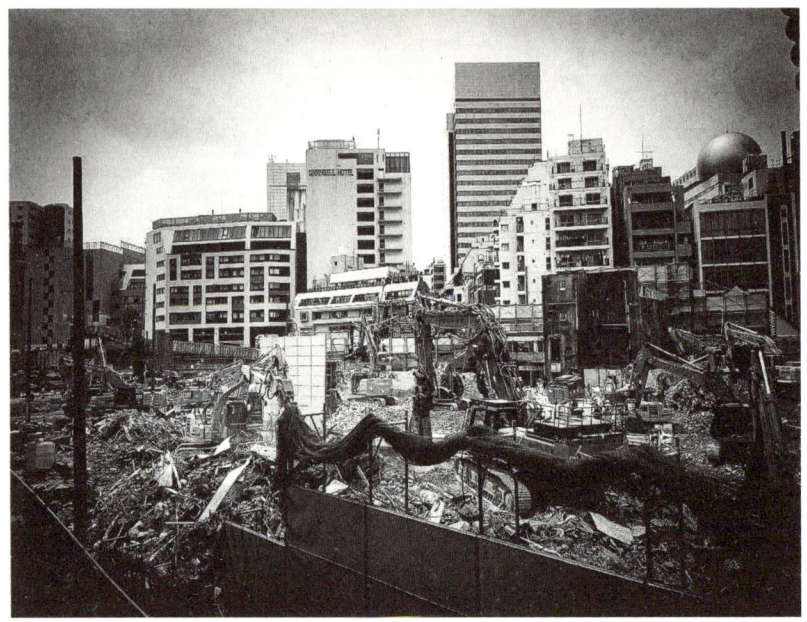

Shibuya, Tokyo, under construction or destruction, it's your choice . . .

All these dreams and rude awakenings played out against the surreal backdrop of a global pandemic that turned the world upside down. Many businesses cataloged in this book closed for good, some people in these pages left or vanished from the scene. Not everyone made it out alive. But life goes on.

Three years later, the tourists are starting to come back to Japan, people (myself among them) are starting to cautiously reemerge from self-imposed isolation back into the city streets. And what do we find there?

A blank page.

A strange new place to explore and discover.

It's time to make the next map of Mondo Tokyo.

Thanks to:

Izumi Evers, Julia Macias, Masaya Honda, Tomohiro Machiyama, Yoshiki Takahashi, Denki Watanabe, Takuma Sugi, Takeshi Ota, Hiroyuki Mistume Takahashi, Matt Alt, W. David Marx, Jean Snow, Dara Hyde, Matthew Bucemi, Vincent Shortino, Tim, Molly, and the music of Outrageous Cherry.

Author biography

Patrick Macias is the editor in chief of *Otaku USA* magazine, the founding editor of Crunchyroll News, and the author of numerous books about Japanese pop culture, including *TokyoScope: The Japanese Cult Film Companion*. In addition to contributing liner notes to the Criterion Collection and Arrow Video, he also wrote the original story for the anime series *URAHARA* which was simulcast globally in 2017. Born and raised in Sacramento, California, Patrick now lives in Tokyo, Japan.